Reading Law Forward

Other Books by Peter Charles Hoffer

Daniel Webster and the Unfinished Constitution
The Federal Courts: An Essential History
A Nation of Laws: America's Imperfect Pursuit of Justice
Roe v. Wade: *The Abortion Rights Controversy in American History,*
    Third Updated Edition
The Supreme Court: An Essential History, Second Edition

Reading Law Forward

THE MAKING OF A DEMOCRATIC JURISPRUDENCE FROM JOHN MARSHALL TO STEPHEN G. BREYER

Peter Charles Hoffer

University Press of Kansas

Published by the University Press of Kansas (Lawrence, Kansas 66045), which was organized by the Kansas Board of Regents and is operated and funded by Emporia State University, Fort Hays State University, Kansas State University, Pittsburg State University, the University of Kansas, and Wichita State University.

Library of Congress Cataloging-in-Publication Data

Names: Hoffer, Peter Charles, 1944– author.
Title: Reading law forward : the making of a democratic jurisprudence from
　John Marshall to Stephen G. Breyer / Peter Charles Hoffer.
Description: Lawrence, Kansas : University Press of Kansas, 2023. | Includes index.
Identifiers: LCCN 2022053988 (print) | LCCN 2022053989 (ebook)
　ISBN 9780700635085 (cloth) | ISBN 9780700635092 (ebook)
Subjects: LCSH: Jurisprudence—United States.
Classification: LCC KF380 .H64 2023 (print) | LCC KF380 (ebook) |
　DDC 349.73—dc23/eng/20230505
LC record available at https://lccn.loc.gov/2022053988.
LC ebook record available at https://lccn.loc.gov/2022053989.

British Library Cataloguing-in-Publication Data is available.

Printed in the United States of America

10　9　8　7　6　5　4　3　2　1

The paper used in this publication is acid free and meets the minimum requirements of the American National Standard for Permanence of Paper for Printed Library Materials Z39.48–1992.

Contents

Introduction

Reading Law Forward

Classical jurisprudence asks: "What is the function of law?" How are judges supposed to decide cases? Modern jurisprudence adds: What is the relationship between society and law, and how can law improve that relationship? In a democracy like ours, this last project is vital. Philosopher Ronald Dworkin's 1986 treatise *Law's Empire* introduced a superhuman judge he called Hercules. Hercules engaged the puzzles of both classical and modern jurisprudence. Hercules "knows that other judges have decided cases that, although not exactly like this case, deal with related problems; he must think of their decisions as part of a long story he must interpret and then continue, according to his own judgement of how to make the developing story as good as it can be." The key word was "continue." When the statute law was clear, other judges might "loyally enforce" the will of the legislature, but Dworkin's Hercules was not bound down by conventionalism, chained to precedent, history, and tradition. Nor was he simply pragmatic, taking the law where he wanted it to go, an activist on the bench. He was constrained by the "canons" of judging. So Dworkin hedged his bets: "Judges may not read their own convictions into the Constitution . . . no matter how much that judgement appeals to them." Instead, "they must regard themselves as partners with other officials, past and future, who together elaborate a coherent constitutional morality." Hercules's struggle remains at the center of our jurisprudence. We honor the judge constrained by existing law, but should we also admire the judge who seeks in existing law the promise of a better world—"a future," as good as it can be?[1]

Why should Hercules's task concern us—us being outsiders looking in at the realm of jurisprudence? Rather than reading another academic discourse on jurisprudence, do we not want better law from our judges? That better law is the best outcome of cases, outcomes in which the parties to the case and the public are all winners. In his *Active Liberty* (2005), a work much shorter than Dworkin's but destined to stand alongside it as a classic text of jurisprudence, Justice Stephen G. Breyer offered a way to such a better law. He wrote, "Through examples, my thesis illustrates how emphasizing the democratic objective can bring us closer to achieve the proper balance between" active and restrained constitutional interpretation, a method "by which judges, when they interpret a legal text, will yield better law—that helps a community of individuals democratically find practical solutions to important contemporary social problems."[2]

Reading Law Forward incorporates the spirit, though not the entire substance, of doctrines like judicial pragmatism, consequentialism, instrumentalism, and their jurisprudential cousins. According to this cluster of doctrines, judges sometimes engage in some form of policy making, applying law to particular cases on the basis of perceived best outcomes. Reading law forward goes beyond this—not only applying law according to needs of a changing world, but interpreting law according to those changing needs. Reading the law forward, the judges in this book not only applied the existing precedent, but looked ahead to future (anticipated) conditions. Like the pilgrim in T. S. Eliot's "Little Gidding" (1942), the judges return from the future to the place where they began and come to "know the place for the first time." To be sure, advocates of this forward-looking jurisprudence readily provide complex qualifications. For example, even the foremost defender of pragmatic judging concedes that the doctrine is pretty "squishy."[3]

Forward-looking variants of jurisprudence have their critics. It is not just the softness of pragmatism/consequentialism/instrumentalism that worries these faultfinders. It is the fear that such lawmaking from the bench creates a gap between legal reality and the judge's vision of the law that would leave us with "dissociative and incoherent" legal precedents. More telling, it is a concern that judges who substitute their ideas of better law for a more objective reading of existing law violate the most sacred canons of professionalism. Justice Horace Gray of the Massachusetts Supreme Judicial Court, ruling in 1867 on a charitable bequest to Wendell Phillips, and others, as trustees for the benefit of runaway slaves, put it succinctly: "But it is the duty of the judicial department to expound and administer the laws as they exist."[4]

That concern echoes in more modern times. US Supreme Court

Justice Antonin Scalia reminded his readers that "the common law is precedent bound" and those precedents, rooted in long years of judicial reasoning, were not to be cast aside lightly. Applying that doctrine, Justice Samuel Alito has argued in his opinion striking down *Roe v. Wade* that constitutional rights must be "deeply rooted in this nation's history and tradition." Justice Clarence Thomas agreed in a decision voiding New York State's gun regulations: "The government must demonstrate that the regulation is consistent with this nation's historical tradition of firearm regulation."[5]

Judge Robert Bork went a little further when he criticized what he saw as the liberal politics of some judges. His *The Tempting of America* (1989) scorned those on the bench who engaged in judicial activism: "Professions and academic disciplines that once possessed a life and structure of their own have steadily succumbed in some cases almost entirely to the belief that nothing matters beyond politically desirable results, however achieved." Bork believed that constitutional law had yielded to this seduction, and legal writing and judicial opinions had become openly politicized. Bork called on all judges to return to the safe harbor of originalism.[6]

Originalism has many followers and many formulas, but central to all of them is strict fidelity to constitutional text. Critics ask whether this is ever possible when the intent of the text's authors cannot be determined with certainty. Defenders reply that contemporary understandings of the language of the texts suffice to fix their meaning. Whichever position one adopts, precedent—the authority of older cases—is central to common-law jurisprudence; reading the law forward is unorthodox, but actually part of the common-law tradition. That is, the common law has proven itself capable of growth from within. This tension is present in constitutional adjudication. A conservative, Chief Justice Warren Burger wrote, "the choices we discern as having been made in the Constitutional Convention impose burdens on governmental processes that often seem clumsy, inefficient, even unworkable, but those hard choices were consciously made" and they must be followed. The foremost advocate of "the living constitution," Justice William Brennan, agreed that "the line we must draw between the permissible and the impermissible is one which accords with history and faithfully reflects the understanding of the Founding Fathers." But both men signed on to decisions that expanded existing precedent to cover conditions wholly unanticipated by the framers, for example, mandated school busing in *Swann v. Charlotte Mecklenburg Board of Education* (1971).[7]

This then is Hercules's dilemma once again—how to justify reading the law forward, to find in law its best outcomes, while not imposing the judge's own values on the law. And once again, it devolves into an academic quarrel over complex theories of law. I propose that an answer to Hercules' dilemma lies not in more finely spun debates over theories of jurisprudence, but in an empirical study of how in practice one particular jurisprudence of textual interpretation can lead to better law. In the following pages I examine how a group of America's foremost judges read the law forward. By assessing their contribution to our store of legal ideas, I believe we can approach a judgment about what kinds of jurisprudence have a beneficial impact on American law.[8]

But first, let me offer two examples of reading law forward to show how it worked. In writing his opinion striking down the Pennsylvania antikidnaping law of 1826 in *Prigg v. Pennsylvania* (1842), Justice Joseph Story was torn between his personal antipathy to chattel slavery and a federal statute that protected the property interests of slaveholders. His answer was to read law forward. The Fugitive Slave Act of 1793, based on the Rendition Clause of the federal Constitution, seemed to mandate free-state assistance to the slavecatcher. Story agreed with counsel for Maryland (and Prigg) that the federal act was constitutional. Story then read the 1793 act forward, that is, looking at likely consequences (obliquely phrased as "the prejudices of some portions of the non-slaveholding states"), to find that mandating state assistance would cause all manner of problems for state laws and state legal officials. He found that the best interpretation of it applied only to federal government and struck down the Pennsylvania act. He then went back to the case to relieve state officials of any positive duty to abet the slave catcher.

Each state is at liberty to prescribe just such regulations as suit its own policy, local convenience, and local feelings. . . . To guard, however, against any possible misconstruction of our views, it is proper to state, that we are by no means to be understood in any manner whatsoever to doubt or to interfere with the police power belonging to the states in virtue of their general sovereignty. That police power extends over all subjects within the territorial limits of the states; and has never been conceded to the United States.

Applying the very doctrine of states' rights that undergirded domestic slavery, realizing that requiring free states to assist slave catchers would open a Pandora's Box of troubles, Story revised the reach of the Fugitive Slave Act of 1793.[9]

In *Hynes v. New York Central Railway* (1921) a boy jumping into a river where boys routinely swam died when a pole on the railway behind the plank from which the boys jumped loosed and sent a cable that knocked him into the water. The law of trespass was clear. The boy was trespassing and the company owed no duty of care to trespassers. It was not liable for his death. The lower courts found for the company. New York Court of Appeals judge Benjamin Cardozo read the law forward to see that the growing density of city life, through which the railroads ran their tracks, would present many more cases like this one, to which he thought older ideas of liability were ill suited. He opined that "the law of bathers does not depend on these nice distinctions . . . land owners are bound to regulate their conduct in contemplation of the presence of travelers upon the adjacent public ways." Comparing the river bathing spot to a public highway and the swimmers to travelers was Cardozo rewriting the law of liability that had existed from long before the republic existed. He convinced the New York Court of Appeals to reverse the lower courts' decision and in the process revised the law of tort liability.[10]

The choice of seven judges herein who read the law forward was easy in one sense and difficult in another. If there is a hall of fame of judges in America, all seven in the pages that follow would be elected on the first

ballot. Though different in many ways, and coming from distinct pe-
riods in our history, John Marshall, Joseph Story, Lemuel Shaw, Louis
Brandeis, Benjamin Cardozo, William O. Douglas, and Stephen Breyer
all made signal contributions to our public life. But leaving out other
candidates was painfully hard. Why, for instance, are Oliver Wendell
Holmes Jr., Earl Warren, and William Brennan absent? Surely concepts
like Holmes's "Market Place of Ideas," Brennan's "Living Constitution,"
and Warren's "All deliberate speed" read the law forward. Sandra Day
O'Connor's formulation of "undue burden" in abortion rights cases and
Ruth Bader Ginsburg's blistering opinions in gender discrimination
cases secure their places in any scholarly history of the High Court.
Other judges could be added to the list of the missing. But to repeat,
those who are included belong.[11]

In somewhat parallel fashion, the choice of cases, and the opinions
therein, required serious thought. Opinions, the somewhat mislead-
ingly named reasoning of appellate judges in cases, can be quite long.
The seven judges in the present essay wrote thousands of opinions,
and one wants to do justice to their efforts. Some of their cases were
landmarks in our constitutional landscape, and lay obvious claim to
inclusion, but even in these one cannot reproduce the entire opinion.
One has to select key passages. Some cases discussed here are less well
known, but the judges' opinions in them are striking examples of their
thinking. To be sure, other genres of legal scholarship epitomize cases,
offering brief summaries, or "string" citations of cases in reference
notes. This method of presentation is suitable if one is concerned with
substantive outcomes of cases, but less valuable if one is examining the
reasoning of the judge. Every case in this book belongs in the book,
although many others might have been added.[12]

John Marshall, 1832. Library of Virginia. Portrait by Henry Inman.

1. John Marshall

Eighteenth-century lawyers and judges on both sides of the British Atlantic were wary of innovation. The Anglophone common law changed slowly over the centuries. In prevailing Anglo-American colonial jurisprudence, law was separate from politics, judges were not to be politicians, and political policy (future public arrangements) was separate from private law (resolution of past disputes between individuals). Law looked backward, sometimes all the way back to medieval times, for precedent and precept. Then the protests challenged all of these assumptions.[1]

But the American Revolution had little patience for such snail-like change. Over the course of the seven years that they waged war against Britain, American legislators and jurists passed hundreds of new laws and ratified new constitutions. Lawyers routinely engaged in a forward-looking law, for some form of reading the law forward was necessitated by the birth of the republic. In effect, it became the default jurisprudence of federal nation building. Although the French aristocratic visitor Alexis de Tocqueville would lament that American lawyers concerned themselves with what had been done rather than with what one ought to do, that was not so in the founding era of the nation.[2]

True, from the first days of the Continental Congress, legal innovations of the revolutionary variety faced criticism. In England and the colonies, defenders of parliamentary acts and the king's rights argued that revolutionary concepts of law were themselves violations of law. Joseph Galloway, a Philadelphia lawyer not unsympathetic to the colonial cause—at first—in 1775 decried "a lawless power established throughout the colonies, forming laws for the government of their conduct, depriving men of their natural rights, and inflicting penalties more severe than death itself, upon a disobedience to their edicts." This species of conservatism regarded legal texts as fixed in their meaning, and looked to the intent of the (English) framers of the law. But the innovators and the American framers were now those in power.[3]

Their innovative, forward-looking view of law carried into the state-making era and through the framing of the federal Constitution. The new system of government was an experiment in federalism. Although much of the text was borrowed from state constitutions and the Articles of Confederation, as a whole, the document was innovative. At its core was a dual federalism, in which both the central government and the state governments were sovereign. But that very novelty again pressed judges to read the law forward. Foremost among the jurists who grew to intellectual and professional prominence in the revolutionary age was John Marshall of Virginia.[4]

In person Marshall was a remarkable combination of entrepreneur and speculator (he had a huge law practice and invested in land), deep thinker, principled believer in the prospects of the new nation, and political opportunist. In short, he embodied many of the contradictions and ironies of early national America. He was born to the gentry and inherited a plantation, but preferred to live and work in Richmond. He saw combat as a young officer in the Revolution, and served as a diplomat, in Congress, and later as secretary of state. Though briefly a member of the House of Representatives, he never sought high elective office. Simple in dress and manner, he rarely stood on ceremony and had little attachment to the aristocratic pretensions of the great Virginia Tidewater aristocracy. Not bookish or pedantic, he had a great store of common sense and personal charisma. When he passed away, the judges of the district court and the Maryland state courts gathered in Baltimore to honor him. They resolved "to wear the badge of mourning for two months." As Missouri Senator Thomas H. Benton wrote of Marshall, "he was supremely fitted for high judicial station—a solid judgment, great reasoning powers, acute and penetrating mind . . . attentive, patient, laborious . . . grave on the bench, social in the intercourse of life, simple in his tastes, and inexorably just."[5]

Marshall gave little clue to his personal or political beliefs when he wrote for the Court. He opined as though the law dictated the course of his pen, worked hard for consensus on the Court, based his writing on the broadest possible grounds, and pioneered in switching the Court from "seriatim" opinions, in which every justice read his own, to "opinions for the Court" in which justices "signed on" to one another's opinions. In this, and in many other ways, he worked to insure harmony, if not uniformity of opinion, on his court. But as much as Marshall wanted to take the federal courts out of partisan politics, or at least defend their independence by appearing to take them out of partisan politics, Republican President Thomas Jefferson's efforts to purge the courts of Federalists like Marshall posed an almost insuperable obstacle.[6]

In the 1800s, as Jefferson and his successors were changing the political composition of the federal judiciary from Federalist to Republican, John Marshall was reasserting the centrality of the federal courts in the interpretation of federal law. To do this, he had to make the federal courts the best readers of the Constitution, and to do that, he cautiously but resolutely read law forward. Once one sees that, apart from Jefferson's personal animosity against Marshall, the Jeffersonians and their successors did not pose a fundamental threat to the operation of federal courts, one can view Marshall's contributions to the federal courts' story in a new light. Rather than battling against the Jeffersonians, who looked backward to an older, agrarian, states' rights world, he saw himself carrying on the efforts of the framers into an uncertain future.[7]

In a series of seminal cases Marshall and his court faced and passed critical tests of separation of powers and judicial federalism. The answer for Marshall was a forward-looking reading of law, albeit one forced on him by the exigencies of his, and the nation's, situation, then a return to the text with its meaning newly and firmly fixed. He did not see law as an instrument of reform. He was a social and economic conservative. John Marshall's jurisprudence was structural, that is, according to Marshall it was built into the very columns and beams of the Constitution. But it was never that simple. One had to read that text forward in order to fill in the gaps the framers left in constitutional texts.

The first of these cases, *Marbury v. Madison* (1803), allowed Marshall to define the relationship between the federal courts and Congress with more precision, giving new meaning to the concept of judicial independence in a checks and balances system. The second case, the first of two treason prosecutions of Aaron Burr (1807), again raised separation of powers questions, this time the courts' relations with the president. The third case, *Fletcher v. Peck* (1810), required a reading of the meaning of the Contracts Clause. The next cases, *McCulloch v. Maryland* (1819), and *Osborn v. Bank of the U.S* (1824), surveyed the Necessary and Proper Clause. The last of the cases, *Gibbons v. Ogden* (1824), asked the Court to define the Commerce Clause. Marshall did all of this by reading the Constitutional text forward.

Because it came in the midst of the controversy over the Judiciary Acts of 1801 and 1802, and because Federalists suspected Jefferson of seeking to destroy the federal court system in order to undermine their party, *Marbury* was seen by some politicians and jurists then (and now) as a test of the independence of the judiciary. As framed by Marshall, it was a much narrower matter—whether Congress could confer on the Supreme Court a procedural authority not included in section 2 of Article III. But on that narrow foundation, Marshall's opinion built a great edifice. He used the case to explain the role of the Supreme Court in constitutional interpretation. In so doing, he established in the Court a check on Congress that was not in the letter (text) of Article III. He did not invent judicial review, but nothing in the Constitution explicitly conferred on the Supreme Court the power to declare federal law unconstitutional.[8]

The facts of the case were relatively simple: William Marbury, an Annapolis financier, Federalist supporter, and tax collector for the state of Maryland, was supposed to receive a commission as a justice of the peace for the District of Columbia. Marshall, still performing the secretary of state's duties, failed to send it on and incoming Secretary of State Madison, with the assent of President Jefferson, did not remedy Marshall's oversight. When he did not get the commission, Marbury filed suit with the clerk of the Supreme Court under the provisions of the Judiciary Act of 1789. Its section 13 authorized the Supreme Court to issue a writ (a judicial command) "of mandamus, in cases warranted by the principles and usages of law, to any courts appointed, or persons holding office under the authority of the United States," to perform some act—in this case requiring Secretary of State Madison to send the commission to Marbury. Thus the case went directly to the Court. Over the long course of the Marshall Court, fewer than 1 percent of its cases were based on its original jurisdiction under Article III, section 2.[9]

The issue before the Court, as Marshall framed it, was whether the

Court had jurisdiction over Marbury's case. He intentionally ignored the political context of the suit. In a very long opinion for that day (twenty-six pages), Marshall wrote for a unanimous Court. He ruled that the justices could not issue the writ of mandamus because it was not one of the kinds of original jurisdiction given the Court in Article III of the Constitution. The Constitution controlled or limited what Congress could do, and in particular prohibited the Congress from expanding the original jurisdiction of the Court. Congress had violated the Constitution by giving this authority to the Court. Marshall struck down that part of the Judiciary Act of 1789 as unconstitutional. The power that Marshall assumed in the Court to find acts of Congress unconstitutional, and thus null and void, was immensely important. First, it protected the independence of the Court from Congress. Second, Marshall implied that the Court was the final arbiter of the meaning of the Constitution. This vital pronouncement of judicial supremacy would be elaborated and extended in the coming years to include state legislation and state court judgments. The other branches of the federal government might engage in some sort of constitutional self-scrutiny when they acted, asking themselves if they had exceeded their power, but the final voice in contested cases must be the Supreme Court's. Finally, Marshall reminded everyone that the Constitution was the supreme law, and that every act of Congress had to be measured against it. All three of these conclusions looked to a future in which the Court would be a fully equal third branch of the federal government. To be sure, the Court had no intention of involving itself in the everyday details of the other branches' operation, for example, how the secretary of state ran his office, and giving the Supreme Court the power to do this through writs of mandamus would violate basic tenets of separation of powers.[10]

None of this was explicit in the text of Article III. Marshall reread that text, returning to it after examining a future in which the Court's original jurisdiction was left to Congress. He did not suggest that he was revising Article III to include judicial review in it, but that is what he did.

Marshall knew that his opinion would be viewed as a slap at Jefferson. Jefferson certainly felt it to be. But Marshall had covered this base as well. In what seemed at the time almost an aside, he wrote that "questions in their nature political" would be rejected by his court "without hesitation." He then qualified that blanket denial of jurisdiction by adding, "but where" an official of an elected branch of government acted outside of the law, or did not perform an act that the law commanded, it was the duty of the courts to intervene. To fail to do so would ignore the legal rights of a complainant. Marshall's dictum would in the fullness of time become both the basis for the abstention of the Court from political questions and the intervention of the Court in matters of voting law and redistricting. It was a near-perfect example of reading existing law forward to anticipate and deal with new problems, and then returning to text to fix its meaning. He wrote as if the very structure of the Constitution forced his hand—he had to deny any political questions, because he knew that these would recur.[11]

The second case in which Marshall read law forward to define the boundaries of separation of powers found him at the circuit court meeting in Richmond, Virginia, in the spring of 1807. In February 1807 Aaron Burr had been arrested in Mississippi by order of the Territorial Governor General James Wilkinson, and without a grand jury indictment or the chance to defend himself was hustled back to Richmond. To the circuit court there what amounted to a federal posse comitatus had brought Aaron Burr, and there he was charged by Jefferson's handpicked team of prosecutors with treason. Earlier in Burr's travels through the West, similar charges were brought and he was not indicted on them. But Jefferson was convinced that his former vice president had intended to sever the trans-Appalachian West from the rest of the nation, and had already told Congress that Burr was guilty.[12]

John Marshall presided on circuit with district court judge Cyrus Griffin. In the course of the trial, Burr, a fine attorney himself, assisted by Maryland's Luther Martin, the state's former Federalist attorney general, turned the tables on Jefferson, and left Marshall in a quandary: Could he issue a subpoena on Jefferson commanding the production of Wilkinson's letters about the alleged Burr conspiracy along with Jefferson's replies? If Wilkinson's correspondence with Jefferson might be material in Burr's defense, could Marshall deny the motion? For four days, counsel for both sides argued the permissibility of Burr's motion.

Finally, on June 13, 1807, Marshall ruled on the request for the papers. "When this subject was suddenly introduced, the court felt some doubt concerning the propriety of directing a subpoena to the chief magistrate, and some doubt also concerning the propriety of directing any paper in his possession, not public in its nature, to be exhibited in court." After all, there was no precedent for it under the federal Constitution. But as in *Marbury* Marshall claimed that his hands were tied. "The practice in this country has been, to permit any individual, who was charged with any crime, to prepare for his defense, and to obtain the process of the court, for the purpose of enabling him so to do." Was the president subject to such process? No man was above the law, Marshall determined, and the "Constitution and laws of the United States" made plain the president's duty to the court. Actually, it was Marshall reading the Federal Crimes Act of 1790 defining treason forward that permitted this rule, creating an exception to strict separation of powers when read back into the Constitution.

According to Marshall, neither Congress nor the president could rescind the rights so precisely laid out in the Federal Crimes Act of 1790, to which Marshall added the Sixth Amendment: "'every such person or persons accused or indicted of the crimes aforesaid [including treason], shall be allowed and admitted in his said defense to make any proof that he or they can produce by lawful witness or witnesses, and shall have the like process of the court where he or they shall be tried, to compel his or their witnesses to appear at his or their trial as is usually granted to compel witnesses to appear on the prosecution against them.'" The 1790 act placed both sides at trial "on equal ground." Marshall continued: "A subpoena duces tecum, then, may issue to any person to whom an ordinary subpoena may issue, directing him to bring any paper of which the party praying it has a right to avail himself as testimony." Marshall promised that all such evidence from the president would be handled with the care and decorum that Jefferson's high station required, but he must comply with the subpoena.[13]

Marshall was firm but not unaware of the delicate nature of this subpoena. "Much has been said about the disrespect to the chief magistrate, which is implied by this motion ... These observations will be very truly answered by the declaration that this court feels many, perhaps, peculiar motives for manifesting as guarded a respect for the chief magistrate of the Union as is compatible with its official duties." Jefferson's reply was frostily formal, but he bowed to the court's order. "In answering your [i.e., Marshall's] letter . . . I informed you . . . that I had delivered [Wilkinson's letter], with all other papers respecting the charges against Aaron Burr, to the attorney general [of the United States, Caesar Rodney] when he went to Richmond." Jefferson assumed that Rodney would share them with the court, but Rodney was no longer in Richmond, and Jefferson promised to write Rodney "to forward that particular letter without delay." Jefferson instructed the heads of his departments to send to Richmond "two letters from the secretary at war, which appeared to be within the description expressed in your letter." Both men knew that the subject would reappear, and it did. The law must be read forward to create the appropriate precedent, which then would govern future cases under the Sixth Amendment.[14]

In *Fletcher v. Peck* (1810) the Marshall Court explored how the Contracts (Obligations) Clause might settle the issue of private versus public grants. The clause, part of Article I, section 10, read, "no state shall . . . pass . . . any law impairing the obligation of contracts." The case was collusive, Peck being a holder of western (Yazoo) lands sold by Georgia, whose legislature later rescinded the sales for fraud. The sale created a vested right; the retraction was based on public interest. After he could not get Georgia to repay what he had paid for a parcel, Peck turned to a lawsuit in federal court. In order to sue in federal court under the diversity provisions of the Judiciary Act, he needed the other party to the suit to be a resident of a different state. (A second requirement was monetary, but the land was worth more than the $500 minimum.) He found Robert Fletcher, a New Hampshire real estate developer. Peck conveyed to Fletcher lands in the Yazoo sale for the price of $3,000. Filed in 1803 in the circuit court of Massachusetts, the suit was decided in 1807 in favor of Fletcher. In 1809, Peck appealed to the US Supreme Court.[15]

The first time the case came to the Supreme Court, John Quincy Adams, recently resigned from the US Senate, argued for Peck that the grant was a "contract executed" when the sale was made, and subsequent acts by the legislature could not extinguish Peck's title. Persuaded by Luther Martin, counsel for Fletcher, that there was a technical defect in the pleading, Chief Justice Marshall sent the case back to the circuit court, instructing it to consider that argument. Perhaps the justices were bothered by the manifest collusion of the parties, or perhaps they were stalling, hoping that Congress would step in and indemnify the Yazoo lands' purchasers. Congress had debated that proposition already. When the case returned to the Supreme Court on Fletcher's appeal, the argument made for the defendant in error (Peck), by his counsel, Joseph Story, was that "the legislature was forbidden by the constitution of the United States to pass any law impairing the obligation of contract. A grant is a contract executed, and it creates also an implied executory contract, which is, that the grantee shall continue to enjoy the thing granted according to the terms of the grant."

Chief Justice Marshall, writing for the Court, agreed with Story. Georgia could rescind the land sales. But the state constitution was not the only fundamental law in question. The federal Constitution also bore on the question of the constitutionality of rescinding the land sales. Land sale disputes would be a future of federal lawsuits for years to come. Marshall had to read the Contracts Clause of the Constitution forward to resolve the issue. "The question, whether a law be void for its repugnancy to the constitution, is, at all times, a question of much delicacy, which ought seldom, if ever, to be decided in the affirmative, in a doubtful case." This was pure Marshall—first, show the gravity of the case and its difficulty. The Court did not jump to conclusions, particularly in such momentous cases. Next, assert the paramount role of the Court in deciding cases: "The court, when impelled by duty to render such a judgment, would be unworthy of its station, could it be unmindful of the solemn obligations which that station imposes." Then thrust the facts into the opinion: "But it is not on slight implication and vague conjecture that the legislature is to be pronounced to have transcended its powers, and its acts to be considered as void." Finally, he explained that the Court had reached the conclusion that "the opposition between the constitution and the [state] law should be such that the judge feels a clear and strong conviction of their incompatibility with each other." Hidden in the corner of this litany was the prospect that such state laws conflicting with constitutional provisions would recur.[16]

Georgia could annul its own legislation. But here there was a third party, for Peck had purchased the land from an original grantee without knowledge of the fraud in the original grant. Fraud would set aside a land conveyance, "but the rights of third persons, who are purchasers without notice, for a valuable consideration, cannot be disregarded." This was an old common law prescription, but nothing in the Constitution incorporated or "received" the common law. Marshall simply read it into the Contracts Clause. Even though it was an old prescription, here, as a matter of constitutional law, it was given renewed life. As a matter of policy as well as of law, "Titles, which, according to every legal test, are perfect, are acquired with that confidence which is inspired by the opinion that the purchaser is safe. If there be any concealed defect, arising from the conduct of those who had held the property long before he acquired it, of which he had no notice, that concealed defect cannot be set up against him." Let the seller beware; the buyer is not at fault. "He has paid his money for a title good at law, he is innocent, whatever may be the guilt of others, and equity will not subject him to the penalties attached to that guilt." All titles would be insecure, and "the intercourse between man and man would be very seriously obstructed, if this principle be overturned." Recognizing the future impact of allowing this to happen, Marshall foresaw the danger, and interpreted the law to forestall that danger.[17]

The state was not just any party to a contract, of course, but the state of Georgia was part of the federal union and so bound by the federal Constitution. "The validity of this rescinding act, then, might well be doubted, were Georgia a single sovereign power"—that is, if one regarded the Constitution as merely a compact among fully sovereign states. "But Georgia cannot be viewed as a single, unconnected, sovereign power, on whose legislature no other restrictions are imposed than may be found in its own constitution." More than Marshall's nationalism was on display here. For him, and for the unanimous Supreme Court, Georgia "is a part of a large empire; she is a member of the American union; and that union has a constitution the supremacy of which all acknowledge, and which imposes limits to the legislatures of the several states, which none claim a right to pass." It had not escaped his attention that when Georgia was called to account for its failure to pay a revolutionary war debt, in *Chisholm v. Georgia* (1793), the state did not even bother to send counsel to take part in the case. The strong, repetitive language of his opinion was as close to scolding as he would ever come. "The constitution of the United States declares that no state shall pass any bill of attainder, ex post facto law, or law impairing the obligation of contracts." The covenant (contract) had been breached by the state of Georgia, in violation of the Constitution.[18]

At stake in *McCulloch v. Maryland* (1819) was the jurisdiction of federal courts when state statutes appeared to violate provisions of an act of Congress. The case raised the federalism issue directly. By rooting the jurisdiction of the federal courts in the Constitution and reminding the states that the Constitution was the supreme law of the land, Marshall not only protected a congressional act from a state's interference, he reasserted the privileged role of the federal courts in interpreting the relationship between his court and state statutes.

In 1819 the United States was mired in one of its worst economic panics. Land speculation had overheated the economy, and banks all over were failing. The Second Bank of the United States, chartered in 1816 after the federal government's financial troubles during the War of 1812, was supposed to prevent such collapses before they occurred, but the overseers of the bank were themselves speculators, and many of the bank's practices were both inefficient and corrupt. A number of states, including Maryland, passed laws regulating the bank branches in the state. James McCulloch was the cashier of the Maryland branch of the Bank of the United States and he was fined for trying to do its business without paying the licensing fee of $15,000 to the state. When his conviction was upheld by the state supreme court, he appealed to the US Supreme Court.[19]

There was an ominous hint of something more than states' rights in the arguments that Maryland's counsel made. Joseph Hopkinson and Walter Jones, appearing for the state, proposed that the Constitution was "a compact between the States, and all the powers which are not expressly relinquished by it, are reserved to the States." While one might conclude that Hopkinson and Jones were simply repeating

James Madison's Virginia Resolutions' incautious reference to a "compact" theory of the Constitution, in the chamber above the Supreme Court's courtroom, members of Congress were furiously debating whether Missouri could come into the Union as a slave state. Neither of the Maryland lawyers mentioned slavery, but everyone in the courtroom was aware that Maryland was a slave state, and its congressional delegation supported the admission of Missouri. If antislavery forces prevented the admission of Missouri, could the compact theory be redeployed as the basis for severing the Union? The case had already generated "great excitement" and Marshall's decision for the Court would become a landmark defense of constitutional nationalism.[20]

The decision of the Court was unanimous. Writing for the Court, Marshall rejected the compact theory of the Constitution. It looked back to the time when the states' sovereignty was all but untrammeled. Instead, he looked forward. There he found that the Constitution was a new form for government that reflected the will of an entire people. It followed that the federal government spoke for that people, not for the concurrent will of the independent states. The federal government could not be bound by the narrowest confines of strict construction of the Constitution because it could not then respond to exigency or take advantage of opportunity. The Bank of the United States was constitutional; it enabled the federal government to tax, to borrow, and to carry out other economic policies; it fit the very definition of "necessary and proper." Insofar as "the power to tax involves the power to destroy," and the state licensing fee would "annihilate" the Bank, Marshall had no choice but to strike down the Maryland law. Not to do so would be to subject the whole of the Constitution to the whims of state legislatures—a very likely future. The power to strike down a state statute expanded the jurisdiction of the federal courts to the full extent prescribed in the Constitution's Supremacy Clause, attaching it to Article III, section 2's opening words—"The judicial power shall extend to all cases, in law and equity, arising under this Constitution." Marshall read the law forward to see the necessity of the bank, and from that vision, gave full effect to the Necessary and Proper Clause.[21]

In a reaction to the Court's pronouncement, defenders of strong states' rights sought to revise the Judiciary Act of 1789. Led by jurists like Virginia Court of Appeals Judge Spencer Roane, they found the line of decisions beginning with *McCulloch* and continuing with *Cohens v. Virginia* (1821) "disastrous in its consequences," as violating the "boundaries between the powers of two sovereign and independent governments." Advocates of revising section 25 of the Judiciary Act of 1789, which gave the Court jurisdiction over appeals from the state supreme courts, made their case in Congress from 1820 to 1831, when the House of Representatives voted down the last of the proposals, 138 to 51. Nevertheless, the gap between Marshall's vision of the role of the federal courts in the federal system and his critics' views would not be easily bridged. The effect of the criticism of his opinions, however, was to make Marshall appear to be an advocate of a central government so strong it would engulf state sovereignty. That was never Marshall's intent. Instead, he deployed future prognostications piecemeal, as required to protect the federal vision of national governance.[22]

In two cases with a common nexus of fact and law, one from Ohio, *Osborn v. Bank of the United States*, and the other from Georgia, *Bank of the United States v. Planters Bank of Georgia*, the Supreme Court had to decide the reach of the "arising under" clause of Article III and its decision was as important to federalism questions as *McCulloch*. In 1819 the Ohio legislature authorized Ralph Osborn, the state treasurer, to collect a tax on the state branch of the Second Bank of the United States. The tax would relieve the state banks of some of their own indebtedness to the tune of some one hundred thousand dollars. In effect it was a state-mandated transfer of funds from a federal bank to the local banks. The Bank asked the circuit court to enjoin the collection of the tax. The circuit court for the district of Ohio, in 1819, refused the request. The Bank then sued for recovery of the taxes from the state in the circuit court, and it found in favor of the Bank. The state appealed to the Supreme Court. In the Georgia case, the Bank went after a local bank owing it money. In both cases, defendants pleaded that the federal courts in which the suits were brought lacked jurisdiction to hear the cases, despite the fact that the enabling act creating the Bank allowed such suits in federal court.

Marshall went directly to the jurisdictional questions. The statute rechartering the Bank of the United States allowed suits against it in state as well as federal courts. "These words seem to the Court to admit of but one interpretation." To be sued meant the capacity to bring a suit. The decision of the circuit court should have prevented collection of the tax. The more important point was that the jurisdiction of the circuit court was not that conferred by the act creating the Bank. It was the jurisdiction conferred by the Constitution itself. "The 3d article . . . declares 'that the judicial power shall extend to all cases in law and equity arising under this constitution, the laws of the United States, and treaties made, or which shall be made, under their authority.' This clause enables the judicial department to receive jurisdiction to the full extent of the constitution, laws, and treaties of the United States." The Constitution conferred the jurisdiction on the circuit court whenever a federal law was at issue. If the Bank could sue officers of Ohio in federal court, it could sue the officers of a bank chartered by the state of Georgia. In these cases, once again, Marshall read the law forward into an area not specifically covered by the Necessary and Proper Clause, then returned to the clause to affirm an expansive interpretation.[23]

Another occasion for Marshall to read constitutional text forward—this time the Commerce Clause—came in 1824, with *Gibbons v. Ogden*, "the great steamboat case." The Hudson River had been a major commercial thoroughfare from the time that the Dutch West Indian Company contracted with Henry Hudson to navigate the river. With the construction of the Erie Canal, the Hudson became the gateway to the Great Lakes (via the Lake Ontario–Lake Erie connection) and thus to the Midwest. None of this was lost on entrepreneurs in New York City, the entrepôt of imports and exports. The use of the Hudson was made even more valuable by Robert Fulton's perfection of the steamboat, although the idea was older, with various experimental versions of the craft predating Fulton's boat by decades. Fulton died in 1815 before realizing the value of his efforts, but his patents were defended by Aaron Ogden, governor of New Jersey and himself a partner in the Fulton company. If potential shippers could gain control of the Hudson, in effect monopolizing the route, they could expect a windfall in profits with the new form of transportation. This is exactly what John R. Livingston, whose family had been a major power in New York politics since the early eighteenth century, brought to the

Fulton-Ogden enterprise. In 1808 the state legislature granted a thirty-year monopoly of steamboat navigation of the Hudson to their North River Company.[24]

Under the Articles of Confederation, states were relatively free to restrict their own businessmen's rivals' river trade. The issue was the formal reason for the Annapolis Conference of 1786, whose leading voices (Hamilton and Madison) in turn called for a constitutional convention. At the Philadelphia meeting the next year, delegates addressed the problems of proprietary state control of riverways with the Interstate Commerce Clause. As finally framed in Article I, section 8, clause 3, it gave to Congress the authority "to regulate commerce with foreign nations, and among the several states, and with the Indian tribes." Did it also give to Congress an exclusive right to that regulation, or could states continue to regulate river trade wholly within the state? Did Congress have to act for the clause to rise from sleep? The problem was one of meaning of the clause, and Marshall, by reading the law forward, would then return with his answer to set the meaning of the Commerce Clause.[25]

Ogden had secretly entered into an arrangement with a New Jersey rival, Thomas Gibbons. Gibbons, an adventurous investor, had been one of the disappointed grantees of Yazoo lands—and found steamboat trade appetizing. He was highly litigious, fiercely competitive, and well schooled in law. Together, the two men persuaded the New Jersey legislature to pass a law fining foreign businesses (for which read the Fulton-Livingston steamboat company) plying New Jersey waters. Failure to pay the fines meant forfeiture of the vessels. After a personal squabble, Gibbons, dissatisfied with his deal with Ogden, formed his own steamboat company in 1816 and sought legal aid to undo the New York state monopoly. Ogden, similarly, tried to convince New Jersey to drop its retaliatory legislation.[26]

In the meantime, the Fulton-Livingston company was fighting rivals within the state, and in 1812 it sought an injunction, a court order against all rivals navigating the Hudson, from the court of chancery (an injunction being one equitable remedy the court offered). Chancellor John Lansing declined to issue it. The waters, like the air, he thought belonged to everyone. Petitioners appealed to the Court of

Impeachments and Errors, which issued the injunction. The three judges of that court agreed that the New York law was constitutional, and that an injunction rather than a trial at law was the proper way to protect property rights from diminution. One of the judges, James Kent, who could rightly be classed with Marshall as a jurist, added that Congress had not yet passed any law regulating the use of waterways, and until it did, the Commerce Clause of Article I did not apply.[27]

Gibbons's attempt to undo the injunction made no headway against such a combination of political muscle and juridical logic. His appeal in 1820 to the New York high court only succeeded giving subsequent federal litigation the name by which it was known: in the court's terse opinion, basically repeating what Kent had opined, the case became *Gibbons v. Ogden*. The important point is that in the 1810s, before slavery became the fulcrum of states' rights thinking, chief justices and courts in the North were recurring to states' rights to protect the commercial regulations of their jurisdictions.[28]

With Gibbons unable to break the injunction in New York courts, he turned to federal court and the redoubtable Daniel Webster. When it was finally heard, at the winter 1824 session, Webster was joined by William Wirt, and New York's case, as well as Ogden's, was presented by Thomas Oakley, formerly New York's attorney general, and Thomas A. Emmet, whose brother Robert had been attorney general of New York ten years earlier. But the real opponent in Webster's mind was Kent himself.[29]

In the meantime, an economic war of each against all raged. New York refused to let anyone navigate any of the waters within the state without a license from the state. The violator would lose his vessel. Connecticut had the same law regarding steamships. New Jersey imposed a reciprocal law—if anyone lost a ship under the New York law, he could bring an action for triple damages, in New Jersey, against "the party who thus restrains or impedes him under the law of New-York." Presumably that meant New York magistrates hailed into New Jersey courts because they enforced a New York law in New York. What a tangle, and with no resolution in sight so long as states' wounded sovereignty commanded the issue. What was more, without a clear resolution this kind of interstate commercial combat would become common.[30]

The war of each against all that seventeenth-century English political philosopher Thomas Hobbes had seen in the wilds of the New World, and the framers of the Constitution had seen in the confederation period, would return. States would again impose burdens on one another, and national trade would suffer. Counsel for Ogden might argue that "the States may legislate, it is said, wherever Congress has not made a plenary exercise of its power, But who is to judge whether Congress has made this plenary exercise of power?" For Congress's regulatory power to work, it must be exclusive. "All useful regulation does not consist in restraint; and that which Congress sees fit to leave free, is a part of its regulation, as much as the rest." Noncommercial state regulations, for example, health and welfare, were—as before— left to the states unless Congress intervened. Even then, for example, in the construction of roads, there could be concurrent activity.[31]

Marshall listened closely, according to contemporary accounts, as Webster made the argument for the federal license under the Commerce Clause. The laws of New York "were void, still, as against any right enjoyed under the laws of the United States, with which they came in collision; and that, in this case, they were found interfering with such rights." The Coasting Act rested on the Interstate Commerce Clause. "The power of Congress to regulate commerce, was complete and entire, and, to a certain extent, necessarily exclusive." *Exclusive* sounded absolute, but the "to a certain extent" was a hedge that would reappear in Marshall's opinion for the Court. Webster "did not mean to say that all regulations which might, in their operation, affect commerce, were exclusively in the power of Congress; but that such power as had been exercised in this case, did not remain with the States." Navigation of waterways that ran between states was within the exclusive federal commerce power.[32]

Marshall's opinion for the appellants agreed that the Interstate Commerce Clause was more important than the patents issue. He recognized as well the need to read the clause forward, see how it could resolve the question, and then return to the text with the broadest possible rereading. First came the boilerplate acknowledgment of how well the case was argued and its importance:

> No tribunal can approach the decision of this question without feeling a just and real respect for that opinion which is sustained by such authority [i.e., a bow to Chancellor Kent's opinion and his reputation], but it is the province of this Court, while it respects, not to bow to it implicitly, and the Judges must exercise, in the examination of the subject, that understanding which Providence has bestowed upon them, with that independence which the people of the United States expect from this department of the government.[33]

Next came recognition and recapitulation of Webster's history lesson, Marshall agreeing with every point. "This instrument contains an enumeration of powers expressly granted by the people to their government. It has been said that these powers ought to be construed strictly. But why ought they to be so construed? Is there one sentence in the Constitution which gives countenance to this rule?" So much for the Republican's canon of strict construction of the Constitution, a stance that Marshall had dismissed in many prior opinions, but this time, instead of simply discarding strict construction, Marshall jumped up and down on the corpse.

> We do not, therefore, think ourselves justified in adopting it. What do gentlemen mean by a "strict construction?" If they contend only against that enlarged construction, which would extend words beyond their natural and obvious import, we might question the application of the term, but should not controvert the principle. If they contend for that narrow construction which, in support of some theory not to be found in the Constitution, would deny to the government those powers which the words of the grant, as usually understood, import, and which are consistent with the general views and objects of the instrument; for that narrow construction which would cripple the government and render it unequal to the object for which it is declared to be instituted, and to which the powers given, as fairly understood, render it competent; then we cannot perceive the propriety of this strict construction, nor adopt it as the rule by which the Constitution is to be expounded.

The opposite of strict construction was loose construction, in which the meaning of the text lay in its best future application, in other words, let the text look ahead.[34]

Marshall then offered a disquisition on the meaning of the word *commerce.* This exploration too had a forward-looking purpose. "The subject to be regulated is commerce, and our Constitution being, as was aptly said at the bar [i.e., by Webster], one of enumeration, and not of definition, to ascertain the extent of the power, it becomes necessary to settle the meaning of the word." New York had contended that commerce meant buying and selling, and nothing more. It did not mean the transportation of goods. "This would restrict a general term, applicable to many objects, to one of its significations." That made no sense to Marshall. Commerce was intercourse of all mercantile kinds, "in all its branches." These included kinds of commerce not yet practiced. After all, the provision in the Constitution included commerce with other nations. How could this be performed without shipping? Overseas trade, so vital to the American economy, could hardly be excluded from commerce even if the Constitution had not included trade with other nations. "The convention must have used the word in that sense, because all have understood it in that sense, and the attempt to restrict it comes too late." In short, the members of the convention were sensing the unforeseen needs of the new federation. "All understood it" is a form of originalism in the service of Marshall's own reading of the text. That is, one understands the meaning of terms in the Constitution by reference to the intent of the framers. Marshall was not at the Constitutional Convention, but he was practicing law in Virginia at the time and he knew all of the Virginia signers and all of the ratification convention members because he was one of the Henrico County delegation to it. (He voted aye.) But he understood that the original intent of the framers included an open-ended invitation to accommodate the future.[35]

Marshall found other parts of the Constitution whose plain sense supported his consequentialist reading of the Commerce Clause. Take, for example, the embargo of 1808, so hated by the merchants of New England. They objected to it on many practical grounds, "Yet they never suspected that navigation was no branch of trade, and was therefore not comprehended in the power to regulate commerce." In other words, they read the plain meaning of the term. "They did, indeed, contest the constitutionality of the act. They denied that the particular law in question was made in pursuance of the Constitution not because the power could not act directly on vessels, but because a perpetual embargo was the annihilation, and not the regulation, of commerce." In other words, the New England Federalists "admitted the applicability of the words used in the Constitution to vessels. No example could more strongly illustrate the universal understanding of the American people on this subject. It was always understood to comprehend navigation within its meaning."[36]

By following the waters, as much as the logic of his own argument, commerce among the several states had become commerce that reached into a single state—including New York's Hudson River. After all, "Can a trading expedition between two adjoining States, commence and terminate outside of each? And if the trading intercourse be between two States remote from each other, must it not commence in one, terminate in the other, and probably pass through a third? Commerce among the States must, of necessity, be commerce with the States." This rested on a reading of future problems—that is, if "commerce" were not read broadly. Marshall saw the constitutional text in its future context.[37]

Congress had passed laws regarding navigation. Did these preclude the New York monopoly the appellees claimed was permitted by the absence of explicit federal law on steamboat traffic? "The power to regulate, that is, to prescribe the rule by which commerce is to be governed like all others vested in Congress, is complete in itself, may be exercised to its utmost extent." Because Congress had not yet done so, however, did this allow for a concurrent exercise of state and federal riverine regulation? Marshall had already established that the congressional regulatory power extended to commerce within the states. Nothing in the sovereignty of the states, which Marshall conceded, diminished Congress's power to regulate river traffic, for concurrent power would automatically diminish the authority of Congress. Webster had argued, and Marshall repeated, "Full power to regulate a particular subject implies the whole power, and leaves no residuum; that a grant of the whole is incompatible with the existence of a right in another to any part of it." What about the concurrent power states had to tax? Was this not analogous to regulation of commerce? How about the right to inspect goods coming into the state? Marshall again turned to recent history to reject these analogies:

> The idea that the same measure might, according to circumstances, be arranged with different classes of power was no novelty to the framers of our Constitution. Those illustrious statesmen and patriots had been, many of them, deeply engaged in the discussions which preceded the war of our revolution, and all of them were well read in those discussions. The right to regulate commerce, even by the imposition of duties, was not controverted.[38]

Historians have noted that the issue of federal intervention in states' regulations was raised during the Missouri Compromise debate. Advocates of slavery feared that Congress would adopt laws for Missouri effectively barring slavery. Marshall weighed in on this question on the side of a robust nationalism. "In making these provisions [for regulation of importation of goods, and prohibition of the importation of slaves] the opinion is unequivocally manifested that Congress may control the State laws so far as it may be necessary to control them for the regulation of commerce." Indeed, the slavery issue lurked in the shadows at every junction of Marshall's opinion, for the slave states treated the internal, interstate slave trade as commerce in persons, rather than things, and hotly resented any federal interference. If the federal government, whether Congress or the High Court, could define an exclusive regulatory power of commerce in the federal government, might not Congress or the Court, in some future time, outlaw the internal slave trade?

> If this inference were correct, if this power was exercised not under any particular clause in the Constitution, but in virtue of a general right over the subject of commerce, to exist as long as the Constitution itself, it might now be exercised. Any State might now import African slaves into its own territory. But it is obvious that the power of the States over this subject, previous to the year 1808, constitutes an exception to the power of Congress to regulate commerce, and the exception is expressed in such words,

as to manifest clearly the intention to continue the preexisting right of the States to admit or exclude, for a limited period."[39]

States exercised some concurrent powers with the federal government, for example, the licensing of pilots, the building of lighthouses, and of course taxation, but none of these could be extended to the regulation of commerce generally. "These acts were cited at the bar for the purpose of showing an opinion in Congress that the States possess, concurrently with the Legislature of the Union, the power to regulate commerce with foreign nations and among the States." Marshall and his brethren rejected the analogy of these state powers to the present case. "Upon reviewing them, we think they do not establish the proposition they were intended to prove. They show the opinion that the States retain powers enabling them to pass the laws to which allusion has been made, not that those laws proceed from the particular power which has been delegated to Congress."[40]

Marshall was not the most brilliant of constitutional thinkers, more a hedgehog than a fox, but like the hedgehog, he knew where he was going. That objective was to protect the past achievements of the framers by finding room for the Constitution in a rapidly evolving American society.

There is one glaring absence in Marshall's looking into the future that bears comment. One would suppose that in the early antebellum period, reading the law forward would have a good deal to say about slave law. After all, slavery was a major topic at the Constitutional Convention, and slavery nearly brought the federal government to its knees during the Missouri statehood debates. Abolitionists were beginning to argue that the Constitution could not be read as a pro-slavery document, as the word *slavery* did not appear in it, but every lawyer knew that the three-fifths compromise, the Rendition Clause, and the decision not to bar importation of "such persons" until 1808 in the Constitution were about slaves. Marshall himself lived and worked in Richmond, Virginia, a major slave-trade marketplace, and he had economic interests in slaves on his nephews' plantations. Marshall said little about slavery, regarding it as a matter for the states, a stance in clear contrast to his views of banks and commerce. His reticence was a common feature of slaveholders of his class, including his great political opponent, Thomas Jefferson.[41]

Marshall's colleague, friend, and supporter on the Court, Joseph Story, also read the law forward when the case seemed to call for it, in the process reinterpreting the relevant law. In this, his primary concern was the increasing prospect of national disunity, ending in the breakup of the Union. He did not own slaves, or engage in the slave trade. How to read the law forward in slavery cases, and then recur to the constitutional text to save the Union from both abolitionists and secessionists, was for him a matter of grave importance.

Joseph Story, 1844–1845. Library of Congress Prints and Photographs
Division. Photo by Mathew Brady's Studio.

2. Joseph Story

Joseph Story was born in Salem, Massachusetts, the cockpit of the American Revolution during its most perilous year. If there was a model New England nationalist in the formative years of the new nation, Story could claim the title, along with John Quincy Adams. A moralist in his personal views, and a republican who believed that the protection of private property and personal liberty was the greatest purpose of all law, Story would become the foremost jurist of the early antebellum period. He attended Harvard College from 1795 until 1799 and then read law with Samuel Sewall, later chief justice of the Supreme Judicial Court of Massachusetts, and then Samuel Putnam, in Salem. He began private practice in 1801, and was elected to Congress as a Jeffersonian Republican in 1808. After one term in Congress, Story ran for and won a seat on the state assembly, and was named its speaker. In 1811, after the seat for the first circuit on the US Supreme Court had remained empty for fourteen months, president James Madison named Story to it, joining Chief Justice John Marshall and his brethren on the bench. Story would serve until his death in 1844.[1]

One would expect from a New England conservative like Story a powerful commitment to the past, and a view of interpreting law that comported with that commitment. That is indeed what one finds, but the project of securing the federal government was not yet complete. Story hesitatingly read the law forward because he could see on the horizon a great danger to the enterprise that Marshall championed: a secure and permanent Union resting on a puissant Constitution. From his earliest days Story believed in that project, but the fate of the nation was uncertain in his time. Two wars with Britain, endless conflict on the edges of the nation, and tenuous diplomatic relations with neighbors and distant powers made the future of the United States perilous. Law could help secure that future, but like Hamilton and Marshall, Story believed that the law must recognize and be prepared to deal with the unforeseen and the unpredictable. His Constitution was thus a supple and powerful tool rather than a fixed and rigid set of rules. Like all law, it changed over time, and should. As he told the bar of Suffolk County, Massachusetts, in 1821, "We can here trace a regular progress from age to age in the laws, a gradual adaptation of them to the increasing wants and employments of society, and a substantial improvement, corresponding with their advancement in the refinements and elegancies of life."[2]

In 1831, he wrote a brief autobiographical memoir for his son, William Wetmore Story, that related the story of his life. His father was "a sturdy Whig" and a thoroughgoing revolutionary of the Samuel Adams type. Story admired the modest but firmly republican manners of his father, his "plain practical sense," and his control of his emotions. Judge Story was religious, but not bigoted. Instead, his views were liberal and tolerant. His own belief in religious freedom came from that source.[3]

Unlike many boys of his generation and background, Story had little interest in military affairs and showed no martial ardor. What he had instead, his passion, was a love of books, learning, and reading. He carried this through his entire life, and into his legal practice.[4]

The "memoir" demonstrated a genuine diffidence, part modesty, part conservativism in Story's view of his own abilities. As he told the families of other members of the Harvard faculty in 1830,

> If [such a lecturer as he] should indulge in such a vain and dreamy self-complacency, he would painfully learn, that other minds had already anticipated almost all his peculiarities of opinion and comment; that antiquity had exhausted them in its captivating literature, never yet excelled, and perhaps never to be excelled; or that modern science, by its exact experiments, had put to flight whatever of theory might float round his own physical researches.

He simply did not regard himself as a pioneer in legal or political thought. For it was "a profession whose lessons enlighten and enlarge" the mind and the spirit. The "science of the law claims me as a fixed devotee, it rules me." But he had little praise for the "dark and mysterious elements" of older law, and the "repulsive and almost unintelligible forms of processes and pleadings."[5]

Story was one of the few republican lawyers in a forest of Federalists in the first decade of his practice. But by his own efforts, learning, and diligence, he soon rose to the very top of the bar in Massachusetts. Madison appointed him to the High Court in 1811 (over Thomas Jefferson's objections) in part because the president thought that Story's learning and political leanings would act as something of a brake on Marshall's dominance of the tribunal and because Madison appreciated the scholarly bent in Story's background. Thus, Story's first assays in reading the law forward followed Marshall's example. Story understood that reading the law forward belonged primarily to Congress. As he wrote in *The Brig Alexander* (1813), "I admit that Congress can only declare what the law shall be for the future," and it was not the task of the courts or the judge to "strain language in support" of novel interpretations of law. But sometimes it was necessary—that is, it was compelled by the language of existing law—to provide for future exigencies.[6]

One sees this hesitancy in the first of Story's many immensely detailed opinions, *Martin v. Hunter's Lessee* (1816). There is some question whether the chief justice, having a personal interest in the case and thus recusing himself, had more than a little to do with the opinion. The issue was a familiar one to him, in any case. The Court of Appeals of the State of Virginia refused to execute a writ from the US Supreme Court, claiming, "The court is unanimously of opinion that the appellate power of the supreme court of the United States does not extend to this court under a sound construction of the constitution of the United States; that so much of the 25th section of the act of congress, to establish the judicial courts of the United States, as extends the appellate jurisdiction of the supreme court to this court, is not in pursuance of the constitution of the United States." Allowed to stand, the result would have been a body blow to the appellate power of the High Court, and to the Supremacy Clause and Article III, under which Congress had passed the Judiciary Act of 1789. Note how Story seemed to be resting his argument on the intent of the framers, but in fact it rested on the future sovereignty of the national courts. Although a conservative, Story's argument was not—nor could it be. He had to look ahead to the danger lurking in the concession to Virginia—the Union could fall apart piece by legal piece.[7]

Story spoke for the Court: "The questions involved in this judgment are of great importance and delicacy. Perhaps it is not too much to affirm, that, upon their right decision, rest some of the most solid principles which have hitherto been supposed to sustain and protect the constitution itself." The "delicacy" was a call out to Marshall, whose conventional usage it was. Then came a reminder, embedded in the federalist history of the constitution. Although 1816 was less than two generations removed from the framing, Story's account was as much hagiography as biography. "The constitution of the United States was ordained and established, not by the states in their sovereign capacities, but emphatically, as the preamble of the constitution declares, by 'the people of the United States.'" In fact, as Story no doubt knew, the replacement of the original preface "we the states . . . " with "we the people of the United States" was the work not of the convention, but of Gouverneur Morris on the Committee of Style and Arrangement at the tail end of the meeting. It was something of a coup by the nationalists. Still, "there can be no doubt that it was competent to the people to invest the general government with all the powers which they might deem proper and necessary; to extend or restrain these powers according to their own good pleasure, and to give them a paramount and supreme authority."[8]

This was pure Marshall. From it flowed "that the people had a right to prohibit to the states the exercise of any powers which were, in their judgment, incompatible with the objects of the general compact; to make the powers of the state governments, in given cases, subordinate to those of the nation, or to reserve to themselves those sovereign authorities which they might not choose to delegate to either." Now came a hint of reading law forward: "These deductions do not rest upon general reasoning, plain and obvious as they seem to be. They have been positively recognized by one of the articles in amendment of the constitution, which declares, that 'the powers not delegated to the United States by the constitution, nor prohibited by it to the states, are reserved to the states respectively, or to the people.'"[9]

Although Story conceded that the Tenth Amendment limited the powers of the federal government, he continued, "On the other hand, this instrument, like every other grant, is to have a reasonable construction, according to the import of its terms; and where a power is expressly given in general terms, it is not to be restrained to particular cases, unless that construction grow out of the context expressly, or by necessary implication. The words are to be taken in their natural and obvious sense, and not in a sense unreasonably restricted or enlarged"—a warning and simultaneously an invitation to Madison's future "liquidation" of constricted texts. As Marshall himself repeatedly intoned,

> The constitution unavoidably deals in general language. It did not suit the purposes of the people, in framing this great charter of our liberties, to provide for minute specifications of its powers, or to declare the means by which those powers should be carried into execution . . . the instrument was not intended to provide merely for the exigencies of a few years, but was to endure through a long lapse of ages, the events of which were locked up in the inscrutable purposes of Providence.

Likening the Constitution to an instrument was not only a metaphor—it was a formula for reading the document's text.[10]

Over this course of years, "It could not be foreseen what new changes and modifications of power might be indispensable to effectuate the general objects of the charter; and restrictions and specifications, which, at the present, might seem salutary, might, in the end, prove the overthrow of the system itself." Who were the legitimate modifiers of these plans? The Congress. And that meant that the Court could read the Judiciary Act of 1789, although it was founded on Article III, beyond its text to do what the act's text allowed Congress to do: not only to establish lower federal courts, but to enable appeal from the state courts to the US Supreme Court. This was an example of reading the law forward, "leaving to the legislature, from time to time, to adopt its own means to effectuate legitimate objects, and to mould and model the exercise of its powers, as its own wisdom, and the public interests, should require."[11]

Now it was the Court's turn to read the law forward. Missing from Story's, as from Marshall's, formulation was the agency of the lawgiver. They knew that the law evolved, but the cause of the evolution they believed necessity or exigency itself, not the active judges or lawyer. This was more than a little misleading, because Story knew that the judge played an active rather than a passive role in reading law. But the assumption then, as for many years previously, was that the judges did not make law, they found it. Story did not reveal that the guiding hand belonged to the judge. Instead, the interpretation of the law was almost automatic, guided not by the desire of the judge to read the law, but by the principles inherent in the law itself. He concluded, "With these principles in view, principles in respect to which no difference of opinion ought to be indulged, let us now proceed to the interpretation of the constitution, so far as regards the great points in controversy."[12]

The two texts in question were Article III of the Constitution and the Judiciary Act of 1789, undertaken by Congress in its first session. "Such is the language of the article creating and defining the judicial power of the United States. It is the voice of the whole American people solemnly declared, in establishing one great department of that government which was, in many respects, national, and in all, supreme." None of this mattered, of course, if the 25th article of the Judiciary Act was not part of the appellate jurisdiction given the court, or was not part of the power given Congress to elaborate Article III. Story elided these questions. The Article acted "upon states . . . to deprive them altogether of the exercise of some powers of sovereignty, and to restrain and regulate them in the exercise of others." What was more, "The language of the article throughout is manifestly designed to be mandatory upon the legislature. Its obligatory force is so imperative, that congress could not, without a violation of its duty, have refused to carry it into operation." Of course, the article did not mandate a judiciary act. That was the decision of the lawgivers in Congress. That is, seeing the need for a lower federal judiciary, they read their powers under the Article to create that judiciary. Then they added to the act the authority of the Supreme Court to hear appeals from the state supreme courts. There was nothing in the Article's text requiring this—"The judicial power of the United States shall be vested (not may be vested) in one supreme court, and in such inferior courts as congress may, from time to time, ordain and establish"—but Story read the Article's text forward: "Could congress have lawfully refused to create a supreme court, or to vest in it the constitutional jurisdiction?" Well, it could have, or it could have declined the invitation. The forced nature of Story's reading law forward was here on full display. Congress could not decline the invitation, and Story could not fault them for accepting it. His hand, like theirs, was forced by the language of Article III, or so he wrote.[13]

The precatory mode "shall extend" was the platform on which Story built his claim. "We are of opinion that the words are used in an imperative sense. They import an absolute grant of judicial power." History itself dictated that Article III be read forward. "They cannot have a relative signification applicable to powers already granted; for the American people had not made any previous grant. The constitution was for a new government, organized with new substantive powers, and not a mere supplementary charter to a government already existing."[14]

Thus far, Story's reading of law mirrored Marshall's—one had to read the Constitution and congressional legislation expanding it forward because there was no backward. Here the crucial term was "extend": "As the mode is not limited, it may extend to all such cases, in any form, in which judicial power may be exercised." While one way to read the reach of the term was reference to the intent of the framers, Story did not rely on that interpretive mode. "It may well have been the intention of the framers of the constitution imperatively to extend the judicial power either in an original or appellate form to all cases; and in the latter class to leave it to congress to qualify the jurisdiction, original or appellate, in such manner as public policy might dictate." But "may" was not enough. What mattered was future exigency. "It would, therefore, be perilous to restrain it in any manner whatsoever, inasmuch as it might hazard the national safety." Any other course would jeopardize national sovereignty.[15]

The application of general grants of power, that is, the movement from the constitutional text to the congressional act could not be limited by the former. "The judicial power is delegated by the constitution in the most general terms, and may, therefore, be exercised by congress under every variety of form, of appellate or original jurisdiction. And as there is nothing in the constitution which restrains or limits this power, it must, therefore, in all other cases, subsist in the utmost latitude of which, in its own nature, it is susceptible." It was that absence of limitation, made necessary by an unpredictable future, that required interpretation of the original grant. "To extend to all cases" meant just that, including future cases. This included cases in the state courts, or cases brought into the state courts by suitors in federal court.[16]

Where did Story's reading law forward lead him? In other words, how important was it to his view of the Constitution? One clue lay in the way that Story faced the states' rights argument. "It has been argued that such an appellate jurisdiction over state courts is inconsistent with the genius of our governments, and the spirit of the constitution." Against this, Story's face was unyielding. "We cannot yield to the force of this reasoning; it assumes principles which we cannot admit, and draws conclusions to which we do not yield our assent." The Constitution was replete with clauses that limited and intruded into the power of states. "It is crowded with provisions which restrain or annul the sovereignty of the states in some of the highest branches of their prerogatives." One of these was the power of the Supreme Court to hear appeals from state courts, and another of these powers was the requirement that state courts obey federal writs. "The language of the constitution is also imperative upon the states as to the performance of many duties. . . . And in these, as well as some other cases, congress have a right to revise, amend, or supersede the laws which may be passed by state legislatures."[17]

Story concluded that "it is certainly difficult to support the argument that the appellate power over the decisions of state courts is contrary to the genius of our institutions." By looking forward to the needs of the nation Story was able to look back to its spirit, in which "The courts of the United States can, without question, revise the proceedings of the executive and legislative authorities of the states, and if they are found to be contrary to the constitution, may declare them to be of no legal validity. Surely the exercise of the same right over judicial tribunals is not a higher or more dangerous act of sovereign power." Did looking forward miss the possibility of the abuse of power? "It is always a doubtful course, to argue against the use or existence of a power, from the possibility of its abuse. It is still more difficult, by such an argument, to ingraft upon a general power a restriction which is not to be found in the terms in which it is given. From the very nature of things, the absolute right of decision, in the last resort, must rest somewhere—wherever it may be vested it is susceptible of abuse."[18]

Once again he hid the active role of judges who read the law forward behind the machinery of government, much like the wizard in *The Wizard of Oz*. "The constitution has presumed (whether rightly or wrongly we do not inquire) that state attachments, state prejudices, state jealousies, and state interests, might sometimes obstruct, or control, or be supposed to obstruct or control, the regular administration of justice." It was the document that lent itself to reading law forward, not Story, he insisted. "It cannot be believed that they could have escaped the enlightened convention which formed the constitution. What, indeed, might then have been only prophecy, has now become fact; and the appellate jurisdiction must continue to be the only adequate remedy for such evils."[19]

From the forward reading of the constitutional text, it was a short step to the reading of the 25th article of the Judiciary Act. "The next question which has been argued, is, whether the case at bar be within the purview of the 25th section of the judiciary act, so that this court may rightfully sustain the present writ of error." Clearly the answer was yes, if, as Story had proven, the Judiciary Act followed from the Constitution, and "a final judgment or decree in any suit in the highest court of law or equity of a state, where is drawn in question the validity of a treaty or statute of, or an authority excised under, the United States, and the decision is against their validity." This was true of the Virginia court refusal to obey an order from the federal circuit court concerning a statute of Congress. "The case, then, falls directly within the terms of the act." Let this one go, and in future no writ issued to a state court under the Judiciary Act would be efficacious. The writ was the proper one, issued in the proper fashion. But unlike Marshall, whose patience wore thin quickly in such challenges, Story was willing to consider a collateral issue. "In this case, however, from motives of a public nature, we are entirely willing to wave all objections, and to go back and re-examine the question of jurisdiction as it stood upon the record formerly in judgment. We have great confidence that our jurisdiction will, on a careful examination, stand confirmed as well upon principle as authority." He then rehearsed the substantive nature of the case. While this recounting of the facts of the original case was not necessary to resolve the issue before the High Court, and courts of appeal were supposed to accept the facts from trial courts below (courts of appeal dealt with legal, not factual, issues) Story indulged it. "The recital of facts contained a regular deduction of the title of Lord Fairfax until his death, in 1781, and also the title of his devisee. It also contained a regular deduction of the title of the plaintiff, under the state of Virginia, and further referred to the treaty of peace of 1783, and to the acts of Virginia respecting the lands of Lord Fairfax." This was a case entirely within the "express purview of the 25th section of the act."[20]

Story had engaged in two sweeping asides, the first on the nature of the jurisdiction of the Court and the second on the facts of the case, neither of which was necessary to get to the issue actually presented— whether the writ was within the purview of the Judiciary Act. But the case was a momentous one—the High Court facing the supreme court of Virginia. Remember this was before *McCulloch*. Story, in his fifth year on the Court, with Marshall standing off to the side, believed that he bore the entire burden of establishing its appellate jurisdiction. Virginia alleged that the appellate jurisdiction was limited. "If this be the true construction of the section, it will be wholly inadequate for the purposes which it professes to have in view, and may be evaded at pleasure. But we see no reason for adopting this narrow construction." After all, it was the construction of the meaning of the Treaty of Paris that was at the heart of the matter.

> If the court below should decide, that the title was bad, and, therefore, not protected by the treaty, must not this court have a power to decide the title to be good, and, therefore, protected by the treaty? Is not the treaty, in both instances, equally construed, and the title of the party, in reference to the treaty, equally ascertained and decided? . . . We are, therefore, satisfied, that, upon principle, the case was rightfully before us, and if the point were perfectly new, we should not hesitate to assert the jurisdiction.

In the end, it was the authority that the Supreme Court had as the final arbiter of its jurisdiction. "We have thus gone over all the principal questions in the cause, and we deliver our judgment with entire confidence, that it is consistent with the constitution and laws of the land."[21]

Although Story was busy teaching, riding circuit to hear and decide cases in New England, and meeting with the Court twice a year, he found time to write a series of commentaries on law. Story was also the first Dane Professor of Law at Harvard Law School from 1829 until his death. Lecturing was the pedagogical tradition at the law school, and Story turned his lectures into a series of commentaries on the substantive law, as well as the first prototype casebook. These commentaries remain important sources for the ideas of the generation after the framers. They included *Commentaries on the Law of Bailments* (1832); *Commentaries on the Constitution of the United States* (3v., 1833), and a short version for the classroom, *Constitutional Class Book* (1834); *Commentaries on the Conflict of Laws* (1834); *Commentaries on Equity Jurisprudence* (2v., 1835–1836); *Equity Pleadings* (1838); *Law of Agency* (1839); *Law of Partnership* (1841, 1846); *Law of Bills of Exchange* (1843, 1847); *Law of Promissory Notes* (1845, 1851); and *A Familiar Exposition of the Constitution of the United States* (1847), the last three posthumously. While most of these resemble the later "hornbook" or law textbook, *Commentaries on the Constitution* was more. They were the continuation of a type of legal writing that went back to William Blackstone's *Commentaries on the Laws of England* and St. George Tucker's *Commentaries on Blackstone*, among others. Commentaries were more than recitals of existing law. They gave the author the chance to comment on that law, including reasons for its weaknesses and suggestions for its improvement.

Commentaries on the Constitution was, like Blackstone's work, multivolumed. Volume 1 was the start of an exhausting and uninviting labor, filled with "dry research," but the major sources were the recent publication of the Federalist essays and Marshall's opinions on the Court. Story denied any originality. "The reader must not expect to find in these pages any novel views, and novel constructions of the Constitution. I have not the ambition to be the author of any new plan of interpreting the theory of the Constitution, or of enlarging or narrowing its powers by ingenious subtleties and learned doubts." But the Union had to be preserved against those who (like John C. Calhoun) had proposed ingenious subtleties like the compact theory of the Constitution, and that required more than just plain text analysis. But even in renouncing that theory, Story offered a theory of reading the text: "A constitution of government is addressed to the common sense of the people; and never was designed for trials of logical skill, or visionary speculation."[22]

If not "visionary speculation," at least some thoughtful musing on the immediate future? The *Commentaries* were not written in a political vacuum. They were composed in the time when South Carolina, objecting to a raise in the tariffs on imported textiles, sought a legal way to prevent the collection of the tariff in its harbors. The answer was nullification, a doctrine derived at least in part from objections Thomas Jefferson and James Madison authored to the Alien and Sedition Acts of 1798. They had proposed that the states had the power to interpose themselves between their citizens and the operation of federal law. Calhoun, in 1828 then vice president, secretly composed a constitutional basis for nullification. This was the compact theory of the Union, and thus of the Constitution. Calhoun likened the Union to a contract among the various states, whose stipulations the states were free to accept or decline. Story did not mention Calhoun, but he did cite Jefferson's views (before Jefferson became president and sidled closer to the Story line) and the views of St. George Tucker to refute them. "They go to the extent of reducing the government to a mere confederacy during pleasure; and of thus presenting the extraordinary spectacle of a nation existing only at the will of each of its constituent parts." In fact, that is pretty much what Calhoun's Exposition and Protest (1828) suggested. To refute this, Story looked back to the intentions of the framers and the evils of the Confederation era, and forward, in which the past was prologue: "Consequences like these, which place the dissolution of the government in the hands of a single state, and enable it at will to defeat, or suspend the operation of the laws of the union, are too serious, not to require us to scrutinize with the utmost care and caution the principles, from which they flow, and by which they are attempted to be justified."[23]

An even more general and sweeping argument for reading law forward closed the first volume:

> Every form of government unavoidably includes a grant of some discretionary powers. It would be wholly imbecile without them. It is impossible to foresee all the exigencies, which may arise in the progress of events,

connected with the rights, duties, and operations of a government. If they could be foreseen, it would be impossible *ab ante* to provide for them. The means must be subject to perpetual modification, and change; they must be adapted to the existing manners, habits, and institutions of society, which are never stationary; to the pressure of dangers, or necessities; to the ends in view; to general and permanent operations, as well as to fugitive and extraordinary emergencies.

In short, existing fundamental law must be read forward, if the document, and the nation on which it was built, were to survive. But then, another waffle, for Story was by inclination and dedication a conservative:

> Temporary delusions, prejudices, excitements, and objects have irresistible influence in mere questions of policy. And the policy of one age may ill suit the wishes, or the policy of another. The constitution is not to be subject to such fluctuations. It is to have a fixed, uniform, permanent construction. It should be, so far at least as human infirmity will allow, not dependent upon the passions or parties of particular times, but the same yesterday, today, and forever.[24]

Over and over, he reserved to the future investigations of wise men how the Constitution might be read to deal with new circumstances. For it was "wisest and safest to leave all future questions . . . to be judged by future conditions and exigencies of the Union." And "Congress ought to be left free to exercise a sound discretion according to future exigencies of the nation." To Congress, then, was to be left the job of reading the Constitution's text forward? But there the wars of the two parties had made such readings of the text into intractable controversies, for example, in the meaning of the Necessary and Proper Clause. Here "the advocates of states' rights and the friends of the Union will meet in hostile array." Who then was to decide the outcome of the combat? The reader of *Martin v. Hunter's Lessee* need not guess.[25]

Slavery was not prominent in *Commentaries on the Constitution*, its volumes meant for lawyers. But *Constitutional Class Book* (1834), designed for upper-level students, a condensation of the three volumes of the *Commentaries*, offered Story a chance to revisit some of his opinions on the subject of slavery for a more impressionable audience. It was an age of unalloyed patriotism, and Story meant "to awaken in the bosoms of American youth a more warm and devoted attachment to the National Union, and a more deep and firm love of the National Constitution." The native peoples had a right to their lands, which the European newcomers did not respect, instead asserting their own, by right of discovery. Like Roger Williams, Story did not buy this explanation. "But their real object was to extend their own power, and increase their own wealth, by acquiring the treasures, as well as the territory of the New World. Avarice and ambition were at the bottom of all their enterprizes." Remember that this was two years after the Court, in an opinion by the chief justice that Story supported, argued that the Cherokee were the lawful possessors of their lands by treaty. That decision notwithstanding to the contrary, Georgia militia, aided by federal troops, began the long dispossession of the Indians. Then Story waffled, conceding the right of discovery, and the subordinate position of the Indian nations in the United States.

After the independence of the colonies was established, the Revolution was followed by a confederation of the new states, but by all it was conceded that "here were many other defects in the Confederation, . . . sufficient to establish its utter unfitness, as a frame of Government for a free, enterprizing, and industrious people." Defense of the Confederation was impossible, as "it became apparent that the Confederation, being left without resources and without powers, must soon expire of its own debility. It had not only lost all vigor, but, it had ceased even to be respected."

None of this was quite true; Story was writing law office history. None more so than his description of the Constitution: "Thus was achieved another, and still more glorious triumph in the cause of liberty, than even that by which we were separated from the parent country. It was not achieved, however, without great difficulties and sacrifices of opinion. It required all the wisdom, the patriotism, and the genius of our best statesmen." Throughout his exposition of the parts of the Constitution, derived from the far longer *Commentaries on the Constitution*, a single theme stood out: "We shall treat it, not as a mere compact, or league, or confederacy, existing at the mere will of any one or more of the States, during their good pleasure; but, (as it purports on its face to be) as a Constitution of Government, framed and adopted by the people of the United States, and obligatory upon all the States, until it is altered, amended, or abolished by the People." Again, recall that secession had already been mentioned during the Missouri Statehood debates. The very view of the Union as a compact, and the Constitution as a mere contract, was the heart of the South Carolina Exposition and Protest of 1828. With ideas that would weaken the Union like nullification already in play, Story had much to fear. The severing of the Union was at all costs to be prevented. But the purposes of the Union were only discussed in generalities. Thus, the blessings of liberty in the Preamble meant only that "Its duties, and its powers, thus naturally combine to make it the common guardian and friend of all; and in return, the States, while they may exercise a salutary vigilance for self-protection, are persuasively taught, that the blessings of liberty, secured by the National Government, are far more certain and extensive, than they would be under their own distinct sovereignties."[26]

Story's view of more controversial subjects was subdued but not hidden. For example, on the restrictions on importation of slaves, "It is to the honor of America, that she should have set the first example of interdicting and abolishing the slave trade in modern times." But the right to own, sell, buy, and otherwise carry on domestic traffic in slaves was not. "But it was indispensable to yield something to the prejudices, wishes, and supposed interests of the South." So too was the three-fifths compromise on representation in the lower house: "It was seen to be unequal in its operation, but was a necessary sacrifice to that spirit of conciliation, on which the Union was founded." So, too, the Rendition Clause, providing for the forced return of runaway slaves from one state to another, "was introduced into the Constitution solely for the benefit of the slave-holding States, to enable them to reclaim their fugitive slaves, who should escape into other States, where slavery is not tolerated. It is well known, that, at the common law, a slave escaping into a State, where slavery is not allowed, would immediately become free, and could not be reclaimed."[27]

Considerations on the future of law in these lessons were clearest in the section on the judiciary. Story had no doubt that "it has always been deemed a function indispensable to the safety and liberty of the people, that courts of justice should have a right to declare void such laws, as violate the Constitution." As contemporary and modern commentators on judicial review agree, there is nothing in the Constitution that guarantees this function to the judiciary. To reason to it, as Story did, from the establishment of a Supreme Court and from the Supremacy Clause was not original (Marshall got there before him), but more than hinted that such a power was necessary to prevent all the evils that had preceded the Constitution. "Unless a Supreme Court were established, there would be no adequate means to ensure uniformity in the interpretation and operations of the Constitution and laws." The judiciary must have this power for "It is obvious, that no human Government can ever be perfect; and it is impossible to foresee, or guard against all the exigencies, which may in different ages require changes in the powers and modes of operation of a Government, to suit the necessities and interests of the people." As the past had proved, "The future is that, which may well awaken the most earnest solicitude, both for the virtue and the permanence of our republic."[28]

Story disliked slavery. It was not just a private opinion. He shared it widely. In an October 1819 grand jury charge in Boston, he told the jurors that "the existence of slavery under any shape is so repugnant to the natural rights of man and the dictates of justice that it seems difficult to find for it any adequate justification." There was a cure, gradual emancipation, but that cure did not lie in the hands of the courts— except in the case of the international slave trade.[29]

The slave trade provisions of the Constitution brought slavery into the federal courts. Although Congress could not entirely ban the trade until 1808, Congress barred American shippers from engaging in overseas slave trading in a series of acts, beginning in 1794 (Americans could not supply slave ships); 1800 (forfeiture of the vessel violating the 1794 act); 1807 (expanding the 1800 act to cover any vessel engaging in the trade in American waters); 1818 (forbidding any participation in the international slave trade by American vessels); 1819 (empowering the president to use the US Navy to interdict vessels violating the 1818 act); and finally 1820 (making violation of the earlier acts the capital offense of piracy). All of these violations of federal law were tried exclusively in federal courts. Some federal judges were friendly to slavery. South Carolina district judge Thomas Bee read the statutes so strictly that defendants got off easily. South Carolina's economy depended on the external and internal slave trade, as well as the labor of slaves. As Bee wrote in *U.S. v. Kitty* (1808), dismissing the charges against a slaver for violating the 1807 ban on importation of slaves, "especially as the act of congress upon which the suit is grounded expressly gives the court a discretionary power in extreme cases, of which this is surely one," the court could lean toward leniency. The slaves were sold on the Charleston auction block. In the meantime, the burden in time and effort of these slave trade cases induced Bee to write to the South Carolina congressional delegation seeking additional pay. As Story indicated to the Boston jurors, he viewed the acts, and their violators, in a different light: "and yet there are men among us who think it no wrong to condemn the shivering Negro to perpetual slavery."[30]

U.S. v. Ship Amistad (1841) was the first of the great trilogy of opinions Story wrote in the final years of his life. It concerned the overseas slave trade. Here the forward reading of law was far less obvious than in *Martin v. Hunter's Lessee*, but the need to read law forward had a new and even more frightening exigency. The debate over slavery was tearing the nation apart. One of the institutions holding it together was the High Court. The influence of the slave power on the Court was obvious in its composition—already shifted from the Federalist to the Democratic parties and from the North to the South. Story had shown his fear of the prospect of the breakup of the Union in his *Commentaries on the Constitution.* That fear had, if anything, grown in the six years since his three volumes had appeared. Thus, the conservatism of his earlier writings wore, and had to wear, a new face.

Story had become more cautious, if that were possible, in his *Amistad* opinion for the case was watched carefully and widely, by both defenders of slavery and abolitionists. "This is the case of an appeal from the decree of the Circuit Court of the district of Connecticut, sitting in admiralty." The facts were a tangle of claims and counterclaims by the ship owners and Spain on the one side, and on the other by the next friends of the Africans whose rebellion on board the slaver *Amistad* in Cuban waters brought it into American waters. By the time the case reached the High Court, the claims were reduced substantially. By 1840,

> the only parties now before the Court, on one side, are the United States, intervening for the sole purpose of procuring restitution of the property, as Spanish property, pursuant to the treaty [with Spain], upon the grounds stated by the other parties claiming the property in their respective libels. The United States do not assert any property in themselves, nor any violation of their own rights, or sovereignty or laws, by the acts complained of. They do not insist that these negroes have been imported into the United States, in contravention of our own slave trade acts. They do not seek to have these negroes delivered up for the purpose of being transferred to Cuba, as pirates or robbers or as fugitive criminals found within our territories who have been guilty of offences against the laws of Spain. They do not assert that the seizure and bringing the vessel and cargo and negroes into port by Lieutenant Gedney for the purpose of adjudication is a tortious act. They simply confine themselves to the right of the Spanish claimants to the restitution of their property upon the facts asserted in their respective allegations.

On the other side were the Africans. They claimed to be free natives of Africa kidnapped in their own land illegally and carried to Cuba.[31]

The federal government argued that the Africans were slave cargo, and must be delivered up to Spain according to the treaty of 1795 as modified by the 1819 treaty. Under it, property taken within the other nation's waters illegally were to be given to the nation that owned the ships. The same was true when a ship belonging to nationals of one nation was forced to harbor in the other nation's waters or were taken by pirates, in time of peace. But none of this mattered so much to Story as the fact, proven by evidence (to his satisfaction) at the trial courts, that "these negroes, under all the circumstances, fall within the description of merchandise, in the sense of the treaty." Or that they "themselves are pirates and robbers." And that depended on the fact that "these negroes were, at the time, lawfully held as slaves under the laws of Spain and recognised by those laws as property capable of being lawfully bought and sold."[32]

Presented with the occasion to read the treaty backward, he

demurred: Although "we see no reason why they may not justly be deemed, within the intent of the treaty, to be included under the denomination of merchandise," they were not goods to be bought or sold. Instead "It is plain beyond controversy, if we examine the evidence, that these negroes never were the lawful slaves of Ruiz or Montez or of any other Spanish subjects. They are natives of Africa, and were kidnapped there, and were unlawfully transported to Cuba in violation of the laws and treaties of Spain and the most solemn edicts and declarations of that government." Now came reading the treaty and other laws forward. "By those laws and treaties and edicts, the African slave trade is utterly abolished; the dealing in that trade is deemed a heinous crime; and the negroes thereby introduced into the dominions of Spain are declared to be free." Nothing in the treaty itself said this. Story arrived at it by putting together evidence that the Spanish slave traders had "full knowledge of all the circumstances." So did the attorney general of the United States when he argued their part in court. "If then, these negroes are not slaves, but are kidnapped Africans who, by the laws of Spain itself, are entitled to their freedom, and were kidnapped and illegally carried to Cuba, and illegally detained and restrained on board the *Amistad*, there is no pretense to say that they are pirates or robbers." While Story might "lament the dreadful acts by which they asserted their liberty and took possession of the *Amistad* and endeavored to regain their native country," they were justified in their actions.[33]

Story then doubted, in court, that the documentary evidence presented on behalf of the Spanish claimants was genuine. He did not give "full faith and credit" to the documents purporting to show that the slave ship was merely traveling between Cuban ports, instead of bringing the men from Africa to Cuba. He rejected the argument that this "Court have no right to look behind these documents. . . . To this argument we can in no wise assent." He continued, "We do not here meddle with the point whether there has been any connivance in this illegal traffic on the part of any of the colonial authorities or subordinate officers of Cuba because, in our view, such an examination is unnecessary," as indeed it was. Story had made the point already. For such documents were "always open to be impugned for fraud, and whether that fraud be in the original obtaining of these documents or in the subsequent

fraudulent and illegal use of them, when once it is satisfactorily established, it overthrows all their sanctity and destroys them as proof."
Again, where was fraud a matter discussed in the treaty? Story was
reading the law of fraud, one of the most important categories by which
equity cases were determined every year on his circuit, into international law. As he told suitors in Massachusetts, New Hampshire, and
Connecticut, "Fraud will vitiate any—even the most solemn—transactions, and an asserted title to property founded upon it is utterly void."
Connecting this to the ninth article of the treaty, requiring owners of
disputed ships to offer sufficient proof of ownership, he impugned the
character and conduct of the Spanish owners and, by implication, of
the Spanish governments and, finally of the US attorney general who
represented them in court.[34]

He then read into the case, and the law, material from his own *Commentaries on the Conflict of Laws.* "The conflict of rights between the
parties under such circumstances becomes positive and inevitable,
and must be decided upon the eternal principles of justice and international law." Above all, "the doctrine must apply where human life
and human liberty are in issue, and constitute the very essence of the
controversy. The treaty with Spain never could have intended to take
away the equal rights of all foreigners who should contest their claims
before any of our Courts to equal justice, or to deprive such foreigners
of the protection given them by other treaties or by the general law of
nations." Upon the merits of the case, then, there does not seem to us
to be any ground for doubt that these negroes ought to be deemed free,
and that the Spanish treaty interposes no obstacle to the just assertion
of their rights.[35]

But Story could not ignore the elephant in the room. The United
States had entered the case not out of an abstract interest in the treaty
with Spain, but because the administration of John Tyler wanted to
protect the rights of parties not at the bar—that is, the rights of Americans to their slaves. Story knew this—everyone in the courtroom in the
basement of the US Capitol that day knew this. Were the Africans now
free? Were they to be taken back to Africa? "The United States do not
now insist upon any affirmance of this part of the decree, and, in our
judgment, upon the admitted facts, there is no ground to assert that

the case comes within the purview of the act of 1819, or of any other of our prohibitory slave trade acts." Story then concluded that "the said negroes be declared to be free, and be dismissed from the custody of the Court, and go without day."[36]

The second of the trilogy, *Prigg v. Pennsylvania* (1842), imposed on a reluctant Story another round of reading law forward. Story's detestation of slavery had not abated since *Amistad*, but domestic slavery remained the law in half the nation. As he had written in his *Commentaries on the Conflict of Laws*, among all nations, "the state of slavery will not be recognized in any country whose institutions and policy prohibit slavery." Slavery was "strictly territorial." But the United States presented a different case, for although the individual states were sovereign, and slavery was a matter of domestic law in those states, the federal government had, at the behest of the slave states, taken a hand in questions of runaway slaves. As he wrote in his opinion in *Le Jeune Eugenie* in the circuit court meeting in Boston, that same Boston circuit session of 1822, "sitting therefore, in an American court of judicature, I am not permitted to deny that under some circumstances it might have a lawful existence . . . and the practice may, form a part of the domestic policy of a nation." It might seem to Story that the Rendition Clause and the Fugitive Slave Act of 1793 made no sense on their face. After all, was the labor of the unborn "owed" to anyone? Still, no free state could deny to citizens of the slave states their right to their property, and the Rendition Clause of the Constitution, as explained in the 1793 Fugitive Slave Act, barred states from interfering. At the same time, states like Pennsylvania believed that they had the duty and the right to protect due process for their free black citizens. The question then became how Pennsylvania might do this in the face of federal law. The answer was the antikidnaping act, which provided that slave catchers must bring suspected runaways before a state magistrate, where the captured party could provide evidence that he or she was in fact not a runaway.[37]

The procedural story of *Prigg* was, after a fashion, the same as in *Martin*: an appeal from a state supreme court, this time from Pennsylvania's to the US Supreme Court. The appellant was a Maryland slave catcher named Prigg, and he sought relief from a criminal charge of kidnaping an African American named Margaret Morgan, allegedly

with the intent of selling her as a slave. The Pennsylvania antikidnaping act of 1826 required that he bring her before a state magistrate for
a hearing. He did, but when the magistrate did not rule on the matter
Prigg simply carried her back to her putative owner in Maryland. Actually, he took her children as well (one of whom was born in Pennsylvania, and by its law was free). Tried in Pennsylvania, he was found
not guilty by a jury. This time, he convinced a jury that Morgan was
actually a slave belonging to Margaret Ashmore, a citizen of Maryland;
that the slave escaped and fled from Maryland into Pennsylvania in
1832. But without the approval of the magistrate, Prigg had still violated
the Pennsylvania law.

Now came a special circumstance. Maryland harbored Prigg and
kept the Morgan family. The two states' governments agreed that rather
than battle over extradition of Prigg and return of the Morgans (Margaret's husband had attempted to rescue her but drowned during the
effort), they would submit the matter to the US Supreme Court. While
it would appear unlikely that the Court would find in favor of Pennsylvania, the case went far beyond its fact pattern to a national importance. Did states have to assist slave catchers, or could they demur. Did
Congress have exclusive authority in the area of rendition of fugitives,
or did the federal courts have to pay free state law some regard?[38]

Story was worried about "the agitations on this subject in both
States, which have had a tendency to interrupt the harmony between
them, may subside, and the conflict of opinion be put at rest." Again,
he was looking forward, this time to resistance to whatever decision he
made. He had hoped, he reported, that the willingness of both states to
put the questions to the Court would become a model for other states
and for the nation as a whole. Law read forward, that is, existing federal
law read forward to deal with new state laws and interstate conflict,
would resolve problems that kept arising. It was a chance for forward-
looking reasoning to work; but Story could not pull it off. Instead, he
fell back on a reading of the Constitution and the Fugitive Slave Act
that was rooted in past, inefficient, and confusing understandings. In
the approaching maelstrom, Story's vision of future peace was buffeted
and swept from side to side.[39]

Story conceded that "Few questions which have ever come before this Court involve more delicate and important considerations, and few upon which the public at large may be presumed to feel a more profound and pervading interest." But the concession was more than a little disingenuous because the question was not a new one, and could have been answered by a recitation of precedent. Instead, Story took refuge in first principles, "in the exposition of this part of the Constitution, we shall limit ourselves to those considerations which appropriately and exclusively belong to it, without laying down any rules of interpretation of a more general nature." He was not going to innovate or invent. But that is exactly what he did. For

> It will indeed probably be found, when we look to the character of the Constitution itself, the objects which it seeks to attain, the powers which it confers, the duties which it enjoins, and the rights which it secures, as well as the known historical fact, that many of its provisions were matters of compromise of opposing interests and opinions, that no uniform rule of interpretation can be applied to it which may not allow, even if it does not positively demand, many modifications in its actual application to particular clauses.

In short, Story found no fixed interpretation of the Rendition Clause or the Fugitive Slave Act in the past.[40]

Thus, "the safest rule of interpretation, after all, will be found to be to look to the nature and objects of the particular powers, duties, and rights with all the lights and aids of contemporary history." This was an invitation to a weighing of future considerations, but Story waited to issue that invitation. Instead, he rehearsed the conventional view of Constitutional text. "There are two clauses in the Constitution upon the subject of fugitives, which stands in juxtaposition with each other and have been thought mutually to illustrate each other." Note that only one concerned slavery. The first was the rendition of felons, a very old provision of both domestic and international law. The second was much newer, and read, "No person held to service or labor in one State, under the laws thereof, escaping into another, shall, in consequence of any law or regulation therein, be discharged from such service or labor, but shall be delivered up on claim of the party to whom such service or labor may be due." Its origins lay in the history of the Constitutional

Convention. "Historically, it is well known that the object of this clause was to secure to the citizens of the slave-holding States the complete right and title of ownership in their slaves, as property, in every State in the Union into which they might escape from the State where they were held in servitude." Whether the clause was necessary to keep the slave South in the Union was a question that Story elided. He simply asserted that "The full recognition of this right and title was indispensable to the security of this species of property in all the slave-holding States, and indeed was so vital to the preservation of their domestic interests and institutions that it cannot be doubted that it constituted a fundamental article without the adoption of which the Union could not have been formed." Note how he seemed to shove abolitionism, gaining strength at that time in domestic politics and already the rule in the rest of the Anglophone world, to one side. "Its true design was to guard against the doctrines and principles prevalent in the non-slaveholding States, by preventing them from intermeddling with, or obstructing, or abolishing the rights of the owners of slaves." This was a reference to the North's free soil future, for in 1787, antislavery opinion was not so potent in the North.[41]

To reinforce that point, Story introduced material not relevant to the case at hand, to wit, his own reading of international law.

> By the general law of nations, no nation is bound to recognize the state of slavery as to foreign slaves found within its territorial dominions, when it is in opposition to its own policy and institutions, in favor of the subjects of other nations where slavery is recognized. If it does it, it is as a matter of comity, and not as a matter of international right. The state of slavery is deemed to be a mere municipal regulation, founded upon and limited to the range of the territorial laws.

It would seem, at this point, that Story was laying the groundwork for finding the Pennsylvania law constitutional. Why else lug in international law? After all, England and France had abolished slavery and their ships policed the waterways to prevent the international slave trade. But this apparent aside had a purpose, as he then reiterated his earlier point in the new context of growing international condemnation of slavery. "It is manifest from this consideration that, if the

Constitution had not contained this clause, every non-slaveholding State in the Union would have been at liberty to have declared free all runaway slaves coming within its limits, and to have given them entire immunity and protection against the claims of their masters." If only. But then, this "course . . . would have created the most bitter animosities and engendered perpetual strife between the different States." So, the free states made a concession to the "safety and security of the southern States." It was a concession of "intrinsic and practical necessity," but it was a concession against the grain of liberty and history. Not history, actually, but the future. Story has been accused of bowing to the slaveocracy. Actually, though pressed hard by the proslavery tenor if not the explicit language of the Constitution, Story wanted his views on slavery etched into the opinion.[42]

Still, avid defenders of slavery on the Court like Chief Justice Roger Taney and Justice Peter Daniel would strongly dissent from all but the decision. As Story's would be the opinion of the Court, they were left with an unpalatable choice—and they swallowed hard, accepting a portion of Story's reasoning. With this mind, one can explain why so much of what Story wrote was tortuously convoluted—giving and taking back with the same hand, over and over again, sometimes in the same passages.

Note that Story did not defend slavery itself. He did not say, as the proslavery advocates of the time were insisting, that slavery was good for anyone. He merely said that the language of the Rendition Clause must be interpreted clearly, and its objective completely effectuated. This was the prologue to his claim that the Clause gave to Congress, and the federal government, the exclusive authority to enforce the Clause and legislation based on it. "No court of justice can be authorized so to construe any clause of the Constitution as to defeat its obvious ends when another construction, equally accordant with the words and sense thereof, will enforce and protect them." That purpose was "the existence of a positive, unqualified right on the part of the owner of the slave which no state law or regulation can in any way qualify, regulate, control, or restrain. The slave is not to be discharged from service or labor in consequence of any state law or regulation."[43]

Story's logic was irresistible, but it did not lead where advocates of

slavery might expect. If "any state law or state regulation which inter-
rupts, limits, delays, or postpones the right of the owner to the immediate possession of the slave and the immediate command of his
service and labor operates *pro tanto* a discharge of the slave therefrom,"
it must fall. Which meant, for him, that any state action to abet the
slave catcher was not mandated by the Constitution and the Act. This
was a "positive and absolute" exclusion of the state's power, for "If this
be so, then all the incidents to that right attach also." It the owner's
right was absolute, it was because "the local laws of his own State confer
upon him, as property, and we all know that this right of seizure and
recaption is universally acknowledged in all the slaveholding States."
Again, the hidden or not so hidden implication was that slavery was
limited to the states whose laws permitted it. It was not national at all.
So, if slavery was not national, but the rights of the slaveholder to his
property were guaranteed by federal law only, fugitive slave law was at
war with itself. It was a nice point, and one can see Story working hard
to place it at the very center of his opinion.[44]

The next step in Story's opinion made the contradiction even
clearer. "Upon this ground, we have not the slightest hesitation in holding that, under and in virtue of the Constitution, the owner of a slave
is clothed with entire authority, in every State in the Union, to seize
and recapture his slave whenever he can do it without any breach of
the peace or any illegal violence." Whenever he can do it without any
breach of the peace or illegal violence was exactly what the Pennsylvania legislation was meant to prevent. Prigg had used force to carry
the Morgans away from their Pennsylvania homes. How could a slave
catcher not breach the peace? What was illegal violence? Was it a measure of the extent of the force used or merely a definition of what was
illegal? More and more local communities were resisting the actions
of slave catchers, sometimes violently. Note again the contradiction in
the middle of the next passage: "In this sense and to this extent, this
clause of the Constitution may properly be said to execute itself, and to
require no aid from legislation, state or national." "In this sense and to
this extent" is a qualifier in a passage that began with an absolute. The
engine driving the contradiction was the conjunction of the past—the
language of the Constitution—and the future—the prospect of more

violence. In projecting the law forward Story had created the contradiction, but by maintaining that states did not have to help the slave catcher, Story reread federal law to avoid conflict between states and the federal government.[45]

This escape from the essential contradiction of a nation half slave and half free was the central contribution of his final passages. From this discussion of slave states' rights, Story segued into the opposite side of the question of slave law.

> The [free] state legislation may be entirely silent on the whole subject, and its ordinary remedial process framed with different views and objects, and this may be innocently, as well as designedly, done, since every State is perfectly competent, and has the exclusive right, to prescribe the remedies in its own judicial tribunals, to limit the time as well as the mode of redress, and to deny jurisdiction over cases which its own policy and its own institutions either prohibit or discountenance.

Again, this was a tangent, since Story had already said that states could not interfere with slave owners' right to recapture a runaway. What exactly was Story doing? He was coming at the exclusivity of federal law from another angle. "If, therefore, the clause of the Constitution had stopped at the mere recognition of the right, without providing or contemplating any means by which it might be established and enforced, in cases where it did not execute itself, it is plain that it would have been, in a great variety of cases, a delusive and empty annunciation." Hence the need for the Fugitive Slave Act of 1793. But see what that act did, and what it did not do. It was a complete ("perfect") remedy. It did not require the assistance of any state. Indeed, were it "left to the mere comity of the States to act as they should please, and would [slavery] depend for its security upon the changing course of public opinion, the mutations of public policy, and the general adaptations of remedies for purposes strictly according to the *lex fori*" there might be no remedy at all for the slave owner. Again, the hint, each time broader, that growing anti-slavery opinion in the North was making slave catching difficult: What else would mandate mention of "the changing course of public opinion"? Looking forward to growing free soil resistance to slave catching added consequences to his considerations.[46]

Story was not done pulling the chain of the slavery advocates by saying one thing and implying its opposite. The law said that the slave shall be delivered up on the claim of the putative master or his agent, but "we think it exceedingly difficult, if not impracticable, to read this language and not to feel that it contemplated some further remedial redress than that which might be administered at the hands of the owner himself." By whom? On what claim? For who was to determine the claim "of right, made by one person upon another, to do or to forbear to do some act or thing as a matter of duty." Some form of due process must be implied, surely.

> The slave is to be delivered up on the claim. By whom to be delivered up? In what mode to be delivered up? How, if a refusal takes place, is the right of delivery to be enforced? Upon what proofs? What shall be the evidence of a rightful recaption or delivery? When and under what circumstances shall the possession of the owner, after it is obtained, be conclusive of his right, so as to preclude any further inquiry or examination into it by local tribunals or otherwise, while the slave, in possession of the owner, is *in transitu* to the State from which he fled?

All of this, phrased as question rather than statement, seemed to imply that some form of due process had to exist. This is exactly what Pennsylvania was arguing. On whose side was Story?[47]

In the final pages of the opinion, Story's forward reading of law came clear. Nothing in the constitutional clause or in the enabling legislation of 1793 said or even implied that states were not to aid and abet the recaption. This was Story reading the law forward, finding the best consequence, then returning to reinterpret the Constitution and the law of 1793. Supposedly, if free states were not compelled to assist in recaption of runaways, the agitation in the free states against recaption would die down and the Union would be safe. "If, indeed, the Constitution guaranties the right, and if it requires the delivery upon the claim of the owner (as cannot well be doubted), the natural inference certainly is that the National Government is clothed with the appropriate authority and functions to enforce it." It followed that "where the end is required, the means are given; and where the duty is enjoined, the ability to perform it is contemplated to exist on the part of the functionaries to whom it is entrusted." Put more simply, actually repeated, was the exclusivity of the duty. "The clause is found in the National Constitution, and not in that of any State. It does not point out any state functionaries, or any state action, to carry its provisions into effect." From this he reasoned, "The States cannot, therefore, be compelled to enforce them, and it might well be deemed an unconstitutional exercise of the power of interpretation to insist that the States are bound to provide means to carry into effect the duties of the National Government, nowhere delegated or entrusted to them by the Constitution." It would thus be unconstitutional for states to interfere, or for federal officials to force state officials to assist the slave catcher.[48]

In *Swift v. Tyson* (1842) Story's reckoning of the future of commercial transactions was unmistakable. It was the fulcrum of his opinion. Federal courts heard a wide variety of fraud cases in the antebellum years and the courts played a vital role in preventing scoundrels from escaping justice by crossing state borders or carrying their misdeed across state lines. In these, there was always the potential for friction between competing state and federal courts. *Swift* was one such case of interstate fraud demonstrating judicial federalism.[49]

One of the most important sectors of antebellum commerce was the exploitation of natural resources. Forest products were an important export in the colonial period, and domestic demand for wood for building materials, paper, furniture, and firewood grew apace with the new nation. Sale of the bounty of the forests to foreign countries as well as for use on the domestic market made the lumber industry one of the most profitable in the antebellum period. With the lure of profits came swindlers. As Bangor, Maine, emerged as a major center of the lumber industry, unscrupulous speculators in Maine along with conspirators in commercial entrepôts like New York City and Boston engaged in fast and loose deals to sell timberland to which they had no title.[50]

In earlier years, Maine land shenanigans had led to gunplay, but by the 1830s, the lumber merchants' schemes had become more sophisticated. They used commercial paper (in this case "bills of exchange") that were endorsed (a promise to pay, like endorsing a bank check) and circulated far beyond the circle of original entrepreneurs, to kite their speculation. The problem came when a creditor received an endorsed bill of exchange, without notice of the underlying fraud, and tried to pass it on for payment. If the original drawer "dishonored" it, that is, refused to accept it and pay it, the entire chain of transactions could come under the scrutiny of the courts. That is what happened with increasing frequency after the Panic of 1837 brought banks crashing down and spurred creditors to demand payment on notes.[51]

George W. Tyson, a New York resident, had given the bill as payment for land in Maine. Unbeknownst to him, the sellers did not have title to the land. He had been duped. The bill of exchange passed through a series of hands until it arrived in Swift's hands, and when he demanded payment on it, Tyson refused. Tyson removed the suit from the state court to the federal circuit court in the Southern District of New York, where, under New York law, Tyson could (and did) offer proof of the original fraud as a defense to Swift's demand for payment. Presumably, as the federal court was bound by the Rules of Decision Act to use the law of the state in which it sat, that would end the matter.[52]

Hearing the case at the beginning of May 1836, District Judge Samuel Betts and Justice Smith Thompson disagreed, however, and on the division of opinion the case automatically sent the case to the US Supreme Court. There it changed character and significance. From a pretty typical and straightforward (in law, if not in its facts) case of fraud, it became the basis of the doctrine of federal common law. Justice Story, writing for a unanimous court, knew all about these frauds from his travels on the New England circuit. He also knew that the negotiability (legal circulation) of commercial paper was vital for business dealings. "It is for the benefit and convenience of the commercial world to give as wide an extent as practicable to the credit and circulation of negotiable paper."

How then to promote the flow of business across the country without violating the strictures of the Judiciary Act of 1789? Story found a way to get around the New York law imposed by its courts, and with it, the vagaries that state court interpretations of state law imposed on interstate commerce. "It is, however, contended, the . . . judiciary act of 1789 . . . furnishes a rule obligatory upon this Court to follow the decisions of the state tribunals in all cases to which they apply," but "in the ordinary use of language it will hardly be contended that the decisions of Courts constitute laws. They are, at most, only evidence of what the laws are; and are not, of themselves, laws." This was instrumental reasoning at its most daring: in short, federal courts were only bound to follow state statutes, not the precedents of state courts.

If it appeared that Story had, with a wave of the hand, dismissed the entire Anglo-American common law concept of precedent, in which the state appeals courts' interpretations of statutes had the status of law, what he had caused to disappear with one hand he re-created with the other. The Supreme Court's decisions, themselves no more or less precedent than the state supreme courts' decisions, were binding on the state courts.

> It becomes necessary for us, therefore, upon the present occasion to express our own opinion of the true result of the commercial law upon the question now before us. . . . Undoubtedly, the decisions of the local tribunals upon such subjects are entitled to, and will receive, the most deliberate attention and respect of this Court; but they cannot furnish positive rules, or conclusive authority, by which our own judgments are to be bound up and governed.

Note that under the *Swift* regime, two identical fact pattern cases might be resolved differently, because one was adjudicated in state court and the other in federal court. What happened to precedent? "But, admitting the doctrine to be fully settled in New York, it remains to be considered whether it is obligatory upon this court if it differs from the principles established in the general commercial law." General commercial law? That was Story's reading of section 34 of the Judiciary Act of 1789. In it, federal courts were bound to follow the laws of the state in which they sat, but "The laws of a state are more usually understood to mean the rules and enactments promulgated by the legislative authority thereof, or long-established local customs having the force of laws," not state court precedent. "In all the various cases which have hitherto come before us for decision, this court have uniformly supposed that the true interpretation of the 34th section limited its application to state laws, strictly local that is to say, to the positive statutes of the state, and the construction thereof adopted by the local tribunals," not the outcome of state court cases.[53]

In what was surely the most succinct and yet forceful enunciation of reading law forward in his day, Story continued, "It becomes necessary for us, therefore, upon the present occasion, to express our own opinion of the true result of the commercial law upon the question now before us." Recall that in *Commentaries on the Constitution* he had avowed no intention to introduce new or obscure interpretations of law of his own. In *Swift*, he did just that. The basis of his decision was then "the known usual course of trade and business." Long before Karl Llewellyn and the other authors of the Uniform Commercial Code in 1942 reached the same conclusion, Story arrived there. Of course, he found in English precedents, in particular the law merchant as adopted by Lord Mansfield and others, enough to make his forward reading of law look almost conventional.[54]

Despite its growing centrality in his opinions, Story's forward reading of the law was a defensive posture, a way to ward off novel ideas that would return the nation to the time before the Constitution. As he told the lawyers of Suffolk County, Massachusetts, after *McCulloch* was decided, but while the debate over the admission of Missouri was in full swing,

> and what, let me ask, with becoming solemnity, what would be the consequence, if these attempts, repudiating the old and settled doctrines of the constitution, should succeed? What but to subject it to the independent and uncontrollable interpretation of twenty-four sovereign states; to give it in no two states the same power and efficiency; to weaken its salutary influences, and subdue its spirit; to increase the discords and rivalries of contending states; to surrender its supreme judicial functions into the hands of those, who feel no permanent interest to exercise or support them; in short to drive us back to the old times, and the old practices under the confederation.

The only safety in the future lay in the forward reading of the Constitution, then back again to secure it and the Union's future.[55]

Lemuel Shaw, c. 1856. Museum of Fine Arts Boston. Photo by Southworth & Hawes.

3. Lemuel Shaw

State supreme court judges are rarely accorded the respect and are rarely as cited as US Supreme Court justices, with a few exceptions. The reason may be that a state supreme court decision is compelling precedent for the state, but not for other states. It may, however, be persuasive, and widely adopted. For this reason, at the head of this list stands Massachusetts Supreme Judicial Court's Lemuel Shaw. For thirty years, from 1830 to 1860, Shaw presided as the chief justice of that court, a period when Massachusetts law set the pattern for much of the free North. A man of robust appetites and powerful opinions, Shaw not only sat at the center seat of the court, he led it through over two thousand opinions in fifty-six volumes of the state court reports. His contributions in labor law, negligence, and property law were the high-water marks of the classic age of American jurisprudence. His trilogy of cases on slavery foresaw the coming national crisis, although from a different perspective than his fellow Massachusetts jurist Joseph Story. A Federalist and then a Whig in politics, Shaw was nevertheless willing and able to read the law forward when novel situations presented themselves in his court.[1]

Shaw's and Story's judicial service ran along parallel lines. Shaw attended Harvard College a year after Story, and the two men must have known each other there, but a friendship did not form. Story's famous energy had already manifested itself. Shaw was far more placid. In later years, Shaw never sat on a federal court. Story was a federal judge. Story turned down the chief justiceship of the Massachusetts Supreme Judicial Court just before Shaw was offered it, and accepted. Shaw was junior counsel to Daniel Webster when the Charles River Bridge case was first argued at the bar of the US Supreme Court, in 1829, but before oral argument commenced, Shaw took his seat on the state supreme court. He never did argue that or any other case before Justice Story. Both men worked with Daniel Webster, but Webster did not bring them together. Thus, as in parallel lines, the two men moved through the same space but do not seem to have moved in the same social or political circles. Shaw's court sat within a stone's throw of Boston's port. Story's circuit service brought him to Boston every year. When Shaw refused to issue the habeas corpus in the Latimer case discussed below, counsel for the runaway slave turned to Story, whose circuit court was then in session. (He too declined.) The two men nevertheless respected each other's talents. When Story was nominated for the new Dane Chair at the Harvard Law School, Shaw, a member of the Harvard Corporation (the board of overseers), commended Story for his "brilliant talents, enlightened zeal, and indefatigable exertions." Shaw often quoted Story opinions, for example, *Prigg v. Pennsylvania* (1842), when fugitive slave questions came to his court. For appearing to turn away from their extrajudicial opposition to slavery when on the bench, both men were the targets of antislavery leaders' criticism.[2]

Shaw was born to a respectable ministerial family on Cape Cod, in 1781. He entered Harvard College in 1796 and did ably there. He taught school in Boston, and from visits to his uncle, Dr. Lemuel Hayward, a successful doctor, gained a taste for finer things in life than school teaching (or the ministry, to which his father tried to turn his head) could provide. He decided to read law under David Everett and To-mas Selfridge, both luminaries in Boston society, and for three years he studied law in their office. He turned out to be adept at this profession and was admitted to the bar in 1804, in Amherst, New Hampshire. Then he traveled back to Boston, which became his home. He began his practice until 1830, when he was appointed chief justice by Governor Levi Lincoln Jr. Shaw was successful in politics, as a Federalist and then a Whig in the state legislature. A loyal Federalist even after the party was embarrassed by its antiwar stance in the War of 1812, he made important friends like Webster and Harrison Gray Otis, and served on a myriad of city and state commissions. His status grew apace. By the 1820s he was wealthy and politically well connected, but nothing of his legal career suggested the greatness of his judicial career. He had no judicial experience other than legal practice when he was named to the chief justiceship of the supreme judicial court. When the chief justice chair suddenly became vacant, Lincoln, himself a lawyer, of-fered the vacant post of chief justice to Story, who declined. Webster then suggested Shaw. Shaw hesitated, and Webster plied him with the same combination of skill and flattery he had used on Lincoln, and Shaw accepted.[3]

Shaw was not a reformer. He was conservative in his personal beliefs, particularly in his high regard for the rights of private property. As early as his 1815 Fourth of July Speech, in Faneuil Hall, he explained the basic principle of Republicanism (according to the Federalist canon): "It consists in a judicious election of a few, to exercise the powers of government in trust for the whole. . . . this principle has long been recognized and valued, and seems interwoven into the very form and texture of our society." While this principle was wholly out of step with the democratizing fervor of the rest of American politics at that time, it was particularly appropriate to the judiciary, again as Shaw saw it. The judge acted in trust for the better good of the whole. Shaw had no difficulty setting aside jury verdicts, and even lecturing the state's inferior court judges on their duties. He was not an autocrat so much as an authority, self-appointed to be sure, on the judicial function.[4]

A broadly built man, with a flowing mane and a barrel chest, his leonine bearing commanded absolute decorum. He sharply rebuked counsel when they ran too long or interrupted him. He spoke slowly and his deep voice resonated throughout the chamber. His opinions' style was clear and unornamented, like his speech taking time to arrive at his points. When he cited authority, he did so with painstaking detail and thorough research.[5]

One sees this almost imperious manner in his opinion for the court in *Commonwealth v. Kneeland* (1838). Abner Kneeland was an atheist whose newspaper, the *Boston Investigator*, in 1833 published his attack on organized religion. For it, he was indicted for blasphemy. The state constitution provided both for freedom of religious worship and for freedom of the press. Shaw read both of these narrowly in protecting the antiblasphemy state law. The old law was good law. "In all these different descriptions of the offence, one idea is common to them all, which is, that the wilful denial of God, and of his creation and government of the world, with an intent and purpose to impair and destroy the reverence due to him, is the offence intended to be prohibited." The law rested on long usage.

It seems now to be somewhat late to call in question the constitutionality of a law, which has been enacted more than half a century, which has been repeatedly enforced, and the validity of which, it is believed, until this prosecution, has never been doubted, though there have been many prosecutions and convictions under it. It was itself a revision of the colonial and provincial laws, to the same effect, already cited. It was passed very soon after the adoption of the constitution, and no doubt, many members of the convention which framed the constitution, were members of the legislature which passed this law.

They must have believed that the law of blasphemy did not violate the provisions of the constitution they had just fashioned.

The question is not, whether the makers of the constitution were right in this belief, or whether, if the constitution were now to be made, it would be wise to enlarge or restrict the powers of the legislature in this behalf; but if from the article as it stands, taken in connexion with the whole constitution, it cannot be clearly inferred that it was their intention to repeal the laws against blasphemy, and prohibit the legislature from reenacting them, then it cannot be maintained that this act of the legislature is unconstitutional and void.[6]

In *Roberts v. School Board* (1849), Shaw again looked back to the authority that localities had over elementary education in established law. But this time, he sensed that a backward glance was not enough. Kneeland had represented himself, poorly by contemporary accounts, but this time the petitioner, who sought an end to mandated school segregation by race, had a formidable advocate—Charles Sumner. Sumner (already a leading abolitionist and soon to be a US senator) argued that the state had never mandated segregation on the basis of race; that segregation created a caste system repugnant to republicanism; and that the segregation of some children was not legally reasonable, as it had no purpose that the state should pursue. Shaw conceded the learned eloquence of Sumner, but concluded,

It will be considered, that this is a question of power, or of the legal authority of the committee intrusted by the city with this department of public instruction; because, if they have the legal authority, the expediency of exercising it in any particular way is exclusively with them. . . . The power of general superintendence vests a plenary authority in the committee to arrange, classify, and distribute pupils, in such a manner as they think best adapted to their general proficiency and welfare.

More important was the conservative view of the power of law to change social opinions and customs. "It is urged, that this maintenance of separate schools tends to deepen and perpetuate the odious distinction of caste, founded in a deep-rooted prejudice in public opinion. This prejudice, if it exists, is not created by law, and probably cannot be changed by law." The language would echo in Justice Henry Brown's opinion in *Plessy v. Ferguson* (1896), in retrospect, infamous evidence of Shaw's reputation.[7]

But in other areas of the law, Shaw did not look back or defer. He was not an antebellum sentimentalist, not a romantic, and certainly not a friend to the working poor, but he recognized problems that would arise in common law. Though his politics was a throwback, when the case demanded, he looked forward to anticipate novel consequences and then returned to the law to reinterpret or revise its meaning. In some fashion, he could not help but innovate, for the world around him was changing with an almost reckless speed. Railroads were replacing canals as the preferred medium of transportation, and railroad bonds and shares were transforming banking, commerce, and investment. Although the "transportation revolution" and its new commercial face were not quite an industrial revolution, craft workers (artisans) faced the prospect of competing with manufactured goods. He applied his faith in old fashioned freedom—freedom of workers to enter contracts for their labor, and freedom of the market to set prices and wages—to new areas of law by looking ahead and then back.[8]

The vast majority of the two thousand plus cases in which Shaw delivered an opinion were the stuff of common law, that is, disputes by private persons or private businesses over torts, contracts, and property. A few of these cases were "novel" in the sense that they could not be easily settled according to precedent or explicit legislative enactments. A lesser judge would have looked for solutions in the precepts of common law, but Shaw did not view common law as a body of explicit instructions to the judge. Instead, "it is one of the great merits and advantage of the common law, that instead of a series of detailed practical rules, established by positive provisions, and adapted to the precise circumstance of particular cases, which would become obsolete and fail . . . the common law consists of a few broad and comprehensive principles, founded on reason, natural justice and enlightened public policy, modified and adapted to the circumstances" of new cases. Thus Shaw was free to look into the future through the lens of enlightened policy, and reframe the common law as he saw fit.[9]

In *Commonwealth v. Alger* (1851), Cyrus Alger was prosecuted for violating a state law protecting the navigation of Boston Harbor. Alger's counsel insisted he had a property right in the wharf even though it extended beyond the boundary lines permitted for private ventures. Shaw, writing for the court when the case was appealed, agreed with the trial court that the law was constitutional. "The case thus presented, must depend on the construction, validity, and effect of the laws in question, establishing the lines of the harbor, as they affect public and private rights; regarding, as they do, the rights of the public in tide waters and the arms of the sea, and the nature, extent, and limits of the rights of private proprietors in flats and sea-shores." But that was not all the case presented—for the development of the harbor by private interests was going to continue apace as the port of Boston opened its arms to the clipper ships and cargoes from all over the world. Time was when the proprietors of shore land could do what they wanted with it, but that time had passed. While legislative grants to individuals to improve land along waterways were common, the legislatures retained the authority to regulate those usages. "None but the sovereign power can authorize an interruption of such passages, because it has power to judge of what the public convenience requires, and may enact conditions to preserve the natural passages; that all navigable rivers are public property, for the use of all the citizens; and that there must be some act of the sovereign power, direct or derivative, to authorize any interruption of them." The notion of a public convenience was not entirely new, but by looking at the prospect of continued encroachment on shorelands by private developers, Shaw had given a name to legislative protection of public utility. Thus did the state act as the trustee for the general good. "It must be regarded as held in trust for the best interest of the public, for commerce and navigation, and for all the legitimate and appropriate uses to which it may be made subservient." In the very same decision, Shaw defined the "police power" of the state: "The power we allude to is rather the police power, the power vested in the legislature by the constitution, to make, ordain and establish all manner of wholesome and reasonable laws, statutes and ordinances, either with penalties or without, not repugnant to the constitution, as they shall judge to be for the good and welfare of the commonwealth, and of the subjects of the same." Almost offhandedly, Shaw had given birth to two of the most prominent doctrines of later jurisprudence: the public utility and the state's police power. In an age when state legislatures were flexing their regulatory muscles, it was not hard to see a future when state regulations came increasingly to court.[10]

As the shoreline was changing through human activity, so was the landscape. Lines of iron rail now crisscrossed fields and hills. Railroading brought another new activity to the land, and thence to the courts. Take, for example, *Farwell v. Boston and Worcester Railroad* (1842), in which Shaw created the "fellow servant rule" out of whole cloth, protecting the nascent railroad interests in the state against worker injury suits. Nicholas Farwell was an engineer with the line, and in the course of his duties, which he performed correctly, he was thrown from the train to the ground and injured. The cause was the negligence of his fellow workers. Was the line liable? "This is an action of new impression in our courts, and involves a principle of great importance. It presents a case, where two persons are in the service and employment of one company," Shaw began. And with old rules no longer apposite, one had to look to general rules. "The general rule, resulting from considerations as well of justice as of policy, is, that he who engages in the employment of another for the performance of specified duties and services, for compensation, takes upon himself the natural and ordinary risks and perils incident to the performance of such services, and in legal presumption, the compensation is adjusted accordingly." What general rule? Where did it reveal itself in the existing law? Shaw merely foresaw that working on the railroad was dangerous, and would continue to be, and one presumed, looking forward, that the danger was included in the compensation. Where was the proof of that? Nowhere in the law or the facts. Shaw merely added that consideration, and in light of it, the worker should have been aware of the dangers that fellow workers' negligence posed. So, the engineer had come to the danger. In neither of these conditions was the "master," here the railroad owners, responsible for the injury or for the damages that Farwell sought. "But the rule in question seems to be a good authority for the point, that persons are not to be responsible, in all cases, for the negligence of those employed by them."[11]

Shaw was aware that cases of this type would soon flood the courts. The best result was to leave to the injured party a suit against the fellow employee actually responsible for the injury, and hold the employer blameless. Thus the court created something like a subsidy for the struggling lines to protect themselves. The rails had become increasingly important parts of the commercial economy of the state, moving goods and persons more freely and cheaply from place to place, reducing freight and passenger costs, an altogether important part of the economic growth of the region and the nation. All this Shaw had foreseen, and so the law of common carriers and of negligence had to be revisited and revised. The basis for that revision was a return to the older idea of personal responsibility. Everyone was to be responsible in law as in morals for their own actions, including how those actions affected others.[12]

The same willingness to look ahead to likely consequences and then back to older law appeared in *Commonwealth v. Hunt* (1842). Often regarded as the ironic companion case to *Farwell*, the latter antilabor, the former prolabor, *Hunt* actually stood on its own (hence there is no need to reconcile the two outcomes). The case involved an indictment of seven members of a bootmaker's union for criminal conspiracy. Shaw did not think existing law sufficient for this case, although the charge against union members was a familiar one. But the indictment assumed that the purpose of the union was criminal, that is, that the association of workmen was a conspiracy because the object of the association was criminal activity. Shaw rejected this assumption.

The manifest intent of the association is, to induce all those engaged in the same occupation to become members of it. Such a purpose is not unlawful. It would give them a power which might be exerted for useful and honorable purposes, or for dangerous and pernicious ones. If the latter were the real and actual object, and susceptible of proof, it should have been specially charged. Such an association might be used to afford each other assistance in times of poverty, sickness and distress; or to raise their intellectual, moral and social condition; or to make improvement in their art; or for other proper purposes. Or the association might be designed for purposes of oppression and injustice.

The prosecution had to prove what the indictment merely assumed—intended criminal acts. Had Shaw reasoned as he had in *Kneeland*, he would have relied on old case law in Hunt. He rejected this scheme of reasoning.

But when an association is formed for purposes actually innocent, and afterwards its powers are abused, by those who have the control and management of it, to purposes of oppression and injustice, it will be criminal in those who thus misuse it, or give consent thereto, but not in the other members of the association. In this case, no such secret agreement, varying the objects of the association from those avowed, is set forth in this count of the indictment.

Unions of craft workers, like the bootmakers in this case, were increasingly appearing, defending artisans against competition from less skilled workers. The English common law and early American precedent made the simple act of association in restraint of trade a crime. Shaw's decision opened the door to even more widespread union organizing. In the process, Shaw also introduced the concept of freedom of contract. "The case supposes that these persons are not bound by contract, but free to work for whom they please, or not to work, if they so prefer. In this state of things, we cannot perceive, that it is criminal for men to agree together to exercise their own acknowledged rights, in such a manner as best to subserve their own interests." This was the lynchpin of the free states' idealization of free labor, in contrapose to the slave states utilization of slave labor. Shaw also championed free market competition, a notion already widely adopted in American law. "The same thing may be said of all competition in every branch of trade and industry; and yet it is through that competition, that the best interests of trade and industry are promoted." Looking to the future, finding the best outcome, then returning to interpret the law was the feedback loop of reading the law forward.[13]

Shaw is even better known for his slavery cases—freeing sojourners and upholding slave catching. The latter may seem odd in a state whose laws forbade slavery. More irony is that the two kinds of slave cases seemed as much at odds with each other as the *Farwell* and *Hunt* precedents. But again, it was Shaw's reading law forward that made sense of the surface contradictions. Massachusetts was one of the first states to end slavery by law. That end came by a series of lawsuits against slavery between 1780 and 1783. When the cases came to the state's highest court, Chief Justice William Cushing found that slavery was incompatible with the newly ratified state constitution of 1780. In this sense, the Supreme Judicial Court changed the law of slavery by looking ahead to the egalitarian promise of the Revolution, giving substance to its invocation of freedom. But the federal constitution, ratified in Massachusetts in 1788, clearly provided for states' domestic law to retain slavery. Thus, Massachusetts law on slavery was not the same as that of Maryland, Virginia, and other southern states. Shaw was never an abolitionist, but he was never an advocate of slavery either. He thought it morally wrong. Nevertheless, the Missouri statehood battle worried him, as it did Marshall and Story. Sitting in the Massachusetts House of Representatives, he concluded that slavery must be "a question of local jurisdiction."[14]

In *Commonwealth v. Aves* (1836) Shaw faced the question of slavery directly. The slave in question, a six-year-old girl named Med, was brought to Boston from New Orleans by her owner's wife, Mary Slater, and there given to the care of one Thomas Aves, with the purpose of keeping her until Mrs. Slater could return with Med to New Orleans. They had been in Boston for four months when a suit against Aves was brought by the Massachusetts Anti-Slavery Society. Benjamin Robbins Curtis, who as a US Supreme Court justice would later dissent in *Dred Scott v. Sandford* (1857), here represented Samuel Slater. Curtis argued that the Massachusetts Court had to follow the law of Louisiana with respect to a slave owner merely visiting the commonwealth, and that such a decision worked no harm on Massachusetts or its law. What was more, slavery was not immoral in itself. Ellis Loring, representing the state, disagreed. He argued that comity, the full faith and credit clause of the federal Constitution, did not impose an absolute rule on Massachusetts in doubtful cases. Slavery contravened the laws, the sentiments, and the precedents of Massachusetts, and, as a matter of choice of law, Massachusetts, the state in which the case was to be heard, had the authority to prefer its own laws to that of a foreign jurisdiction. On top of which, slavery was repugnant to the people and the laws of Massachusetts.

Lemuel Shaw agreed with Loring.

> The precise question presented by the claim of the respondent is, whether a citizen of any one of the United States, where negro slavery is established by law, coming into this State, for any temporary purpose of business or pleasure, staying sometime, but not acquiring a domicile [i.e., permanent residence], here, who brings a slave with him as a personal attendant, may restrain such slave of his liberty during his continuance here, and convey him out of this State on his return, against his consent."

Med was a little girl, and that is why the state of Massachusetts represented her. "It is not contended that a master can exercise here any other of the rights of a slave owner, than such as may be necessary to retain the custody of the slave during his residence, and to remove him on his return." In other words, no one could be made a slave in the state.[15]

Shaw knew that the case was a novel one, and one of great moment. Federal law did not apply, as Med was not a runaway subject to return under the Rendition Clause of the Constitution and the 1793 Fugitive Slave law. This was a state case decided under state law. "Until this discussion, I had supposed that there had been adjudged cases on this subject in this Commonwealth; and it is believed to have been a prevalent opinion among lawyers, that if a slave is brought voluntarily and unnecessarily within the limits of this State, he becomes free." The reason for this was "not so much because his coming within our territorial limits, breathing our air, or treading on our soil, works any alteration in his *status*, or condition, as settled by the law of his domicile, as because by the operation of our laws, there is no authority on the part of the master, either to restrain the slave of his liberty, whilst here, or forcibly to take him into custody in order to his removal." He looked back to the course of slavery in Massachusetts, and then to the provisions for slavery in the federal Constitution. But that is not where he stopped, or where he found grounds to free Med. This was because slavery had "crept in" to the colony, despite its laws (as he read them), and slavery was customary throughout the colonies. But Massachusetts, he emphasized, had ended slavery during the war "upon the ground that it is contrary to natural right and the plaint principles of justice. . . . The whole tenor of our policy, of our legislation and jurisprudence, from that time to the present, has been consistent with this construction, and with no other."[16]

Without guidance from state law (other than the constitution, which clearly outlawed slavery), Shaw widened his search. He looked to the law of nations, to principles of comity, and, though it was not quite apposite, to federal law. English common law, in particular *Somerset's Case* (1772), was persuasive, but not conclusive. From it, nevertheless, he drew Chief Justice Lord Mansfield's dictum that the domestic law of England did not allow slavery. Indeed, in general he concluded that slavery depended on municipal law, that is, the law of the particular sovereignty. It was positive law, and, being only that, was "so odious, that nothing can be suffered to support it but positive law." Shaw read Chief Justice Marshall's opinion *The Antelope* (1825) as supporting Chief Justice Mansfield's opinion of slavery in *Somerset*.[17]

Still, there was the principle of comity to accommodate. That principle was embedded in the Full Faith and Credit Clause of the federal Constitution as well as in conflicts of laws doctrine. To wit, "each independent community, in its intercourse with every other, is bound to act on the principle, that such other country has a full and perfect authority to make such laws for the government of its own subjects, as its own judgment shall dictate." Given this, "no independent community has any right to interfere with the acts or conduct of another state, within the territories of such state, or on the high seas." But, and here was the big but, within its own territory, each state had the right to use its own precepts with respect to positive law issues, like slavery. He rejected extraterritoriality. The alternative would be that if slavery were legal anywhere, it must be legal everywhere, under the doctrine that property (rights) followed the person wherever he went. This would be the proposition hinted at for territories in Chief Justice Roger Taney's opinion in *Dred Scott* (1857), based on the Fifth Amendment to the federal Constitution. Shaw was again far ahead of the pack.[18]

Recognizing that this was the likely consequence of ruling that the Slaters could take Med anywhere and then return with her to New Orleans, he rejected the doctrine entirely "That slavery is a relation founded in force, not in right, existing, where it does exist, by force of positive law." There was no such law in Massachusetts.

> This affords an answer to the argument drawn from the maxim, that the right of personal property follows the person, and therefore, where by the law of a place a person there domiciled acquires personal property, by the comity of nations the same must be deemed his property everywhere. It is obvious, that if this were true, in the extent in which the argument employs it, if slavery exists anywhere, and if by the laws of any place a property can be acquired in slaves, the law of slavery must extend to every place where such slaves may be carried.[19]

Shaw foresaw that such cases would not be novel ones soon, and anticipating them, tried to read the law of comity to shut the door against claims to the slaves' return. To do this, he invoked the category of sojourner—someone coming into the state who had no intention of remaining, but tarried for a time.

> That by the general and now well established law of this Commonwealth, bond slavery cannot exist, because it is contrary to natural right, and repugnant to numerous provisions of the constitution and laws, designed to secure the liberty and personal rights of all persons within its limits and entitled to the protection of the laws. . . . That, as a general rule, all persons coming within the limits of a state, become subject to all its municipal laws, civil and criminal, and entitled to the privileges which those laws confer; that this rule applies as well to blacks as whites, except in the case

of fugitives, to be afterwards considered; that if such persons have been slaves, they become free, not so much because any alteration is made in their *status*, or condition, as because there is no law which will warrant, but there are laws, if they choose to avail themselves of them, which prohibit, their forcible detention or forcible removal ... the law arising from the comity of nations cannot apply; because if it did, it would follow as a necessary consequence, that all those persons, who, by force of local laws, and within all foreign places where slavery is permitted, have acquired slaves as property, might bring their slaves here, and exercise over them the rights and power which an owner of property might exercise, and for any length of time short of acquiring a domicile; that such an application of the law would be wholly repugnant to our laws, entirely inconsistent with our policy and our fundamental principles, and is therefore inadmissible.[20]

He had borrowed the term *sojourners* from Pennsylvania, whose dealings with slaves and their masters were more common (as neighboring Maryland was a slave state).

Another question was made in that case, whether the slave was free by the laws of Pennsylvania, which, like our own in effect, liberate slaves voluntarily brought within the State, but there is an exception in favor of members of congress, foreign ministers and consuls, and sojourners: but this provision is qualified as to sojourners and persons passing through the State, in such manner as to exclude them from the benefit of the exception, if the slave was retained in the State longer than six months. The slave in that case having been detained in the State more than six months, was therefore held free.

The doctrine did not apply to slaves escaping into Massachusetts or to masters passing through the state on their way to their homes in slave states. Limited as it was, and soon to be tested by the most notorious of all runaway slave cases, *Prigg*, Shaw's was nevertheless an intervention in the interest of freedom. As in *Hunt*, Shaw had foreseen many more cases of this type; he opined that the best solution was to free these slaves, and then read that solution back into conflict of law doctrine.[21]

As much as Shaw valued individual freedom, he insisted on law-abiding conduct. That insistence was tested in the case of George

Latimer in 1842. Accused of running away from his Virginia master, James Grey, Latimer was well known and liked in Boston. When Grey caused a warrant, which the sheriff of Boston executed by jailing Latimer, a crowd gathered at the jail to prevent the hasty removal of Latimer to Virginia. A writ of habeas corpus brought the case before Shaw, who was sitting in session, and Shaw's response was reported in local newspapers. Justice Story, riding circuit in town, agreed, when Grey's counsel asked Story for the writ of rendition. Lawyers for Latimer once again turned to Shaw, seeking to prevent rendition with a writ of personal replevin (to regain property illegally taken by a government official). Shaw decided that there were no grounds to free Latimer on that writ, and the Massachusetts personal liberty law of 1837, requiring due process in rendition, was itself unconstitutional. This was the first law of the commonwealth that Shaw had struck down, here for violating the Fugitive Slave Act of 1793 and the Rendition Clause of the federal Constitution.

Boston's textile and commercial interests were closely aligned with southern cotton production, as it happened, but the antislavery men among the legal profession were determined that Boston not become a handmaiden of the South. These included Richard Henry Dana, who would represent the federal government in the *Prize Cases* during the Civil War. Shaw showed no amenability to these petitions, indeed considered them an affront to his dignity as well as the dignity of his position. When counsel for runaway Thomas Sims sought Shaw's aid in delaying the hearing on Sims's rendition, in 1851, the chief justice not only refused, but brought Story's account up to date. The Necessary and Proper Clause and the Rendition Clause made the Fugitive Slave Act of the preceding year constitutional, and now federal authority was added to the scales against the runaways and the abolitionists. Shaw's views were clear and fixed on the basis of well-settled practice and principle. But the principle was a legal one—the writ would not be returned and the prisoner's case not be heard because it could not, in his mind, prevail.[22]

Shaw was not a pedant. He preferred something like common sense to long-established authority. Conservative in his personal views and character, he deferred to the state legislature, to Congress, and to policy concerns more often than not. Only three times in his term of office did he find legislative acts unconstitutional. The personal liberty law was one of these. By looking back at the reasons for a federal union, Shaw actually looked ahead to the situation if some provision for runaway recapture and rendition were not a part of national law.

> If two states bordered on each other, one a slave state and the other a free state, there would of course be a constant effort of slaves to escape into the free state, and a constant temptation to slave owners to follow and recapture them, which must be done by force, unless sanctioned by treaty. Such acts on both sides must be regarded by each as violations of the exclusive territorial rights of the other, and a justifiable cause of war. There would naturally be a constant border war, leading either to interminable hostility, or to the subjugation of one by the other.

For him, and for all right thinking jurists (in his opinion), "the greater and more appalling evils in prospect" required the state of Massachusetts to cooperate in the return of runaways. There was a limit to this right of recapture and rendition of course. The individual must have "escaped" (a word emphasized in the report of the opinion) from bondage. Shaw had not forgotten *Aves*. Then looking ahead, Shaw could read law forward. Now, the time and opportunity for that intervention had passed.

> If this were a new question, now for the first time presented, we should desire to pause and take time for consideration. But though this act, the construction of which is now drawn in question, is recent, and this point, in the form in which it is now stated, is new, yet the solution of the question depends upon reasons and judicial decisions, upon legal principles and a long course of practice, which are familiar, and which have often been the subject of discussion and deliberation.[23]

Together, Story and Shaw brought Massachusetts to a central station in antebellum lawmaking, a time when lawyers and judges rose to the front rank of the nation's leaders, but a storm was coming, stirred by growing northern resistance to the Fugitive Slave Act of 1850, spurred by the rise of the Republican Party, finally bursting upon the nation with the secession of South Carolina, in December 1860. Lawyers like

Abraham Lincoln, William Henry Seward, and Alexander Stephens of Georgia could not prevent the rupture, though they tried. Shaw had already retired, and in reply to a memorial commemorating his services from the bar, he replied,

> I am happy to bear a strong testimony to my high sense of the influence of power of the legal profession, when honor, integrity and a conscientious regard to duty are its true characteristics. . . . Gentlemen, pardon me in glancing a moment at the future, so far as at last to express a hope and prayer for the continued prosperity of institutions to which our lives have been dedicated.

His last speech was given as if the winds of war were not already blowing harshly on Massachusetts's shores. As Shaw looked into the future his vision, once so clear, had clouded. He died on March 30, 1861, and with him, a legal world of states' rights and slavery began its long, agonized demise.[24]

Louis D. Brandeis, c. 1916. Library of Congress Prints and Photographs Division. Photo by Harris and Ewing.

4. Louis D. Brandeis

Shaw's reading the law forward was of a limited and cautious nature. One could almost miss it in his long recitals of precedent and statute as well as conventional references to principle and general rules. Indeed, one can sense in the bulk of his jurisprudence the rising of a classical or formal style of reading the law. By the end of the antebellum period there were enough American precedents and treatises, whose copies were widely enough circulated, to rest judicial and scholarly interpretation on existing texts. The result was the delegitimization of reading law forward. When new events required new readings of fundamental law, for example, to end slavery, lawmakers amended the Constitution rather than finding ways to extend rights. In other areas of public and private law, "By the middle of the nineteenth century the legal system had been reshaped to the advantage of men of commerce and industry. . . . if a flexible, instrumental conception of law was necessary to promote the transformation of the post-revolutionary American Legal system, it was not longer needed." Its replacement, legal formalism, better suited a market and a society dominated by great interests and "a conservative fear that legislatures might invade 'vested property rights.' "[1]

While not every teacher of law or judge bought into this conservative turn, formalist jurisprudence reassured those who had won the gold ring in the Gilded Age that it was secure in their hands. Even the weaknesses of formalism were recognized as necessary. As Thomas M. Cooley, perhaps the foremost constitutional theorist of the post–Civil War period, wrote, "the weaknesses of a written constitution are, that it establishes iron rules, which, when found inconvenient, are difficult to change." Thus the purposes of the American Revolutionaries were not to establish new laws, but "to maintain old, established principles of the Constitution, instead of overturning them." His contemporary, Harvard Law School dean Christopher Columbus Langdell, adopted a classical justification of rule of law, that law was a science, consisting of "certain principles or doctrines. . . . each of these doctrines has arrived at its present state by slow degrees, in other words, it is a growth, extending in many cases through centuries." There was no room for unanticipated exogenous events in his logically cohesive world.[2]

Not to say that formalism was without flexibility. It could and did incorporate pieces of that past hitherto unincorporated. Foremost among these projects was the reception of a broader set of historical ideas. Led by the revival (or call for the revival) in the law schools of legal history, and by the scholarship of a core of law professors and treatise writers, the infusion of older law into the curriculum of the law schools made formalism more complex and creative than it had been. But common to their varied work was the backward-looking impulse, that law was not to be read forward, even though some in this group were moderate or "mugwump" reformers. "Law was effective only when rooted in custom."[3]

At the end of the century, leading advocates for greater democracy in public law, the Populists and the Progressives, although different in their policies and membership, initiated an attack on judicial formalism. Populists in local and state governments fought a losing battle to protect debtors from creditor banks and corporations. In 1893, infuriated at the imprisonment of state officials by order of federal courts, Governor William J. Stone of Missouri condemned "the usurpation of power by the federal judiciary . . . likewise subversive of the Constitution of the country." William Jennings Bryan, Populist and then Democratic candidate for the presidency, in 1907 warned of "dangerous agitation" if some curb on the conservatism of the federal courts was not applied. Progressives campaigned to control the courts with recall of judges and took aim at the seemingly untrammeled power of federal judges to issue injunctions. For example, Progressive Governor George Sheldon of Nebraska blasted its district court for enjoining a state rate schedule for rail haulage of farmers' grain: "I believe the federal courts have abused the privilege of injunction." He wanted a constitutional amendment to curb judicial use of that power. While the Progressives were not particularly sympathetic to the industrial labor movement, the antilabor injunction's spread aroused the suspicions of liberal politicians, respected jurists, and teachers of law. Such injunctions were sought by manufacturers and businesses to curb or prevent labor union work stoppages. While temporary injunctions of this sort were often issued against organizations, for example, an entire union, they were enforceable against individual officials of the union. Failure to obey led to contempt citations and jail, even when the labor leaders had no notice of the injunction and were not represented in court when the injunction was issued. Theodore Roosevelt admonished the courts on this score. "In this matter of injunctions there is lodged in the hands of the judiciary a necessary power which is nevertheless subject to the possibility of grave abuse. It is a power that should be exercised with extreme care and should be subject to the jealous scrutiny of all men."[4]

While the conservative, classical minded bench resisted, the end-of-the-century political movements' reformism made its way into academic jurisprudence. The sociological jurisprudents, led by Harvard Law School's Roscoe Pound, tried to reattach law to its social, political, and economic roots. After a majority of the Court in *Lochner v. New York* (1905) voided a progressive regulation of bakeshop workers' hours, he told the American Bar Association that "law is often in very truth a government of the living by the dead." That insight demanded a reform of legal teaching, to make it more realistic. It asked for the restatement of the laws, to make them look forward rather than backward, and its tendrils reached into the highest offices of jurisprudence, the US Supreme Court. The next generation of Legal Realists, led by among others Karl Llewellyn, carried this task into the American Law Institute, the Model Penal Code, and a social science commitment to realistic law making. In this context, Louis Brandeis reinvigorated reading law forward as the jurisprudence of liberal democracy.[5]

Brandeis was born in Louisville, Kentucky, a slave trader's city and the first stop on the underground railroad, on November 13, 1856. He was the son of a successful extended family of Jewish merchants. The family was first generation in the United States, but his father favored abolitionism, and an uncle was a continuing source of liberal ideals. The son grew up in an atmosphere of culture, reading, and reformism. Louis attended Harvard Law School and reportedly had the highest grade average on record to that time. He entered law practice in St. Louis, then the legal center of lower midwestern business, and in

1879 relocated to a partnership in Boston with Harvard Law School classmate Samuel Warren. The partnership was very successful, but Brandeis's love of the law had mutated into a vision of the transformative power of law in the public sphere. Typical of successful lawyers of that day, many of his clients were railroads, and he was soon one of the most prominent of the railroads' corporate advisors.[6]

He could have become another John W. Davis of West Virginia, whose professional career path led him to become a spokesman for big business and a major political figure. But Brandeis traveled a different path. When Warren left the partnership, Brandeis began to represent public interest clients. Preparing lecture notes for a course on labor law, he concluded that education in the law was an essential part of a liberal arts education, for law "was a dynamic entity, reflecting social conditions," and must stay ahead of those conditions, or at least foresee them, to be truly democratic. He was the first justice to cite law review articles in his footnotes, which were themselves unique in many ways. He stressed not only the use of legislative history (and legislative intent) but the doctrine of deference to states as laboratories of legal progress. His belief in the limits of judicial law making remains a major theme in constitutional theory. Though he had (and has) his critics, his reputation as a jurist is unsurpassed.[7]

Brandeis battled monopolies, unfair banking and insurance practices, and antiunion lobbies. He was also a conservationist when that movement was getting underway. His defense of conservationist Gifford Pinchot against the accusations of corruption so aroused public opinion that Pinchot's opponent, Richard Ballinger, resigned from his secretary of the interior post and Ballinger's supporter, President William Howard Taft, was embarrassed. The "Pinchot-Ballinger Affair" was one of the reasons that Taft lost his campaign for reelection. He later paid back Brandeis in spite, in 1916 trying to convince the Senate not to confirm Brandeis's appointment to the Supreme Court. Five years later, President Warren Harding would appoint Taft chief justice, and the two men not only made up their personal differences (their different views of law regarding labor and other subjects remained far apart) but Brandeis came to admire Taft's administrative abilities as head of the federal judiciary and manager of the Court's business.[8]

Unlike Marshall, Story, and Shaw, Brandeis believed in government by the people, wanted the little guy to get a fair shake, and battled for banking and insurance regulation and public ownership of utilities. He truly hated corruption, not just in government, but in businesses and unions, and the causes he adopted (often uncompensated for his labors) were on behalf of the victims of this corruption. As he wrote to Massachusetts State assemblyman Norman Hill White, on July 6, 1907, during the campaign to establish savings bank life insurance there, "we have before us the work of putting the law into successful practice." He believed in small government, free of corruption, and feared a powerful central government beholden to great industrial interests. Power must always be supervised and checked by democratic means. In this sense, he was a Woodrow Wilson Progressive, and would become an advisor to Wilson. Wilson's campaign slogan, "new freedom," largely reflected Brandeis's own views, indeed was crafted by the latter man. In turn, Wilson became one of Brandeis's biggest supporters. In the bitterly fought confirmation hearings that brought Brandeis to the U.S. Supreme Court, Wilson's aid was unstinting and crucial. The irony is that Wilson's previous appointment, James Clark McReynolds, would become Brandeis's bitter ideological and personal enemy on the bench.[9]

One of the reasons that the corporate law bar and even former president William Howard Taft lobbied against the appointment of Brandeis to the Supreme Court, setting aside the obvious anti-Semitism in their remarks to the Senate judiciary committee hearings and matters of personal animus, was that Brandeis's speeches and writings saw the law as an "unusual opportunity for usefulness" in promoting reform. The law was a tool to fine-tune democracy. Education of the public in its own interest was a necessity. For views like this, and his role in exposing various and sundry corporate scandals, his critics cried that he lacked judicial temperament. But once on the Court, there was no finer colleague and gentleman than Brandeis. With his sometime ally Oliver Wendell Holmes Jr., Brandeis would carve out a view of a caring Constitution of individual rights.[10]

A nascent version of that view of law found a place in Brandeis's very first publication. Defending his law partner Samuel Warren's family privacy, Brandeis joined with Warren to write "The Right to Privacy" for the *Harvard Law Review* in 1890. The entire premise of the article was that the older law of privacy, resting on property, could not protect a vital emerging interest in personal privacy. "That the individual shall have full protection in person and in property is a principle as old as the common law; but it has been found necessary from time to time to define anew the exact nature and extent of such protection. Political, social, and economic changes entail the recognition of new rights, and the common law, in its eternal youth, grows to meet the demands of society." The very idea of privacy had evolved from the physical to the psychological, "So regard for human emotions soon extended the scope of personal immunity beyond the body of the individual." In the face of new kinds of intrusion into personal space from cameras, news media, and other modern technologies, "now the right to life has come to mean the right to enjoy life,—the right to be let alone." Brandeis was reading the law forward to incorporate a new world of information, in the process finding room in the law for a capacious concept of privacy.[11]

On two other occasions before he joined the Supreme Court Brandeis probed ways that lawyers could read law in this fashion. The first of these was an address at the Harvard Ethical Society on May 4, 1905, a time when a malign partnership of government and business allowed corruption to flourish. The address was titled "The Opportunity in the Law" and came two years before the already-busy Brandeis agreed to prepare litigation for Oregon laundresses and the state law that limited their hours of work. He framed his address as a call to future lawyers to join in the effort to reform law.[12]

Brandeis's rhetorical technique was to show how lawyering should incorporate new opportunities, then circle back to impose those future obligations on the interpretation of existing law. "What you want is this," he told the Harvard undergraduates: "Standing not far from the threshold of active life, feeling the generous impulse for service which the University fosters, you wish to know whether the legal profession would afford you special opportunities for usefulness to your fellowmen, and, if so, what the obligations and limitations are which it imposes." The audience may or may not have shared this impulse with Brandeis, but he did not ask them. Instead, he simply proceeded, "every legitimate occupation, be it profession or business or trade, furnishes abundant opportunities for usefulness." It was not a self-interested usefulness, but service to an unseen future. And "the legal profession does afford in America unusual opportunities for usefulness."[13]

That usefulness ultimately lay in the reinterpretation of law itself. It had always been this way. "The great achievement of the English-speaking people is the attainment of liberty through law. It is natural, therefore, that those who have been trained in the law should have borne an important part in that struggle for liberty and in the government which resulted." Brandeis lumped together the lawyers whom Hamilton and Jefferson divided among themselves. "Nearly every great lawyer was then a statesman; and nearly every statesman, great or small, was a lawyer." What did they share? "With the introduction of a written constitution the law became with us a far more important factor in the ordinary conduct of political life than it did in England. Legal questions were constantly arising and the lawyer was necessary to settle them." How best to do that? Not with arcane or obscure technicalities. But with the facts of everyday life. "The lawyer's processes of reasoning, his logical conclusions, are being constantly tested by experience. He is running up against facts at every point. Indeed it is a maxim of the law: Out of the facts grows the law; that is, propositions are not considered abstractly, but always with reference to facts."[14]

That insight in itself was a departure from the formalist canon that the law was rule-bound, and its shining reason rested on an internal logic. For Brandeis the facts led inexorably to a different reading of the best law, for "The lawyer's investigations into the facts are limited by time and space. His investigations have reference always to some practical end." That practical end was the rethinking of existing law to make it open to future facts. Back and forth the legal mind went, from existing law, to fact, to these facts projected into the future, then back to existing law to read it in a way that accommodated the future. The lawyer must come to a decision, however. He was a doer, not an Olympian contemplator. He must see the future. He must advise. "These are the reasons why the lawyer has acquired a position materially different from that of other men. It is the position of the adviser of men." Facts in themselves do not dictate futures. They represent what has happened in the past. A better jurisprudence recasts facts as predictions of future events, and bades law be read accordingly.[15]

Perhaps in some sense, giving advice to students is inherently futurist. It looks to the best outcome in their futures, then returns to their present to reformat their education. Or so he advised them. Brandeis was noteworthy among lawyers in his day in preferring the role of advisor to that of mere agent of his clients. He stepped in before they went to court, seeing their future as well as the future of the law. He wanted them to see law not as a way to make and win claims rooted in the past, but as a way to improve the future.

> The ordinary man thinks of the Bar as a body of men who are trying cases, perhaps even trying criminal cases. Of course there is an immense amount of litigation going on; and a great deal of the time of many lawyers is devoted to litigation. But by far the greater part of the work done by lawyers is done not in court, but in advising men on important matters, and mainly in business affairs.

Because of his training, experience, and approach, the lawyer (for whom read Brandeis himself) would shape public law. "The magnitude and scope of these operations remove them almost wholly from the realm of "petty trafficking" which people formerly used to associate with trade. The questions which arise are more nearly questions of statesmanship. The relations created call in many instances for the exercise of the highest diplomacy."[16]

Here Brandeis aligned himself (again speaking in a kind of third person) with the lawyers of the founding era. He would make the connection even stronger at the end of this portion of the talk. "The magnitude, difficulty and importance of the problems involved are often as great as in the matters of state with which lawyers were formerly frequently associated." The matters were not those of state making, "but of using law to negotiate among the relations of the great trusts to the consumers or to their employees is like that of feudal lords to commoners or dependents. The relations of public-service corporations to the people raise questions not unlike those presented by the monopolies of old." An American economy and commerce very different from that in the founders' day needed a different kind of lawyer, one whose view of law was robustly consequentialist. "Although the lawyer is not playing in affairs of state the part he once did, his influence is, or at all events may be, quite as important as it ever was in the United States; and it is simply a question how that influence is to be exerted." Alas, some of these lawyers, "Instead of holding a position of independence, between the wealthy and the people, prepared to curb the excesses of either, able lawyers have, to a large extent, allowed themselves to become adjuncts of great corporations and have neglected the obligation to use their powers for the protection of the people." While they might be problem solvers, they did not and would not read the law forward.[17]

Brandeis was prone to sermonizing, and some of these passages resembled the Jeremiads of Puritan ministers at the end of the seventeenth century. They warned against corruption in the clergy, as Brandeis condemned corruption in the law profession. "For nearly a generation the leaders of the Bar have, with few exceptions, not only failed to take part in constructive legislation designed to solve in the public interest our great social, economic and industrial problems; but they have failed likewise to oppose legislation prompted by selfish interests." Why? Their souls had been purchased because they were the leaders of the bar. "In the first place, the counsel selected to represent important private interests possesses usually ability of a high order, while the public is often inadequately represented or wholly unrepresented." Alas, "lawyers have, as a rule, failed to consider this distinction between practice in courts involving only private interests, and practice before the legislature or city council involving public interests. Some men of high professional standing have even endeavored to justify their course in advocating professionally legislation which in their character as citizens they would have voted against."[18]

Now he came to application of the doctrine (another conventional part of the Jeremiad) and a frank invocation to read law forward.

Here, consequently, is the great opportunity in the law. The next generation must witness a continuing and ever-increasing contest between those who have and those who have not. The industrial world is in a state of ferment. . . . The people are beginning to doubt whether in the long run democracy and absolutism can coexist in the same community; beginning to doubt whether there is a justification for the great inequalities in the distribution of wealth, for the rapid creation of fortunes, more mysterious than the deeds of Aladdin's lamp.

The future lay with young and able lawyers who could talk with and act for the workingman in rereading the law. "Nothing can better fit you for taking part in the solution of these problems, than the study and preeminently the practice of law. Those of you who feel drawn to that profession may rest assured that you will find in it an opportunity for usefulness which is probably unequalled. There is a call upon the legal profession to do a great work for this country."[19]

Brandeis took his own advice. He battled against the consolidation of commercial and investment banks, along with unfair practices by insurance companies, public utilities, and corporations. He fought the Boston Elevated Railway's attempt to monopolize the city's traction service, for example, flooding the mail with letters "to supporters," giving them the facts and figures they needed, himself a grey eminence behind the scenes. "He was a fighter who looked ahead," pushing for public ownership of public transportation. He exhibited the same vision, and deployed the same techniques fighting for fair utility rates, and promoted the savings bank life insurance system. That was "an experiment; something quite new" in which law, social planning, and individual activity (in saving as insurance) came together. Small was good; even if the benefits were small, they were saved from the rapacity and intransigent greed of a great insurance company oligopoly. Now the lawyer became the lecturer, promoting the scheme; now he became the counselor of governors and commissions; now he worked tirelessly on the details of the plan. The same energy and vision went to promoting employee participation in management. Unions were good, but the empowerment of workers was even better. So emerged his ideal of industrial democracy, a shared responsibility for output and profits. As he told a Fourth of July gathering at Faneuil Hall in 1915, "What are the American ideals? They are the development of the individual for his own and the common good; the development of the individual through liberty and the attainment of the common good through democracy and social justice."[20]

There was in this, as in Brandeis's other speeches before he was named to the Court, and in his correspondence with Felix Frankfurter, a Harvard Law School professor and younger protégé, a thread of intellectual elitism. The superior men must undertake to protect the public against the corruption of government and big business. Superior men must enter government service. Superior men had superior ability. Superior men would interpret the law under the new conditions of life. As he wrote to Frankfurter on January 28, 1913, "it seems to me that a small group of able, disinterested, well-equipped men, who could give their time to criticism and discussion of legislative proposals, . . . would be of great assistance in the forward movement" in the field of science and invention. Brandeis was always looking for the "first class man" to sponsor.[21]

Brandeis involved himself in local and state political campaigns, but not national politics until he found in Progressive Robert LaFollette a kindred spirit. LaFollette was a reform Republican, and in 1911 announced a campaign for the presidency that Brandeis wholly supported. When that campaign was swallowed by Theodore Roosevelt's decision to return to the presidency, Brandeis found in New Jersey Governor Woodrow Wilson another kindred spirit. Wilson believed in reform from the bottom up, protecting the ordinary citizen through regulation and good government. But Wilson was a Democrat, and that meant that Brandeis had to switch his political horses in midstream. He did and, although he did not personally know Wilson, soon began to speak for and write to Wilson. Many of Wilson's ideas for the "new freedom" came from Brandeis's pen. Soon, the two men formed a friendship, and Brandeis henceforth regarded the new president with respect and warmth. Whether Wilson considered Brandeis for a cabinet post or not, no offer emerged, which was just as well, since Brandeis preferred to remain a private citizen. Nevertheless, Brandeis had soon became the sort of consultant to Wilson as he had been to various reform groups.[22]

The second of the jurisprudential essays came in 1916, shortly before he was nominated for a seat on the Supreme Court. Brandeis addressed the Chicago Bar Association in a major address. The date and the occasion make it a very special contribution to his corpus of writings. But the January 3, 1916, address was also a summation of his views of the law, and its transformative power. The talk seemed to be a review of existing and anticipated law cases, but Brandeis had a lot more on his mind.[23]

Brandeis saw law and government as intertwined, and progress in the latter brought changes in the former. That history began with the Constitution. "The history of the United States, since the adoption of the constitution, covers less than 128 years. Yet in that short period the American ideal of government has been greatly modified. At first our ideal was expressed as 'A government of laws and not of men.' Then it became 'A government of the people, by the people, for the people.' Now it is 'Democracy and social justice.'" From a Progressive point of view, that last phrase might seem obvious—Theodore Roosevelt and Woodrow Wilson were both lawyers and both saw law as a vehicle for reform. But Brandeis was doing a lot more than flashing his Progressive credentials. He was challenging the audience to see the future of both government and law.[24]

Lest they miss the challenge, he doubled down on it. "In the last half century our democracy has deepened. Coincidentally there has been a shifting of our longing from legal justice to social justice, and—it must be admitted—also a waning respect for law. Is there any causal connection between the shifting of our longing from legal justice to social justice and waning respect for law? If so, was that result unavoidable?" Now, when he might have expanded on the notion of law as social justice, Brandeis retreated into what looked like the brief in *Muller v. Oregon.*

> Many different causes contributed to this waning respect for law. Some related specifically to the lawyer, some to the courts and some to the substantive law itself. . . . Many different remedies must be applied before the ground lost can be fully recovered and the domain of law extended further. The causes and the remedies have received perhaps their most helpful discussion from three lawyers whom we associate with Chicago: Professor Roscoe Pound, recently secured for Harvard, who stands preeminently in service in this connection; Professor [John Henry] Wigmore; and Professor [Ernst] Freund.

He did not mention his own contributions. His self-effacement was by now nearly legendary. What is more, he went back in time before he moved forward, another characteristic of his style of argumentation. "The challenge of existing law is not a manifestation peculiar to our country or to our time. Sporadic dissatisfaction has doubtless existed in every country at all times." But the person he named was Jeremy Bentham, an advocate of criminal justice reform (to which Brandeis himself subscribed). Now he brought his audience home: "Since the adoption of the federal constitution, and notably within the last fifty years, we have passed through an economic and social revolution which affected the life of the people more fundamentally than any political revolution known to history." Industrialism, the end of slavery, the emancipation of women, technological advances, all were called into question by the arrival of the great monopolistic corporations. Lawyers served these corporations against the public interest. Small businessmen and laborers lost status and autonomy. To which "legal science—the unwritten or judge-made laws as distinguished from legislation—was largely deaf and blind."[25]

Aiding and abetting the corruption corporations, "Courts continued to ignore newly arisen social needs. They applied complacently 18th century conceptions of the liberty of the individual and of the sacredness of private property. Early 19th century scientific half-truths, like 'The survival of the fittest,' which translated into practice meant 'The devil take the hindmost,' were erected by judicial sanction into a moral law." Worse, "Where statutes giving expression to the new social spirit were clearly constitutional, judges, imbued with the relentless spirit of individualism, often construed them away. Where any doubt as to the constitutionality of such statutes could find lodgment, courts all too frequently declared the acts void." This was law looking backward, where old outmoded doctrines protected new and dangerous institutions, and "constitutional limitations were invoked to stop the natural vent of legislation." He then cited US Supreme Court decisions as evidence, conceding some recession of the high tide of laissez-faire formalist judging. Flickering candles in the night appeared in state court cases, particularly from New York. He read from the cases, again veiling his own strong views by quoting others.[26]

But his message was clear. The struggle continued. Courts must be willing to read the facts of life into the law, look ahead to future needs. The older view that regulatory statutes violated the right to private property construed by courts to lie in the Fourteenth Amendment must fall to "a full knowledge of the facts out of which it arises and to which it is to be applied. But the struggle for the living law has not been fully won." Note the language of struggle. Who is struggling? State legislatures? Lobbyists for the unions? The small businessman? The people themselves? It is the legal profession that carries on the struggle.[27]

There was one adequate remedy. It is not foolproof, but it was appropriate.

> What we need is not to displace the courts, but to make them efficient instruments of justice; not to displace the lawyer, but to fit him for his official or judicial task. And indeed the task of fitting the lawyer and the judge to perform adequately the functions of harmonizing law with life is a task far easier of accomplishment than that of endowing men, who lack legal training, with the necessary qualifications.

Ironically, Brandeis knew that he would soon leave the ranks of the one, and join the ranks of the other. Thus, the challenge was as much to him to find a way to put this jurisprudence into practice, as to his audience. For "The judge came to the bench unequipped with the necessary knowledge of economic and social science, and his judgment suffered likewise through lack of equipment in the lawyers who presented the cases to him. For a judge rarely performs his functions adequately unless the case before him is adequately presented."[28]

Fortunately, the remedy lay not alone on the bench. "Nearly every lawyer of ability took some part in political life. Our greatest judges, Marshall, Kent, Story, Shaw, had secured this training." Brandeis found an unlikely forerunner in Alexander Hamilton.

> [F. S.] Oliver, in his study of Alexander Hamilton, pictured the value of such training in public affairs: "In the vigor of his youth and at the very summit of hope, he brought to the study of the law a character already trained and tested by the realities of life, formed by success, experienced in the facts and disorders with which the law has to deal. Before he began a

study of the remedies he had a wide knowledge of the conditions of human society. . . . With him . . . the law was . . . a reality, quick, human, buxom and jolly, and not a formula, pinched, stiff, banded and dusty like a royal mummy of Egypt."[29]

Recalling his advice to Frankfurter on legislation three years earlier, Brandeis closed with the confident assertion that "Every beneficent change in legislation . . . comes from a fresh study of social conditions, and social ends, and from such rejection of obsolete laws to make room for a rule which fits the new facts." Law was, as he wrote to Frankfurter then, "a field for discovery and invention." It had to be read forward.[30]

The message of "The Living Law," combined with "Opportunities in the Law" and "The Right to Privacy," was not that the law changed itself, but that it must be changed by lawyers looking to the future. Brandeis was not a theorist. He reveled in facts. This, added to his naturally cautious, careful way of revealing his thinking, nevertheless showed an underlying commitment to reading law forward.

On January 28, 1916, Wilson's nomination of Brandeis for a seat on the Court was announced. Within Wilson's official family, and the wider circle of Progressives, the nomination was the consensus choice. No one expected an easy confirmation hearing, but neither did anyone expect the "firestorm" of protests that erupted. For the next six months, agonizingly slowly, the Senate heard testimony. At last, it reported favorably on his fitness. On May 8, Wilson weighed in again in uncompromising support of his nominee. The hearings were divided along party lines; in general progressives supported and conservatives opposed. At least one supporter in the Senate recognized Brandeis's forward-looking jurisprudence. Thomas J. Walsh, a Progressive Democrat from Montana, wrote to the Senate committee on April 3: "The Bar is still the bulwark of the liberties of the people. To it they must look in the future as they have in all our history for fearless champions." Brandeis was one. The Senate voted to confirm the appointment on June 1, 47–22.[31]

The bitterness of the hearings had surprised him (though perhaps they should not have), in particular how critics attacked his lack of judicial temperament (meaning among other things, his reading the law forward). He did not attend the hearings, but wrote letters from

Boston, five and six a day, about it. Outwardly calm, he became even more cautious and even at times deliberately abstruse in his writing. This affected his view of legal process, or at least his willingness to show it openly. In particular, he developed a series of curbs on himself—hiding his proclivity to read law forward in the middle of opinions, sometimes in the middle of paragraphs, and surrounding it with footnotes, or putting it into the footnotes. He expanded the use of law review articles in notes (something that Justice Gray had introduced), to subtly strengthen a particular point. He developed the procedural device of concurring with opinions that were actually dissents. Above all, he imbedded his reform agenda in a hedgerow of facts. When all this did not shield his view of law, he simply concealed his own voice. It was the law, or the court, that was speaking. After all, everyone who read the opinions of the Court over time knew that they "bowed to the lessons of experience and the force of better reasoning." Of course, that was Brandeis writing in dissent.[32]

Brandeis more than shouldered his fair load of writing on the Court. He ceased giving public addresses, publishing law review pieces, and writing books and articles (though he did suggest article material to Felix Frankfurter and other correspondents, and he conceded that "in American law, the next 25 years belong to the [law school] teachers"). But then, the Court was much busier (that is, had a heavier docket load) than today. Litigants could still bring a case to the Court on a writ of error if a federal issue or a constitutional challenge were involved in the state court proceedings. The Court did not control its own case load. This left the High Court with a docket still crammed with nonconstitutional questions. Brandeis routinely wrote (almost always for the majority) around twenty opinions every session of the court (a total of 531 over twenty-three years).[33]

As a justice, Brandeis was conscientious, courteous to the other justices (even to McReynolds), and did not try to rewrite the law according to his prior advocacy. He listened to the bright young law clerks Felix Frankfurter sent him from Harvard Law School, weighed their opinions, even their corrections, but in the end wrote his own opinions. Thus these documents are reflective of his thinking. The active reformist lawyer could not replay that role in robes (at least not Brandeis), so his reading law forward must be teased out from a relatively small number of his opinions, often dissents.[34]

Brandeis was no advocate of judicial activism. But he did engage in it—and one can find it if one tries, for example, in an unpublished opinion in 1922: "Our Constitution is not a straight-jacket. It is a living organism. As such it is capable of growth—of expansion and of adaption to new conditions. Growth implies changes, political, economic, and social." Note, however, how he explained that growth, as though somehow it was coming from the inside of the Constitution, as if it were in the DNA of the text. Thus, "Because our Constitution possessed the capacity for adaption, it has endured as the fundamental law of an ever developing people." What the judge could only hint, the reform lawyer had already revealed.[35]

Sometimes the veil of caution lifted a little. Brandeis believed in "Democracy as a ceaseless process rather than an end," and education, civil responsibility, decentralization of power, experimentation—these were Brandeis's "constant focus." Most of his occasional writings and speeches concerned these interests outside of the profession, although law was always the platform for his reformist stance. Within that sphere, his attention was drawn to legislation. He did not rely on courts, as they looked backward, and in any case he was suspicious of activist courts. Legislatures, properly advised, looked forward. As he wrote in *New State Ice Company v. Liebmann* (1931), albeit in dissent, which freed him from some of the constraints of the robe (his many opinions for the majority were shorter; the dissents were longer), "To stay experimentation in things social and economic is a grave responsibility." This same caution ran through all his opinions, but "Denial of the right to experiment may be fraught with serious consequences to the nation." Who then had the primary responsibility for reading the law forward? "It is one of the happy incidents of the federal system that a single courageous state may, if its citizens choose, serve as a laboratory; and try novel social and economic experiments without risk to the rest of the country." His invitation came with a warning. "This Court has the power to prevent an experiment. We may strike down the statute which embodies it on the ground that, in our opinion, the measure is arbitrary, capricious, or unreasonable." One is reminded of

Ann Green Phillips's admonition to her husband, the radical abolitionist Wendell Phillips: "don't shillyshally." Wendell rarely did. Brandeis habitually shillyshallied. He celebrated reading the law forward and then cautioned against its excess. Then he restrained that caution: "But, in the exercise of this high power, we must be ever on our guard, lest we erect our prejudices into legal principles. If we would guide by the light of reason, we must let our minds be bold."[36]

When a case arose calling for looking into the future, he demonstrated how reading the law forward could lead to better law. For example, in one railroad workers compensation case, the majority agreed with a lower federal court that the state compensations laws had to bow to federal laws, and if the federal law did not provide compensation to an injured worker, then the state could not provide it. Brandeis dissented: In the past, "The wrongs suffered [by railroad workers] were flagrant; the demand for redress insistent; and the efforts to secure remedial legislation widespread. But the opponents were alert, potent, and securely entrenched." In such cases, the dead hand of the past arose from its grave. But

> the promoters of remedial action, unable to overcome the efficient opposition presented in the legislatures of the several states, sought and secured the powerful support of the President. Congress was appealed to and used its power over interstate commerce to afford relief. The Federal Employers' Liability Act was, in a sense, emergency legislation. The circumstances attending its passage were such as to preclude the belief that thereby Congress intended to deny to the states the power to provide for compensation or relief for injuries not covered by it.

For the Court to read the act against its purpose was to substitute the past for the future. It should be read forward to find its best outcomes:

> Later decisions disclose how large a part of the injuries resulting from the railroads' negligence are thus excluded from the operation of the Federal law. For the act was held to apply only to those directly engaged in interstate commerce. This excludes not only those engaged in intrastate commerce, but also the many who—while engaged on work for interstate commerce, as in repairing engines or cars—are not directly engaged in it.

Likewise it excludes employees who, though habitually engaged directly in interstate commerce, happen to be injured or killed through the railroads' negligence, while performing some work in intrastate commerce.

Brandeis read the text of the act differently from the majority. "The scope of the act is so narrow as to preclude the belief that thereby Congress intended to deny to the states the power to provide compensation or relief for injuries not covered by it." The act was part of a reform of worker liability that looks ahead. It was incomplete, but its incompleteness should not be read backward, as the majority had done. Instead, it should be read forward. "Attention should be directed, not to the employer's fault, but to the employee's misfortune. Compensation should be general, not sporadic; certain, not conjectural; speedy, not delayed." The correct reading of law saw its impact on the future. "Society needs such a protection as much as the individual; because ultimately society must bear the burden, financial and otherwise, of the heavy losses which accidents entail." And in this light the act was to be reinterpreted.[37]

Brandeis had supported labor unions but held them responsible for their actions. In an era when businesses sought and federal courts granted antiunion injunctions freely, he had helped Progressives curb the abuse with the Clayton Antitrust Act of 1914. An Arizona law barred such injunctions, but when a business whose former employees picketed and distributed leaflets, the Supreme Court, under new chief justice Taft, reversed the Arizona courts' ruling upholding the statute. In *Truax v. Corrigan* (1921) Brandeis dissented.[38]

In the course of his dissent, Brandeis once again revealed the capacity of a forward-looking jurisprudence. Reviewing the statute law and the precedents of the Court, he reported, "Practically every change in the law governing the relation of employer and employee must abridge, in some respect, the liberty or property of one of the parties—if liberty and property be measured by the standard of the law theretofore prevailing." Then he rehearsed the facts. Finally, in the middle of the paragraph, he read the law forward. "Nearly all legislation involves a weighing of public needs as against private desires; and likewise a weighing of relative social values. Since government is not an exact science, prevailing public opinion concerning the evils and the remedy is among the important facts deserving consideration; particularly, when the public conviction is both deep-seated and widespread and has been reached after deliberation." In other words, read the relevant laws, including the Constitution, in light of the best outcome for the general good. The measure of that lay not in the law itself, or any earlier interpretation of that law, but in how the law would be applied in the future. Then use that best outcome to interpret the meaning of the law.[39]

Justice Brandeis's willingness to read law forward became even clearer in a series of constitutional cases involving the Bill of Rights. Brandeis had not at first realized the importance of "thinking through" freedom of speech cases thrown up by the Espionage and Treason Acts during the First World War. He had agreed with Holmes's opinions for the Court in a series of cases involving dissent against intervention in World War I, then joined Holmes in dissent in the last of the cases. But Holmes's formulations of a marketplace of ideas in which better speech would ultimately win out, and the yelling fire in a crowded theater test, were elegant abstractions. In Brandeis's dissent in *Gilbert v. Minnesota* (1920), his concurrence in *Whitney v. California* (1927), and his dissent in *Olmstead v. U.S.* (1928), he diverged from Holmes's tests.[40]

The Espionage Act of 1917 and the Sedition Act of 1918 were wartime measures. They could not have been passed by Congress without the war, but they remained on the books after the war. In addition to spelling out the varieties of espionage, the first act had an omnibus section 3, part of which read: "Whoever, when the United States is at war, shall willfully make or convey false reports or false statements with intent to interfere with the operation or success of the military or naval forces of the United States or to promote the success of its enemies and whoever when the United States is at war, shall willfully cause or attempt to cause insubordination, disloyalty, mutiny, refusal of duty, in the military or naval forces of the United States, or shall willfully obstruct the recruiting or enlistment service of the United States, to the injury of the service or of the United States" was liable to prosecution, fine, imprisonment, and other penalties. There was in addition a penalty for conspiracy to violate the act so broadly defined that it could include anyone who met with or agreed with someone who acted in furtherance of the conspiracy. The Sedition Act of 1918 added punishment for "any disloyal, profane, scurrilous, or abusive language about the form of government of the United States . . . or the flag of the United States, or the uniform of the Army or Navy."[41]

The cases at issue were *Schenck v. U.S.* (1919), *Debs v. U.S.* (1919), *Frohwerk v. U.S.* (1919), and *Abrams v. U.S.* (1919). They were all short decisions, for the applicable law seemed easy to Holmes. He wrote for a unanimous Court in the first three, then dissented in the fourth. There was no extended First Amendment analysis until Holmes revisited his own views and Brandeis decided to dissent in *Gilbert*.

Charles Schenk was the secretary general of the Socialist Party and oversaw the printing and mailing of circulars to men eligible for the draft. One circular urged that the men not report for the draft and declared the war illegal. It urged that readers petition the government against the Conscription Act. The First Amendment, read literally, explicitly sanctioned petition, free speech, and free press. But the mailing violated the Espionage Act, and went out after the act was passed. Thus the case was a test of the constitutionality of the Espionage Act, not the Conscription Act. By 1919, when the Court heard the appeal, the war was over and the issue might have been mooted. For Holmes, however, the case raised important questions of the relationship of individuals and their government in time of war. "We admit that in many places and in ordinary times the defendants in saying all that was said in the circular would have been within their constitutional rights . . . [but] the character of every act depends upon the circumstances in which it is done. The most stringent protection of free speech would not protect a man in falsely shouting fire in a theater and causing a panic." [42]

Holmes had adopted an "evil tendency" test. The time and place of the speech determined whether it had an evil tendency. In any case, it was unlikely that Schenk's circular would have any impact on the draft. Holmes disagreed. "When a nation is at war many things that might be said in time of peace are such a hindrance to its effort that their utterance will not be endured. . . . The question in every case is whether the words used are used in such circumstances and are of such a nature as to create a clear and present danger that they will bring about the substantive evils that Congress has a right to prevent."[43]

The Debs case was now easily disposed. Eugene V. Debs, a socialist, told a Canton, Ohio, audience that the war was illegal. He was indicted, tried, and convicted under the Espionage Act and sentenced to ten years in jail. Represented by Clarence Darrow, he appealed, resting his case squarely upon the First Amendment. Speech inciting riot, like libel and slander, Darrow conceded, is not protected by the Amendment, but Debs was merely defending socialism and attacking capitalism, a political argument. No riot followed. There was no "clear and present danger" to the nation or the war effort. But the tenor of the speech triggered Holmes's ire. In it "there followed personal experiences and illustrations of the growth of socialism, a glorification of minorities, and a prophecy of success." Notably in this supposed litany of evils was Holmes's reference to the "glorification of minorities." To be sure, Holmes need not have added any of this, for he opined that the case was wholly within the *Schenk* precedent and the Court agreed.[44]

In the third of the quartet of cases, Jacob Frohwerk was a copyeditor at a St. Louis, Missouri, German-language newspaper who prepared for publication articles critical of American entry into the war. What might not be mailed or said in public surely could not be printed in a newspaper, Holmes concluded. Holmes relented a little, admitting that "it might be that all this might be said or written even in time of war in circumstances that would into make it a crime. We do not lose our right to condemn either measures or men because the Country is at war." But even if Frohwerk was merely churning out what his publisher wanted, he was guilty under the act, and subject to ten years at hard labor in a federal penitentiary.[45]

Holmes's dissent in *Abrams v. U.S.*, effectively discarding his prior opinions, was a landmark in First Amendment jurisprudence. Holmes never explained himself (and even refused to concede that he had changed his mind), but a "Red Scare," an antiradical sweep inaugurated by Wilson's attorney general, A. Mitchell Palmer, after the war ended, troubled Holmes. Holmes's young protege, Harvard Law School professor Felix Frankfurter, joined with Harvard Law School dean Roscoe Pound to document the evils of the Red Scare. Leading intellectuals who were not socialists, men like John Dewey, were making the case for a broad reading of First Amendment liberties, and Holmes respected these men. Judge Learned Hand, who had found Schenck innocent, was corresponding with Holmes, as were Harvard Law School professors Zechariah Chafee and Ernst Freund. Freund's blast at the *Debs* decision was as powerful as Pound's blast at *Lochner*. Brandeis, hearing from many of the same men, and worried about the fate of young Harvard law professor Zechariah Chafee, who opposed the prosecution openly, would join in the dissent.[46]

The five defendants in *Abrams v. U.S.*, all young anarchists born in Russia, dropped leaflets in English and Yiddish from a Lower East Side, Manhattan, window criticizing President Wilson's silence about the allies' opposition to the Bolshevik Revolution. Trial in the federal district court, with Henry De Lamar Clayton, an Alabama federal district court judge presiding by assignment, was tainted by the judge's overt animus toward the defendants, but that was not the basis for the appeal to the High Court. Instead, it was based on the "clear and present danger" test. The majority, with Justice John Clarke citing the three Holmes opinions, found that the leaflets violated the Espionage Acts. Clarke found that "the purpose of this [leaflet] obviously was to persuade the persons to whom it was addressed to turn a deaf ear to patriotic appeals in behalf of the government of the United States" and that was tantamount to a conspiracy to defeat the war effort.[47]

In dissent, Holmes found that these leaflets "in no way attack the form of government of the United States," and that the authors did not intend any such act. A strict reading of the Espionage Acts must find real intent. "The principle of the right to free speech is always the same. It is only the present danger of immediate evil or an intent to bring it about that warrants Congress setting a limit to the expression of opinion." These were "silly" publications, and in any case, political speech was privileged. "Congress certainly cannot forbid all effort to change the mind of the country." History—the history of a great democracy—offered a different lesson.

When men have realized that time has upset many fighting faiths, they may come to believe even more than they believe the very foundations of their own conduct that the ultimate good desired is better reached by free trade in ideas—that the best test of truth is the power of the thought to get itself accepted in the competition of the market, and that truth is the only ground upon which their wishes safely can be carried out. That at any rate is the theory of our Constitution.[48]

Nothing in the Constitution included such free marketplaces of ideas, but Holmes added this potent idea to the store of constitutional truths. The Constitution "is an experiment, as all life is an experiment. Every year if not every day we have to wager our salvation upon some prophecy based upon imperfect knowledge." This was a living Constitution, one that grew and embraced larger truths and freedoms. It was a tolerant Constitution that had room for many contradictory opinions. Brandeis concurred.[49]

Brandeis's dissent in *Gilbert v. Minnesota* (1920) went beyond Holmes's dissent in *Abrams*. (Holmes voted with the majority.) It was a powerful argument for the incorporation of the First Amendment freedom of speech into the Fourteenth Amendment's due process requirement for state law because the future held many more instances of suppression. Unlike in the other cases, Joseph Gilbert violated a state sedition law that paralleled the federal law. Gilbert was a leader in the Non-Partisan League, a peace organization, and at a public meeting on August 18, 1917, shortly after the United States entered World War I, he told his audience that a Minnesota law prohibited teaching the doctrine of pacifism. He argued that he had a free speech right to speak on a public matter. There was no riot; no threat to the draft; and the speech, like his views, was entirely peaceable—no call to arms. He was convicted of violating the law. The statute was not a wartime measure—because it applied in peacetime as well. It simply prohibited a certain kind of speech.

Sections 1 and 2 prohibit teaching or advocating by printed matter, writing or word of mouth, that men should not enlist in the military or naval forces of the United States. The prohibition is made to apply whatever the motive, the intention, or the purpose of him who teaches. It applies alike to the preacher in the pulpit, the professor at the university, the speaker at a political meeting, the lecturer at a society or club gathering. Whatever the nature of the meeting and whether it be public or private, the prohibition is absolute, if five persons are assembled.[50]

It did not matter to the state whether Gilbert was suggesting that the young men in the audience enter a different profession than the military, or that the military forces were not right for their best interest, or any other reason that was, well, reasonable. The law singled out content and criminalized it. It did not regard acts, but beliefs and their expression. It did not matter whether the statement was public, for it applied to an utterance in a person's home so long as more than five people heard it. "Thus the statute invades the privacy and freedom of the home. Father and mother may not follow the promptings of religious belief, of conscience or of conviction, and teach son or daughter the doctrine of pacifism. If they do any police officer may summarily arrest them." But the state action was protected against a First Amendment claim because "it is said that the guaranty against abridging freedom of speech contained in the First Amendment of the Federal Constitution applies only to federal action; that the legislation here complained of is that of a State; that the validity of the statute has been sustained by its highest court as a police measure; that the matter is one of state concern; and that, consequently this court cannot interfere." To Brandeis, this made no sense, since the right was a national one, and Gilbert was as much a citizen of the United States as he was of Minnesota.[51]

Brandeis assumed that the right to speak freely concerning functions of the Federal Government is a privilege or immunity of every citizen of the United States that, even before the adoption of the Fourteenth Amendment, a state was powerless to curtail. What was the purpose of the Fourteenth Amendment if not to apply to the states the great rights of the First Amendment? But how to apply them? By analogy of course.

It was held in *Crandall v. Nevada*, . . . that the United States has the power to call to the seat of government or elsewhere any citizen to aid it in the conduct of public affairs; that every citizen has the correlative right to go there or anywhere in the pursuit of public or private business; and that "no power can exist in a State to obstruct this right which would not enable it to defeat the purpose for which the government was established." The right of a citizen of the United States to take part, for his own or the country's benefit, in the making of federal laws and in the conduct of the Government, necessarily includes the right to speak or write about them; to endeavor to make his own opinion concerning laws existing or contemplated prevail; and, to this end, to teach the truth as he sees it.

If people assembled peaceably in petitioning Congress for redress, why would it matter whether they assembled in Minnesota? Were any state to interfere, surely that interference would render the federal right meaningless, and reduce the Constitution to where it was before the Fourteenth Amendment. Next, he offered a sop to his friend and ally Holmes: "There are times when those charged with the responsibility of Government, faced with clear and present danger, may conclude that suppression of divergent opinion is imperative; because the emergency does not permit reliance upon the slower conquest of error by truth. And in such emergencies the power to suppress exists." But Gilbert's words did not amount to a clear and present danger to anyone. Again, "the duty of preserving the state governments falls ultimately upon the Federal Government. . . . And the superior responsibility carries with it the superior right."[52]

Then, Brandeis stopped in his tracks. He would not generalize from his analysis of the case. "As the Minnesota statute is in my opinion invalid because it interferes with federal functions and with the right of a citizen of the United States to discuss them, I see no occasion to consider whether it violates also the Fourteenth Amendment." But he had already found that so. Why step back from it? Well, only a half-step back perhaps. A bocage of case citations should do the trick, together showing that the Fourteenth Amendment and federal law must incorporate the First Amendment. After which he concluded, "I cannot believe that the liberty guaranteed by the Fourteenth Amendment [under the *Lochner* majority opinion] includes only liberty to acquire and to enjoy property." In short, although that doctrine did not appear in any of the cases he cited, or in First Amendment precedent, the existing law must be read forward, to see the danger in such laws as

Minnesota's, and then back to incorporate First Amendment guarantees in the Fourteenth Amendment.[53]

Brandeis's dissent was the first to argue for incorporation of the First Amendment free speech provisions in the Fourteenth Amendment Due Process Clause, hence imposing it upon the states. It would become part of Justice Edward T. Sanford's majority opinion in *Gitlow v. New York* (1925), and would reappear in the next great free speech case, *Whitney v. California* (1927). This time Brandeis wrote a dissent cloaked as a concurrence. In it, the recursive loop of law was again partly concealed, but not easily missed by an alert eye.[54]

A recitation of facts opened Brandeis's opinion. "Miss Whitney was convicted of the felony of assisting in organizing, in the year 1919, the Communist Labor Party of California, of being a member of it, and of assembling with it. These acts are held to constitute a crime, because the party was formed to teach criminal syndicalism." These facts led immediately to the conclusion that "The statute which made these acts a crime restricted the right of free speech and of assembly theretofore existing. The claim is that the statute, as applied, denied to Miss Whitney the liberty guaranteed by the Fourteenth Amendment." The problem with the state statute was that it was rooted in the past—a very distant and different past from Whitney's (and Brandeis's) own. "The felony which the statute created is a crime very unlike the old felony of conspiracy or the old misdemeanor of unlawful assembly." It rendered what was by now a legal assembly into a crime because of the content or subject matter of the gathering. The statute invoked, though Brandeis did not say it, the same doctrine of dangerous tendency that Holmes raised in the first of the Espionage cases of 1919. "Thus the accused is to be punished, not for attempt, incitement or conspiracy, but for a step in preparation, which, if it threatens the public order at all, does so only remotely." Citing recent rulings on analogous state prohibitions, overruled by the Court, Brandeis concluded that "all fundamental rights comprised within the term liberty are protected by the federal Constitution from invasion by the states. The right of free speech, the right to teach and the right of assembly are, of course, fundamental rights." By reading the universal from the particular and applying it to all future cases, Brandeis read the law forward.[55]

Characteristically, Brandeis refused to overgeneralize. "Although the rights of free speech and assembly are fundamental, they are not in their nature absolute. Their exercise is subject to restriction, if the particular restriction proposed is required in order to protect the state from destruction or from serious injury, political, economic or moral." He even qualified that generalization. "That the necessity which is essential to a valid restriction does not exist unless speech would produce, or is intended to produce, a clear and imminent danger of some substantive evil which the state constitutionally may seek to prevent has been settled." In short, there must be activity in furtherance of the speech—words themselves would not do. Nevertheless, this was a major revision of Free Speech doctrine, in fact, a leap forward not fully applied until the 1960s. Then came a tactical retreat, in the form of deference to the competence of the legislative branches, another component of Brandeis's jurisprudence. "The Legislature must obviously decide, in the first instance, whether a danger exists which calls for a particular protective measure." But he did not favor overbroad and vague legislation that assumed facts not in evidence, indeed, not even evident at the time. "Where a statute is valid only in case certain conditions exist, the enactment of the statute cannot alone establish the facts which are essential to its validity." No wonder it was so difficult even for Brandeis's allies to determine where his logic was leading him. It was leading him to the future, where a greater democracy, or at least a commitment to greater democracy, allowed greater latitude in the public expression of political ideas.[56]

Nevertheless, Brandeis wanted to establish the wide and powerful sweep of the First Amendment into the future. "Believing in the power of reason as applied through public discussion, [the framers] eschewed silence coerced by law—the argument of force in its worst form. Recognizing the occasional tyrannies of governing majorities, they amended the Constitution so that free speech and assembly should be guaranteed." These were the tests, and the prosecution of Whitney failed all of them. For now, and in the future, "The wide difference between advocacy and incitement, between preparation and attempt, between assembling and conspiracy, must be borne in mind. In order to support a finding of clear and present danger it must be shown either that immediate serious violence was to be expected or was advocated, or that the past conduct furnished reason to believe that such advocacy was then contemplated."[57]

Brandeis did not finish where one would expect him to finish, with a dissent. "In the present case, however, there was other testimony which tended to establish the existence of a conspiracy, on the part of members of the International Workers of the World, to commit present serious crimes, and likewise to show that such a conspiracy would be furthered by the activity of the society of which Miss Whitney was a member." This was not a stumble, however, but a way to insert a reading of the law into the precedent of the Court. It was similar to what Marshall had accomplished in *Marbury*—protecting the revision of the law by refusing to provide relief. Thus Brandeis's invocation of the deeds not words First Amendment guarantee became part of the majority, hence (theoretically at least) the law. The dissents in *Abrams*, *Gilbert*, and *Gitlow* did not become law; dissents are not law. Only the opinions of the court become law.

The footnotes went along with the concurrence, and they make even clearer his intent. For example, there was Jefferson's first inaugural, which Brandeis read as: "We have nothing to fear from the demoralizing reasonings of some, if others are left free to demonstrate their errors and especially when the law stands ready to punish the first criminal act produced by the false reasonings; these are safer corrections than the conscience of the judge."[58]

In *Olmstead v. U.S.* (1928) Brandeis dissented. The use of wiretapping to convict bootleggers under the Volstead Act was a novelty in the law, and whether it violated the Fourth Amendment against search and seizure without a warrant, and the Fifth Amendment against self-incrimination, came before the court on appeal from the lower federal courts. Brandeis's dissent from Taft's majority opinion contained almost more than any essay can tease out, but the constitutional contribution of the dissent was most evident in the justice's review of history, and the justice read the purposes of the Fourth and Fifth Amendments. As one biographer concluded, Brandeis's opinion "reinvented Fourth Amendment jurisprudence," by looking into the future for a better law.[59]

The key invention was the insertion of Brandeis's concept of the right to privacy in the center of the Amendment. It does not mention privacy, but as in the article on privacy, Brandeis looked ahead to the future intrusions, public and private, on privacy. As he had written in 1890, "Political, social, and economic changes entail the recognition of new rights." In 1928, the rise of electronic surveillance fulfilled that malign prophecy. Thus, the Fourth Amendment had to be revisited and reinterpreted. Facts—greater and greater unrestrained intrusion of the press into private lives, recording what was seen and heard using modern technologies—made the new right of privacy even more important in 1928 than in 1890. For now it was freedom from unwarranted (literally) intrusion into private lives by the government, claiming the law itself as grounds for the intrusion and employing the newer technologies, this time wiretapping telephone conversations.[60]

In *Olmstead*, the facts were stipulated (agreed to by all parties). The defendants were convicted of conspiring to violate the National Prohibition Act. The telephones they habitually used were tapped. There was no warrant. The phones were in the homes of the defendants and in their offices. The agents listened for over five months, and the record of the conversations was 775 pages long. No effort was made to distinguish between criminal and noncriminal conversations or to elide private information. At their trial, the defendants raised objections to the wiretapping as an unreasonable search and seizure, in violation of the Fourth Amendment; and that the use as evidence of the conversations overheard compelled the defendants to be witnesses against themselves, in violation of the Fifth Amendment.[61]

The federal prosecutors, and the majority of the Court in Taft's opinion, simply did not find any right to privacy in the Amendment. This kind of reading of law was formalist originalism. If a right was not mentioned in the text of the Amendment, it could not be inferred from the Amendment. Brandeis was admonitory: "The Government makes no attempt to defend the methods employed by its officers. Indeed, it concedes that if wire-tapping can be deemed a search and seizure within the Fourth Amendment, such wire-tapping as was practiced in the case at bar was an unreasonable search and seizure, and that the evidence thus obtained was inadmissible."

In short, the majority failed to read the law forward to see the problem that new kinds of intrusions posed to privacy, then back, incorporating the protection that the Amendment should have provided against new technologies. In vain did Brandeis insist that the past proved that future malign novelties will require new readings of existing texts. Brandeis cited case after case to show that "Clauses guaranteeing to the individual protection against specific abuses of power, must have a similar capacity of adaptation to a changing world." Note that it was the law that had the capacity of changing, a way to veil the role of the lawyer that Brandeis, before he donned judicial robes, had impressed on Harvard students. Actually, it was lawyers and judges who could, and should, exercise this capacity. His passive language only partially concealed the powerful theme: "Time works changes, brings into existence new conditions and purposes. Therefore a principle to be vital must be capable of wider application than the mischief which gave it birth." In the reading of the Constitution, the judge must see not only what has been, but what may be.[62]

Citations to case law notwithstanding, Brandeis had to concede that precedent did not exactly work for him. The protections of the two Amendments had been limited by the Court. So Brandeis returned to a sweeping invocation of historical principles:

> The protection guaranteed by the Amendments is much broader in scope. The makers of our Constitution undertook to secure conditions favorable to the pursuit of happiness. They recognized the significance of man's spiritual nature, of his feelings and of his intellect. They knew that only a part of the pain, pleasure and satisfactions of life are to be found in material things. They sought to protect Americans in their beliefs, their thoughts, their emotions and their sensations.

As history, this was highly conjectural. As law, it was irrelevant. It looked backward, but it placed Brandeis's reading of the law on the highest ground of moral principle. And once again, no longer hidden, Brandeis inserted that the right to privacy was the best reading of the law. "They conferred, as against the Government, the right to be let alone—the most comprehensive of rights and the right most valued by civilized men."[63]

Finally, an appeal to the purposes of government closed the opinion.

"Decency, security and liberty alike demand that government officials shall be subjected to the same rules of conduct that are commands to the citizen." This was an argument tying government conduct back to individual invasions of privacy described in the 1890 article. "In a government of laws, existence of the government will be imperiled if it fails to observe the law scrupulously. Our Government is the potent, the omnipresent teacher. For good or for ill, it teaches the whole people by its example." Law not only teaching but, in his hands, learning to foresee a dangerous future.[64]

Brandeis's conception of a "living law" was a Progressive version of reading law forward, although sometimes one had to look hard for it in a forest of factual detail and coruscating notes. The silences were also deafening, as when, given the chance to apply the right to be left alone to a woman facing forced state-mandated sterilization for supposedly being an imbecile (she was not as it happened), he demurred. The facts—her intelligence and that of her child—did not matter. But nearing the end of his twenty-three years on the Court and, shortly thereafter, his life, Brandeis had become more conservative about using the law to change the law. Or perhaps his conservative instincts, so often in evidence earlier, simply became more prominent. His desire to curb judicial activism ill fit with the newest need for federal judicial intervention in many areas of civil rights. His deference to state law courts and state legislatures, a part of Wilsonian new freedom, ran directly into the Jim Crow laws of many states, upheld by their courts. Brandeis's preference for long-term democratic solutions to basic wrongs rather than court-ordered solutions and his opposition to great corporations of all kinds, even in reform government initiatives, were consistent elements of his jurisprudence. As he wrote to Felix Frankfurter in 1921, "Bigness is the greatest curse."[65]

Brandeis did not dissent often—some 457 of his 531 published opinions were opinions for the Court. Many of the key ideas of his dissents, for example, the centrality of the right to privacy in the Bill of Rights, became part of constitutional law after his passing. The luminosity of his many dissents, the way they read law forward, would assure him his place as a leading constitutional jurist.

Nearing the end of his service on the Court and contemplating another mind-numbingly busy term, he wrote to Frankfurter, "because of our finite wisdom, and the infinite possibility of error in judgment, we are more likely to be right to turn our thoughts primarily to the simpler problem of means [rather] than directly to hoped for ends." The clutter modifiers in the sentence demonstrate how weary and wary Brandeis was of a Court hearing cases that could and should be decided below. As he wrote in one concurrence near the end of his tenure, "That claim imposed upon the lower court six days of hearings. It imposed upon this Court a reargument and a huge record. With the briefs, it weighs avoirdupois 67 pounds. The narrative statement of the testimony occupies 1,237 pages of the printed record in this Court; the briefs fill 546 pages. There are, besides, 428 exhibits."[66]

As the final years on the bench approached, the approaching finitude of his life reminded him more and more of the limitations of his own powers. But he had done his part to bring the basic freedoms of the Bill of Rights into the new century.[67]

Brandeis's caution was the hallmark of his colleague on the bench and the next of the seven jurists considered here, Benjamin N. Cardozo. Where the former man's caution was a performative choice, a stark contrast to his writing before his elevation, Cardozo's cautious approach was the habit of a lifetime, a facet of a deeply private personality. It could not, however, conceal the brilliance of his reasoning as he read the law forward.

Benjamin N. Cardozo, c. 1932. Library of Congress Prints and Photographs Division. Photo by Harris and Ewing.

5. Benjamin N. Cardozo

Benjamin N. Cardozo's tenure on the US Supreme Court was brief, a mere six years (1932–1938). Though these years saw him write a number of luminous opinions and dissents, his part in the story of jurisprudence begins with his role as a New York State Court of Appeals justice. There he employed a forward-looking approach to rewrite the law of torts and products liability. His 1921 Yale Law School Storrs lectures, published in 1922 as the *Nature of the Judicial Process*, were an instant classic, and with two subsequent volumes of published lectures established the intellectual cache of forward-looking judging. Not least, his concept of an ordered liberty, elucidated in *Palko v. Connecticut* (1937), remains the standard (if not still the precedent) for the incorporation of the Bill of Rights. "This shy, ruminating, self-mocking, morally sensitive, preternaturally acute, large-visioned man of the law," according to Professor Paul Freund, still both attracts and mystifies students of Cardozo's ideas.[1]

The almost lyrical quality of his writing, combined with the frequency of the citations of Cardozo opinions in negligence and other common law cases, over 500 in the New York appellate courts and 170 on the US Supreme Court, has brought him to the foremost rank of American jurists. It has also made him a difficult intellectual subject. There are so many layers one has to peel off in his opinions and his extrajudicial writings, along with so many asides, allusions, and disclaimers, that there may be no real Cardozo jurisprudence at all—only ephemera. Or, as G. Edward White writes of Cardozo, his "strong interest . . . was the preservation of his creative opportunities. He sought to further this interest surreptitiously, by making his exercise of power inconspicuous and by giving his innovation in common law subjects the appearance of doctrinal continuity." In short, he was a jurisprudential magician—now you saw the innovation, now you didn't. Or, as law professor Grant Gilmore concluded, "the more innovative decision to which he had persuaded his brethren on the court [of appeals], the more his opinion strained to prove that . . . no novelty was 'involved.'"[2]

There is another admittedly more speculative way to understand his thinking. For anyone raised in the Jewish learning tradition of the pilpul (Talmud dialectics), questions do not have absolute or straight-forward answers. The Talmud, the source of the pilpul method, features rabbis debating all manner of questions without resolving them. Cardozo had a thorough Sephardic Jewish education. For a biographer of Cardozo, this poses an almost insuperable obstacle to finding the real man; for an intellectual assay, however, perhaps just an examination of the ephemera will do.[3]

Cardozo's New York family was something like Brandeis's, part of a Jewish commercial community of relative newcomers to the city, inter-married and working together in family firms, always aware that they were not in the elite mainstream. Benjamin's father, Albert Cardozo, married well into the Nathan clan and practiced law in the City of New York, part of a thriving Jewish community, until Democratic Party politics reached out to him. A client of Tammany Hall interests, Albert Cardozo did favors on the bench, and was forced to resign in disgrace in the shadow of impeachment, although he continued in private prac-tice until his death in 1885. Born in 1870, Benjamin grew up bearing the reflected shame of the impeachment inquiry into his father's conduct as a New York state judge. "He never forgot his father's fall and what it had done to the family."[4]

At college, in law school, and in his early practice, beginning in 1891, Cardozo "worked hard and socialized little." Serious, thoughtful, intensely inward looking, he was liked and respected by classmates, associates, and teachers, but his graciousness was matched by his secre-tiveness. He did not much care for the classes at Columbia Law School, finding the teaching disjoined and stark, but he took an avid interest in political theory, a specialty of Columbia University. From 1891 to 1914 he lived at home, worked constantly, and fit, for the first time, into something—his family law firm's business. He excelled in appellate court work despite his relative youth and inexperience, but he learned that even the most technically sound argument might not win for his clients. He had to learn to curb his "expressive streak." Still, his reputa-tion grew, and other lawyers began to refer appellate work to him.[5]

The rough and tumble of city and state politics did not attract him, but he ingratiated himself in the reform politics of the city, especially with Jewish interest groups. He sought judicial office when the opportunity presented itself. In 1913, during a time of reform in the city, the reform Fusion party named Cardozo as a candidate for the state supreme court. Cardozo ran a "low-key campaign" and narrowly won the seat. He took office at the start of 1914 and six months later was appointed to the state's highest tribunal, the Court of Appeals, in a temporary slot to help that court clear its backlog of cases. It was not an auspicious beginning to his tenure. In 1917, he was elected to a regular seat on the court, however, and in 1926 was reelected, this time as the court's chief judge.

Cardozo's domestic arrangements during his tenure on the New York Court of Appeals changed only a little from his time in private practice. The court sat in Albany, while home remained New York City. He was still not much of a mixer, preferring work and family to the social activities of the bar and bench, but he had friends in both places. He lived well but not lavishly with his older sister, Nellie. He never married. They were very close emotionally and until her death from heart disease in 1929, he was inseparable from her. His own heart began to fail in 1930, and congestive heart failure would eventually kill him in 1938, in his sixty-eighth year.[6]

The New York State Court of Appeals ordinarily decided cases within two months of hearing them, did not encourage its members to interrogate counsel at oral argument, and did not always issue written opinions (instead, producing "reports" of the court's findings). Cardozo did not always follow these customs, and sometimes his opinions were lengthy and filled with precedents. He was "open minded" and when he was unsure he said so. He would see "a serious principle" in a case where his brethren saw little of note. That principle was "the right of a human being to be treated with dignity and the duty of the law to respond to a violation of rights." When a result was dictated by law, but he was sympathetic to the human side, he might say that the ruling was technically correct but harsh and unfeeling. On top of all this, he had "a photographic memory" for cases. Because, by this time, the Court of Appeals had emerged as the country's foremost commercial tribunal, his reputation as a jurist spread far and wide and his opinions were more often cited than his brethren, and despite the rotation in assignment of cases, he was the author of the court's most important opinions.[7]

Perhaps the best-known example of Cardozo's subtle but powerful creativity on the Court of Appeals is the case that created modern products liability law, *MacPherson v. Buick Motor Company* (1916). In it, Cardozo explored how the law could incorporate the future and then return to reset existing law—but with as many switchbacks and qualifications and as highly selective of a use of precedent as one would come to expect from his writing. The old rule for the liability for a product that was defective was based on privity, a contract doctrine. Here, the buyer of the car sought damages not from the seller, with whom he had privity of contact, but from the manufacturer. He won his suit in the trial court, but the manufacturer appealed, recognizing, as Cardozo did, that these cases would soon flood the docket. Cardozo read the case as an example not of contract law, but of tort law, in particular the law of negligence. What was more, he chose a line of cases from New York courts that held the product manufacturer liable for harm to the purchaser, though they were not in close proximity to one another.

> The defendant is a manufacturer of automobiles. It sold an automobile to a retail dealer. The retail dealer resold to the plaintiff. While the plaintiff was in the car, it suddenly collapsed. He was thrown out and injured. One of the wheels was made of defective wood, and its spokes crumbled into fragments. The wheel was not made by the defendant; it was bought from another manufacturer. There is evidence, however, that its defects could have been discovered by reasonable inspection, and that inspection was omitted.[8]

There was no evidence that Buick knew the tire was defective. It was not liable for fraudulently selling a defective tire. "The question to be determined is whether the defendant owed a duty of care and vigilance to the ultimate buyer." Was the auto inherently dangerous, bringing its manufacturer within the ambit of cases of poison mislabeled, boilers poorly constructed, or firearms? It did not matter. "We are not required to say whether the chance of injury was always as remote as the distinction assumes." If one manufactured a product and put it on the market, one was liable if it did not perform. In *Statler v. Ray Mfg. Co.* (1909), "the defendant manufactured a large coffee urn. It was installed in a restaurant. When heated, the urn exploded and injured the plaintiff. We held that the manufacturer was liable. We said that the urn 'was of such a character inherently that, when applied to the purposes for which it was designed, it was liable to become a source of great danger to many people if not carefully and properly constructed.'" It did not matter if the product was inherently dangerous. "We are not required at this time either to approve or to disapprove the application of the rule that was made in these cases. It is enough that they help to characterize the trend of judicial thought." Cardozo refused to expand on his logic to strict liability for all mass product harms (just as Brandeis declined to expand on his views of free speech). But he did concede, in response to the dissent, that "Precedents drawn from the days of travel by stage coach do not fit the conditions of travel today. The principle that the danger must be imminent does not change, but the things subject to the principle do change. They are whatever the needs of life in a developing situation required them to be." The future needs of life, he might just as well have said, for that was the thrust of his opinion.[9]

Cardozo expanded on this thought in reversing a lower court decision in *Hynes v. New York Central Railway Co.* (1921). Florence Hynes's sixteen-year-old son Harvey was preparing to dive into the Harlem River, on the right of way of the railroad company. He stood on a plank jutting out of the bulkhead owned by the company and was hit by a high tension wire when a pole the company used broke, throwing him to his death. Children had jumped into the water from the plank for years with full knowledge and no complaint from New York Central. The supreme (trial) court found that the son was a trespasser and that the railroad company owed no duty to him unless the injury was willful or wanton. Cardozo, writing for the majority of the Court of Appeals, held that the son was a bather of public waters, not a trespasser, and was entitled to a duty of reasonable care. The railroad's duty did not end just because he was diving from encroaching objects or engaging in the sports common among swimmers. The railroad company was bound to regulate its conduct in contemplation of the presence of travelers upon the adjacent public ways, and here, the structures and ways were so commingled that the fields were brought together. The injury was foreseeable. Thus, liability and duty existed. "Much might be said in favor of another view. We do not press the inquiry, for we are persuaded that the rights of bathers do not depend upon these nice distinctions."

By nice distinctions, Cardozo meant precedent limiting NYC's liability. His tone had changed from the 1916 term—he was less patient with outmoded doctrines.

> We are to ignore the public ownership of the circumambient spaces of water and of air. Jumping from a boat or a barrel, the boy would have been a bather in the river. Jumping from the end of a springboard, he was no longer, it is said, a bather, but a trespasser on a right of way. Rights and duties in systems of living law are not built upon such quicksands.

Living law was pragmatic, but Cardozo's pragmatism did not end with the result of one case—it looped back to liability doctrine and altered it. "The truth is that every act of Hynes from his first plunge into the river until the moment of his death, was in the enjoyment of the public waters, and under cover of the protection which his presence in those waters gave him." Almost poetry, this.[10]

But Cardozo was not done. The opinion ended where it began, with liability of owners to strangers. Cardozo pronounced that the legal protection was that owed to travelers on public thoroughfares that adjacent property owners owed. Trespass did not matter in such cases. And with that conclusion, Cardozo returned to long-established liability rules and overturned them. How did he justify this legerdemain? He attacked the old rule's application to the present case as an example of "the extension of a maxim or a definition with relentless disregard of consequences." This would have been an example of pragmatic consequentialism were Cardozo to stop here. But he did not. Instead, he went on to rewrite the law.

> There are times when there is little trouble in marking off the field of exemption and immunity from that of liability and duty. Here structures and ways are so united and commingled, superimposed upon each other,

that the fields are brought together. In such circumstances, there is little help in pursuing general maxims to ultimate conclusions. They have been framed *alio intuitu*. They must be reformulated and readapted to meet exceptional conditions. Rules appropriate to spheres which are conceived of as separate and distinct cannot, both, be enforced when the spheres become concentric."

Stripped of its geometric metaphors, this was reading law forward.[11]

The publication of Cardozo's Storrs lectures is usually celebrated as the first admission that judges did not find law; they made it, in part based on their own experience, values, and aspirations. Like Columbus's assertion that the world was not flat, Cardozo knew full well that judges' opinions were not mere recitals of law, and so did his audience.

> At what point shall the quest [for the judge's reasons] be halted by some discrepant custom, by some consideration of the social welfare, by my own or the common standards of justice and morals? Into that strange compound which is brewed daily in the caldron of the courts, all these ingredients enter in varying proportions. I am not concerned to inquire whether judges ought to be allowed to brew such a compound at all. I take judge-made law as one of the existing realities of life.

Cardozo did not discard fidelity to precedent or to legislative intent or to the texts of the law, but he continued, "In this perpetual flux, the problem which confronts the judge is in reality a twofold one: he must first extract from the precedent the underlying principle, the *ratio decidendi*; he must then determine the path or direction along which the principle is to move and develop, if it is not to wither and die." One is struck how like this was Lemuel Shaw's view in *Norway Company*. To live, the law must look not only backward, but ahead. To "move and develop" the law must anticipate and progress. Each case offered many paths, those led forward as well as back, and following them ahead would, in the judge's mind, invariably lead back to existing law. Where might these paths ahead lead? Sometimes, the judge "must let the welfare of society fix the path, its direction and its distance" and the party "are to be given such weight as sound judgment dictates. They are constituents of that social welfare which it is our business to discover."

This was social welfare, and it sounded a good deal like utilitarianism, though Cardozo did not quote Mill.[12]

Cardozo then went where others in judicial robes might fear to tread—to the subject of the judge as a legislator. "Legislation has sometimes been necessary to free us from the old fetters." Was Cardozo embracing the doctrine of deference to legislatures? Brandeis had already embraced it. But Cardozo then warned, "Sometimes the conservatism of judges has threatened for an interval to rob the legislation of its efficacy." After all, for the judge, there were limits, constraints, and boundaries imposed by the judicial office and by the canons of judging. Cardozo had already put these to one side in cases like *Hynes*. Cardozo called for a balance between the good of the community and a return to the law as it exists, altering but not abandoning that law. That was the very essence of the common law—forward, then return, keeping the law alive. "In the same way when the question is one of supplying the gaps in the law, it is not of logical deductions, it is rather of social needs, that we are to ask the solution."[13]

A second lecture series, followed by a book, came in 1923, again at Yale Law School. *The Growth of the Law* (1924), the published version of those lectures, refined Cardozo's views. The first set of lectures had an almost elusive quality, as Cardozo made bold statements followed by thoughtful but sometimes overly complex qualifications. Whether the further refinements were necessary or not, the effort reflected Cardozo's manner of reasoning. The problem of the law (and its public reception) was the contrary tugs of stability, hence predictability, and growth, the ability of law to respond to new challenges. The latter was the pole around which Cardozo's prose danced. "We have a filigree of threads and crossthreads radiating from the center and dividing one another into sections and crosssections" was how he described the multitude of potentially contradictory precedents that must be sorted by the new American Law Institute. One almost wishes, as one follows Cardozo's steps, that he would speak more plainly, but that was not his style—or his purpose. "I know there is a vagueness in all this" he conceded. The entire project of judging had come under intense, often unfavorable scrutiny among Progressives. "More and more we are looking to the scholar . . . to the jurist" rather than the judge for the rationale for judicial independence. Perhaps Cardozo was trying to do more than explain. He was trying to defend the judicial profession.[14]

The danger in the single-minded quest for stability was "an intolerable rigidity" in the law and judging. To survive—to retain the trust of the people—law had to grow. That meant that judges had to be open to growth. But the individual judge's presumptions and values, as Cardozo explained in the last chapter of *Judicial Process*, were rooted in the past. Thus, the challenge of good judging was to find a path around that obstacle. "I have made myself today the self-appointed spokesman and defender" of this philosophy of law. It was "creative," rather than mere declaration of what the law had been, and the example he chose to explain this was his own decision in *MacPherson v. Buick* (1916). Of course, the court did not "roam at large" inviting the danger of judicial bias (again thinking of his father) then, any more than was permissible in his philosophy of law.[15]

In this exploration of judging, Cardozo's stance was the reverse of Shaw's. Shaw spoke as the oracle of law; Cardozo was a shadow behind the law, seen for a moment, then gone again behind a wall of other men's thinking. He teased, then withdrew. He said that the judge must choose, but the paths ahead were not clear. Cardozo refused to point the way, only repeating that the way was not dictated by paths already taken. There was only the continual striving for an unseen goal. In the meantime, the many quotations, references, and asides in the text were blinds behind which to hide himself. Shaw bullied his way through cases. Cardozo darted "with averted gaze." The barest hint of where Cardozo stood lay in his repeated invocation of "utility" as "the final test." And then, near his conclusion, one learned that "pragmaticism is profoundly affecting the development of juristic thought." Was this not a bow to a forward-looking jurisprudence? After all, when he ran for election to the Supreme Court in 1913, he was rightly reputed to be a Progressive Democrat, and that meant support for regulatory intervention in the economy among other projects. But "something more" than deference to legislatures was necessary if the law was to be truly future oriented. Here Cardozo broke with Brandeis: deference to legislatures was not enough. Then once again Cardozo covered his tracks by citing Brandeis's dissent in *State of Washington v. Dawson & Co* (1924):

"modification implies growth. It is the life of the law." As it happened, Brandeis found state workers compensation laws constitutional; the state courts of Washington and California and the US Supreme Court disagreed. So did Cardozo, elsewhere, when the New York Court of Appeals struck down that state's workers compensation law.[16]

Cardozo hesitated to join the US Supreme Court when President Hoover asked, then he agreed. It would mean moving from New York to DC, But Nellie was gone, and that impediment removed, the invitation was easier to accept. "Homesick" at leaving New York, Cardozo established something of a homestead in a Mayflower Hotel apartment, and then a rental on Connecticut Avenue. On the Court Cardozo joined with Brandeis, Stone, and Chief Justice Hughes to form something like a liberal bloc. He was cordial with Brandeis (he was cordial with everyone), but the two men did not form the bond that Brandeis had with Holmes or with Frankfurter). McReynolds extended to Cardozo the same discourtesy that he offered Brandeis.[17]

Among the first fruits of this liberal alliance was his opinion in *Nixon v. Condon* (1932). Writing for a majority, Cardozo found that the Texas law barring Blacks from voting in the Democratic Party primary violated the Constitution. (McReynolds dissented.) The state Democratic Party primary was not a private affair. "The petitioner, a Negro, has brought this action against judges of election in Texas to recover damages for their refusal by reason of his race or color to permit him to cast his vote at a primary election." The Texas courts had ruled that political parties were private organizations, and could allow or disallow ballots in the primary election. It was not the first time that the US Supreme Court had intervened. "In *Nixon v. Herndon,* decided at the October term, 1926, this Court had before it a statute of the State of Texas whereby the Legislature had said that 'in no event shall a Negro be eligible to participate in a Democratic party primary election [held in that State]' and that, 'should a Negro vote in a Democratic primary election, such ballot shall be void.'" The Court threw that statute out because, as a state action, it came under the prohibitions of the Fourteenth Amendment.[18]

The all-white Texas state legislature thought it had a way around the decision—put the "state action" doctrine to use. In the *Civil Rights*

Cases (1883) the justices found that the Fourteenth Amendment did not apply to private actors. "Promptly after the announcement of [*Nixon v. Herndon*] the Legislature of Texas enacted a new statute repealing the article condemned by this Court." Instead of good faith compliance, however, the state announced that the political parties in the state were private organizations. Under the new rule, the all-white executive committee of the (now privatized) state Democratic Party reinstituted the old state rule as a housekeeping ordinance for its primary. What the Court had tossed out the front door, by this very obvious subterfuge the state and the Democratic Party of Texas brought the measure back through the rear window.

Lawrence Nixon, an El Paso doctor who had won in the first suit, brought its successor in 1928. He was qualified to vote in all ways, but for his race. The lower court in Texas, as it had in the first suit, dismissed his petition. The Fifth Circuit Court of Appeals sustained the decision of the district court. The Supreme Court agreed to hear Nixon's appeal. Cardozo was less interested in the lower courts' flawed reasoning than the facts—shades of Brandeis. Nixon was "Barred from voting at a primary . . . and this for the sole reason that his color is not white. The result for him is no different from what it was when his cause was here before." Cardozo swept away the distinction between the two laws: their outcome and their purpose were the same. His temper was barely restrained. "We are reminded that the Fourteenth Amendment is a restraint upon the States, and not upon private persons unconnected with a State. . . . This line of demarcation drawn, we are told that a political party is merely a voluntary association . . . as far aloof from the impact of constitutional restraint as those for membership in a golf club or for admission to a Masonic lodge."[19]

Cardozo fumed, the fact of the matter was that "if heed is to be given to the realities of political life, they [nominees of the party] are now agencies of the State, the instruments by which government becomes a living thing. In that view, so runs the argument, a party is still free to define for itself the political tenets of its members, but to those who profess its tenets there may be no denial of its privileges." Having made law by looking ahead at the realities of elections in one-party states like Texas, Cardozo now looped back to the state action doctrine, restricting the scope of his opinion: "A narrower base will serve for our judgment in the cause at hand. Whether the effect of Texas legislation has been to work so complete a transformation of the concept of a political party as a voluntary association we do not now decide." Nixon's right to have his vote counted was confirmed. Cardozo did not apply the full force of his logic to the state action doctrine, however. That would come with litigation over the 1964 Civil Rights Act.[20]

Nevertheless, Cardozo had changed the core meaning of the state action doctrine. He did not use, as later courts would, the interstate commerce clause or the taxing power, but instead swiftly and fully found that the political party was tantamount to a government agency and so its primary was tantamount to state action. Having changed the meaning of the first section of the Fourteenth Amendment, he backed away from any larger or more general application of the doctrine, insulating his intervention from criticism (though Texas would continue to seek ways to exclude Black people from voting).

After the election of Franklin Delano Roosevelt, in 1932, the Court was increasingly faced with a flood of New Deal legislation on national banking, labor, agriculture, and business. Some of these the Court allowed, but by 1936, many of the acts were voided for overreaching the constitutional powers of the executive branch or Congress. Cardozo was sympathetic to the federal government's battle against the Great Depression but did not give a free hand to all of the New Deal legislative initiatives. For example, he concurred when the chief justice and all of his brethren struck down the National Recovery Act in *Schechter Poultry v. U.S.* (1935). But in a series of dissents from the majority view that the federal government exceeded its constitutional powers in regulating industries with a public interest, he showed how subtly transformative his analysis could be. One of these dissents, *Carter v. Carter Coal* (1936), deserves fuller treatment here as it demonstrates how Cardozo deployed a feedback loop to read law forward.

Despite the demise of the National Recovery Act, Congress passed the Bituminous Coal Act (Guffey Act) of 1935 creating a commission of miners and owners to set prices, wages, and the like (similar to what the NRA had done). James Carter, who was a part owner of the Carter Coal Company, brought suit against the government, claiming that coal production was not interstate commerce, and thus was not open to federal regulation. A majority of the Court agreed. Cardozo did not. Joined by Brandeis and Stone, he dissented.[21]

Cardozo did not debate the majority opinion over the tests the Court should use to determine constitutionality. Instead, he simply found that "the Act is within the power of the central government insofar as it provides for minimum and maximum prices upon sales of bituminous coal in the transactions of interstate commerce and in those of intrastate commerce where interstate commerce is directly or intimately affected." Then, being Cardozo, he limited the reach of his dissent. "Whether it is valid also in other provisions that have been considered and condemned in the opinion of the court I do not find it necessary to determine at this time. Silence must not be taken as importing acquiescence." He conceded wryly that "much would have to be written if the subject" before an omnibus ruling on these regulations of manufacturing and mining were possible, and that study would have to explore "all its implications, historical and economic as well as strictly legal," a not-so-subtle jab at the majority opinion's lack of thorough analysis of economic context.[22]

Cardozo began his own analysis with a point-by-point assessment of the petitioner's case. He found that the petitioner had challenged the act on three grounds. First, because the interstate commerce clause did not give the Congress the authority to set prices; second, because the act denied due process under the Fifth Amendment; and third because it entailed an unlawful delegation of legislative power (the *Schechter* argument). The first was easily refuted—the act dealt with interstate commerce, for "to regulate the price for such transactions is to regulate commerce itself, and not alone its antecedent conditions or its ultimate consequences." A neat reverse analogy proved his argument: "Prices in interstate transactions may not be regulated by the states. . . . They must therefore be subject to the power of the nation unless they are to be withdrawn altogether from governmental supervision." What would result (what future calamities would occur) if such a vacuum were permitted? No need to list them—for they lay in the future, but "many a public evil incidental to interstate transactions would be left without a remedy." Having looked into the future and found a multitude of shadowy evils waiting, Cardozo drew back from the prospect of whole-sale government regulation of prices: "This does not mean, of course, that prices may be fixed for arbitrary reasons or in an arbitrary way." Congress did not ignore those questions, and the regulation was not arbitrary (with reference to the legislative history of the act).[23]

Next came a sweeping dismissal of the distinction raised by opponents of regulation between direct and indirect affect. "Sometimes it is said that the relation must be 'direct' to bring that power (over interstate commerce) into play. In many circumstances, such a description will be sufficiently precise to meet the needs of the occasion. But a great principle of constitutional law is not susceptible of comprehensive statement in an adjective." With another sweep of the hand he reduced the long-established distinction to a useless abstraction. "The underlying thought is merely this—that 'the law is not indifferent to considerations of degree.'" Which he replaced with a metaphor: "without an expansion of the commerce clause . . . the waves of causation will have radiated so far that their undulatory motion, if discernible at all, will be too faint or obscure, too broken by cross-currents, to be heeded by the law." Again, he warned of future evils.[24]

Next, he played with the terminology. In the seriousness of the man one sometimes misses the playfulness in his writings. "Perhaps, if one group of adjectives is to be chosen in preference to another, 'intimate' and 'remote' will be found to be as good as any. At all events, 'direct' and 'indirect,' even if accepted as sufficient, must not be read too narrowly." Words were not as important as facts, and the facts here were poorly captured by the distinction between direct and indirect causation. Even if they were employed, "A survey of the cases shows that the words have been interpreted with suppleness of adaptation and flexibility of meaning." It was "need" rather than language that mattered. Need looked to the future, a future in which economic crisis loomed. The old debate over terminology was stuck in the past. Instead, "the power is as broad as the need that evokes it."[25]

Back to the facts. "What has been said in this regard is said with added certitude when complainants' business is considered in the light of the statistics exhibited in the several records." Over 97 percent of the Carter Company's coal was sold in interstate commerce. But other complaining companies had much smaller percentages of interstate sales. "Plainly, it is impossible to say, either from the statute itself or from any figures laid before us, that interstate sales will not be prejudicially affected in West Virginia and Kentucky if intrastate prices are maintained on a lower level."[26]

To brush away the second count of the complaint, a violation of due process, Cardozo cited one of the few cases in which the New Deal Supreme Court upheld a price-fixing statute. "In the pursuit of that inquiry, *Nebbia v. New York* (1934) lays down the applicable principle. There, a statute of New York prescribing a minimum price for milk was upheld against the objection that price-fixing was forbidden by the Fourteenth Amendment." This was not a Fourteenth Amendment case, but a Fifth Amendment case, and *Nebbia* came before the Court voided later federal price-fixing cases, however. It was not really an appropriate precedent as a matter of law, but as a matter of policy it was. Cardozo argued, "We found it a sufficient reason to uphold the challenged system that the conditions or practices in an industry make unrestricted competition an inadequate safeguard of the consumer's interest, produce waste harmful to the public, threaten ultimately to cut off the supply of a commodity needed by the public, or portend the destruction of the industry itself." Need mattered more than precedent. "All this may be said, and with equal, if not greater force, of the conditions and practices in the bituminous coal industry. . . . Overproduction was at a point where free competition had been degraded into anarchy. Prices had been cut so low that profit had become impossible for all except the lucky handful."[27]

The past was also important, when it was a foretaste of the future without the regulation. "Wages came down along with prices and with profits. There were strikes, at times nationwide in extent, at other times spreading over broad areas and many mines, with the accompaniment of violence and bloodshed and misery and bitter feeling. The sordid tale is unfolded in many a document and treatise." These were the studies that Cardozo thought instructive, as opposed to the "strictly legal" ones on which the majority relied. "During the twenty-three years between 1913 and 1935, there were nineteen investigations or hearings by Congress or by specially created commissions with reference to conditions in the coal mines. The hope of betterment was faint unless the industry could be subjected to the compulsion of a code." Needs:

> In the weeks immediately preceding the passage of this Act, the country was threatened once more with a strike of ominous proportions. The plight of the industry was not merely a menace to owners and to mine workers; it was and had long been a menace to the public, deeply concerned in a steady and uniform supply of a fuel so vital to the national economy. . . . Commerce had been choked and burdened.

What could be more relevant to interstate commerce than this parade of horrors, past, present, and future?[28]

Cardozo's opinion was both pragmatic and consequentialist. He deferred to Congress. Then he returned to the Commerce Clause to reread it in light of its best, broadest application.

> After making every allowance for difference of opinion as to the most efficient cure, the student of the subject is confronted with the indisputable truth that there were ills to be corrected, and ills that had a direct relation to the maintenance of commerce among the states without friction or diversion. An evil existing, and also the power to correct it, the lawmakers were at liberty to use their own discretion in the selection of the means.[29]

To defeat the third objection, Cardozo simply cited the provisions in the law. There was no excessive delegation of a legislative-like power to the boards and commissions because of the extensive control the act imposed on the district boards and the commissions the act created. How precisely this avoided the very same line of attack on the NRA was not entirely clear. Cardozo labored mightily to show that these agencies had little discretion, hence they did not have a legislative-like power. Legislatures had great discretion making policy to deal with general problems. (Of course the Court had in the past limited that discretion by striking down wages and price legislation.)

> District Boards and the Commission must conform to the following standards: they must be just and equitable; they must take account of the weighted average cost of production for each minimum price area; they

must not be unduly prejudicial or preferential as between districts or as between producers within a district . . . to the end of affording the producers in the several districts substantially the same opportunity to dispose of their coals on a competitive basis as has heretofore existed.

And so on in excruciating detail. A litany followed by precedents not quite on point (that is, not about pricing).[30]

But the real problem for Cardozo was the same as arose in the NRA: the act set fair wages. It was a union act. Could that most controversial portion of the act be severed—considered separately—from the rest of the act? "The next inquiry must be whether Part I of the statute, which creates the administrative agencies, and Part II, which has to do in the main with the price-fixing machinery as well as preliminary sections levying a tax or penalty, are separable from Part III, which deals with labor relations in the industry, with the result that what is earlier would stand if what is later were to fall." Severability is not just a prudential doctrine. It can be included in the law itself. Here it was. "If any provision of this Act, or the application thereof to any person or circumstances, is held invalid, the remainder of the Act and the application of such provisions to other persons or circumstances shall not be affected thereby." If that were not enough, the format of the statute, with distinct parts, hinted at severability. Finally, "Part III, in some of its most significant provisions, the section or subdivision in respect of wages and the hours of labor, may never take effect at all." It depended on actual conditions after the act went into effect.[31]

How did Cardozo arrive at that? He read the law forward, to anticipate how its provisions would affect the markets, then, taking the best outcome, returned to the law to suggest that since "wages may be fixed by agreement or agreements negotiated by collective bargaining," in any of the districts, "It is possible that none of these agreements as to hours and wages will ever be made. If made, they may not be completed for months, or even years." Better thus to read the law as if Part III were not part of it, until, and unless, it was. In the interval, the rest of the law would work to stabilize the market. Unlike in *Schechter*, in the NRA "Wages and hours in such circumstances were properly described as 'essential features of the plan, its very bone and sinew' . . . which, taken from the body of a code, would cause it to collapse. Here, on the face of the statute, the price provisions of one Part and the labor provisions of the other (the two to be administered by separate agencies) are made of equal rank."[32]

Cardozo was not finished imagining the future under the act. "Employees are to have the right to organize and bargain collectively through representatives of their own choosing, and shall be free from interference, restraint or coercion of employers, or their agents." He had turned the act into the as yet untested in court Wagner Labor Relations Act of 1935. It had the same purpose, applied industry-wide, to even the bargaining power of unionized employees and large industrial employers. If Part III of the Guffey Act were found constitutional, it would have paved the way for the Wagner Act to survive. In fact, the Wagner Act did come to court in *National Labor Relations Board v. Jones and Laughlin Steel* (1937), and with a slender majority including Cardozo, it passed muster.[33]

Near the end of his tenure, Cardozo was able to write two opinions that fundamentally altered the relationship of the federal government to businesses and to the states. The first was *Steward Machine Co. v. Davis*, 301 U.S. 548 (1937). The second was *Palko v. Connecticut* (1937). In *Steward*, Cardozo returned to the long line of cases overturning New Deal legislation, this time writing for the majority upholding the Social Security Act. An Alabama company paid the social security tax, then sued to recover it. The company claimed that the tax violated the Due Process Clause of the Fifth Amendment. The district court and the court of appeals both found for the plaintiff. The Supreme Court disagreed.[34]

Cardozo faced the same set of complaints about the Social Security Act as in the Bituminous Coal Act case.

> The assault on the statute proceeds on an extended front. Its assailants take the ground that the tax is not an excise; that it is not uniform throughout the United States, as excises are required to be; that its exceptions are so many and arbitrary as to violate the Fifth Amendment; that its purpose

was not revenue, but an unlawful invasion of the reserved powers of the states, and that the states, in submitting to it, have yielded to coercion and have abandoned governmental functions which they are not permitted to surrender.

Note that the state of Alabama had not brought nor did it join in the suit. The senators from Alabama, John Bankhead II and Hugo Black, were New Deal Democrats.[35]

Cardozo had little use for the argument from history.

> We are told that the relation of employment is one so essential to the pursuit of happiness that it may not be burdened with a tax. Appeal is made to history. . . . As to the argument from history: doubtless there were many excises in colonial days and later that were associated, more or less intimately, with the enjoyment or the use of property. This would not prove, even if no others were then known, that the forms then accepted were not subject to enlargement.

Cardozo then listed all manner of the enlargements in the text and then the footnotes. "The historical prop failing, the prop or fancied prop of principle remains. We learn that employment for lawful gain is a 'natural' or 'inherent' or 'inalienable' right, and not a 'privilege' at all. But natural rights, so called, are as much subject to taxation as rights of less importance." So much for the past history of excises.[36]

The taxing power of Congress was comprehensive, although if the tax was direct, it had to be apportioned according to the census and uniform throughout the states. Precise terminology did not matter, as the tax could be an excise, or an impost, or a duty. But this was not a direct tax. The argument that Congress lacked the power to tax a privilege "created by state law" was baseless. Congress had taxed corporations chartered by states throughout the nation's history.[37]

Cardozo was sweeping away the objections with broad and swift strokes. Next came the Fifth Amendment. "The excise is not invalid under the provisions of the Fifth Amendment by force of its exemptions." These included agriculture and domestic service. But the Fifth Amendment had no equal protection clause. Rigid uniformity in the tax was thus not required. Cardozo argued by analogy, "if this latitude of judgment [in whom and how to tax] is lawful for the states, it is lawful, *a fortiori*, in legislation by the Congress, which is subject to restraints less narrow and confining." This was reverse federalism, putting Brandeis's idea of the states as laboratories of innovation to use in reading federal law. But how to justify this? "The classifications and exemptions directed by the statute now in controversy have support in considerations of policy and practical convenience that cannot be condemned as arbitrary." Policy and practical convenience were not legal concepts. They were factual matters of future need. Cardozo was racing back and forth between future and present, necessity and convenience, and legal interpretation. And by the way, it was "useless" to repeat that Alabama already had something akin to the exceptions in the federal scheme.[38]

From the grab bag of objections Cardozo now withdrew the argument that the excise coerced states, violating the Tenth Amendment and abridging the division of powers in general. His answer was a matter of future fact: the proceeds went into the US treasury. "No presumption can be indulged that they will be misapplied or wasted." The plaintiff assumed that the act was an example of the federal government's ulterior motive, an unlawful scheme to defraud businesses and the states. There was nothing in the act to substantiate this supposition. Again, future facts mattered. "To draw the line intelligently between duress and inducement there is need to remind ourselves of facts as to the problem of unemployment that are now matters of common knowledge." These were gathered and presented by government counsel. "The roll of the unemployed, itself formidable enough, was only a partial roll of the destitute or needy. The fact developed quickly that the states were unable to give the requisite relief. The problem had become national in area and dimensions." It would only get worse. Cardozo found grounds in the Preamble, "to promote the general welfare." To use the preamble, so long dormant, to sustain a pressing government policy was an example of a feedback loop: see the future problem, find text to support a solution, reinterpret the text to sustain that conclusion. "There was need of help from the nation if the people were not to starve. It is too late today for the argument to be heard with tolerance that, in a crisis so extreme, the use of the moneys of the nation to relieve the unemployed and their dependents is a use for any purpose narrower than the promotion of the general welfare."[39]

Was this extremity—reaching back to the Preamble of 1787—justified? Did the act overleap the bounds set by the Constitution?

> The assailants of the statute say that its dominant end and aim is to drive the state legislatures under the whip of economic pressure into the enactment of unemployment compensation laws at the bidding of the central government. Supporters of the statute say that its operation is not constraint, but the creation of a larger freedom, the states and the nation joining in a cooperative endeavor to avert a common evil.

Cardozo saw the best future of federalism: not states versus the federal government, the constitutional world of Marshall and Story; not states' programs watched over suspiciously, the constitutional world of Brandeis; but states and the federal government working hand in hand to solve common problems. The basis for this was a vision of the common good in the Preamble revisited and given new life as Cardozo returned from his analysis of the best outcome of the Social Security Act. Neither government surrendered its sovereignty. Both fulfilled their purposes.[40]

In *Palko*, Cardozo performed a feat that can only be compared to Marshall's in *Marbury*. He stated a new rule of "ordered liberty" for incorporation of portions of the Bill of Rights in the Fourteenth Amendment, and then protected the intervention by denying Palko's plea for relief. Palko claimed that Connecticut subjecting him twice to trial was double jeopardy, barred by the Fifth Amendment. Cardozo opined that double jeopardy was not part of the regime of orderly liberty.[41]

An old Connecticut statute allowed the Court of Errors to give the prosecution permission to retry a convict for a more serious crime than that for which he had been convicted. Palko was convicted of murder in the second degree by a jury, and the state asked and gained permission from the court to retry him, upon which he was convicted of murder in the first degree. The latter was a capital crime. Palko appealed. His counsel claimed that the Fourteenth Amendment incorporated the portion of the Fifth Amendment against double jeopardy. On its face, this incorporation would have voided the Connecticut law. The state argued that the first trial had not heard his confession. While the jury panel was being assembled for the second trial, he made his appeal. It was overruled, and the second trial jury found him guilty of the more serious offense. The state's Court of Errors affirmed the jury verdict.[42]

A relevant federal precedent had been narrowly decided under the Fifth Amendment. A second trial upon the same indictment at the request of the prosecution was prohibited.

> All this may be assumed for the purpose of the case at hand, though the dissenting opinions show how much was to be said in favor of a different ruling. Right-minded men, as we learn from those opinions, could reasonably, even if mistakenly, believe that a second trial was lawful in prosecutions subject to the Fifth Amendment if it was all in the same case. . . . Even more plainly, right-minded men could reasonably believe that, in espousing that conclusion, they were not favoring a practice repugnant to the conscience of mankind.

Again, Cardozo warned against "The tyranny of labels."[43]

But Palko did not stop there. His counsel argued that the entirety of the guarantees (Amendments 1 through 8) was incorporated. Cardozo was adamant: "There is no such general rule." So what? If the expansive argument was not justified (because incorporation was, after all, prudential) did that rule out the narrower argument about double jeopardy? *Hurtado v. California* (1884) found that trial for capital crimes need not be by indictment. An "information" would suffice. The Fifth Amendment barred self-incrimination, the Court had found in *Twining v. New Jersey* (1908). Trial by jury had similarly been omitted from the list of incorporated rights. As poorly reasoned and offensive to modern law as one today may find these decisions, they were sufficient precedent should the Court apply them in *Palko*. Had Cardozo merely done that, the case would have been of little interest and his opinion far shorter. But then, what would happen to the Court's incorporation of other parts of the Bills of Rights?

> On the other hand, the due process clause of the Fourteenth Amendment may make it unlawful for a state to abridge by its statutes the freedom of

speech which the First Amendment safeguards against encroachment by the Congress . . . or like freedom of the press . . . or the free exercise of religion . . . or the right of peaceable assembly, without which speech would be unduly trammeled . . . or the right of one accused of crime to the benefit of counsel.

What made these rights different? They had been found, according to Cardozo, "to be implicit in the concept of ordered liberty, and thus, through the Fourteenth Amendment, become valid as against the states."[44]

Found? By Whom? By the same court, if not the same justices, as had left other portions of the Bill of Rights by the wayside. Cardozo admitted, "The line of division may seem to be wavering and broken if there is a hasty catalogue of the cases on the one side and the other." This was unacceptable. "Reflection and analysis will induce a different view." For Cardozo, "There emerges the perception of a rationalizing principle which gives to discrete instances a proper order and coherence." One notes the passive voice: "There emerges," from whence? The answer is, from this decision. Cardozo was giving the rules for order and coherence. "The right to trial by jury and the immunity from prosecution except as the result of an indictment may have value and importance. Even so, they are not of the very essence of a scheme of ordered liberty." Essence? As opposed to periphery? "To abolish them is not to violate a 'principle of justice so rooted in the traditions and conscience of our people as to be ranked as fundamental.'" Ask the founders of the nation whether trial by jury was essential, and they would have chorused that it was. If anything was "rooted in traditions," it was trial by jury.[45]

But Cardozo was not concerned with Palko or with double jeopardy. He was concerned with the cases of freedom of speech that were so important to Holmes, Brandeis, and others. These incorporations must be protected. How? "If the Fourteenth Amendment has absorbed them, the process of absorption has had its source in the belief that neither liberty nor Justice would exist if they were sacrificed." Again, note the passive voice—it was the Fourteenth Amendment that was absorbing parts of the Bill of Rights, not the Court or its justices, and certainly not Cardozo.[46]

Now he looked to the future of incorporation. "So it has come about that the domain of liberty, withdrawn by the Fourteenth Amendment from encroachment by the states, has been enlarged by latter-day judgments to include liberty of the mind as well as liberty of action." Again, by what means or process? "The extension became, indeed, a logical imperative when once it was recognized, as long ago it was, that liberty is something more than exemption from physical restraint, and that, even in the field of substantive rights and duties, the legislative judgment, if oppressive and arbitrary, may be overridden by the courts." If the future of incorporation was to be protected, it must be by rereading the Fourteenth Amendment's Due Process Clause, and suiting that to the selective regimen of incorporation. Due Process became Ordered Liberty: those "fundamental principles of liberty and justice which lie at the base of all our civil and political institutions." Individual rights must thus bow to the rights of the polity.[47]

By the end of the 1937 term, Cardozo must have known that his career and his life were coming to an end. He had never cared for the attention that the press paid to members of the Court. Even praise was not welcomed. He felt violated and indignant by prying eyes. His private affairs belonged to no one, and his declining health he kept from all but a few of his closest associates. Cardozo's health failed unrelentingly from the fall of 1937 to the spring of 1938. He died on July 9.[48]

Almost immediately after his funeral, jurists, journalists, and scholars began to debate Cardozo's legacy. Was he a liberal? A conservative? Was he a realist? Or a mystic? Did he prefer judicial restrict? Deference to legislatures? His writing made such sharp distinctions almost impossible, which only added to the eagerness of those who knew him and those who did not to find the real Cardozo. His studied, gracious aloofness gave proof to all manner of judgments. The missing personal correspondence only deepened the mystery. His executors refused to release and then destroyed masses of his papers. The legacy itself became controversial—who was to have charge of it?

There was a picaresque quality in Cardozo's writings, a playfulness with ideas, that he rarely revealed in his correspondence, but one can see it if one is looking closely. Like a magician whose forte is making objects appear and disappear, Cardozo immediately limited or qualified his interventions after making them. He could be severely critical of others' writing, a quality that he also hid behind a formal courtesy (except, again, in correspondence with a few intimates). These qualities of play and solemn judgment became more pronounced as he grew older and more impatient with wrong thinking. Perhaps had he lived to a riper old age, the layers of self-effacement would peel off, and a different, far more sharp-eyed Cardozo would reveal himself to the world. Of his jurisprudence one element is obvious: he was not afraid to read the law forward, find in it a best outcome, and return to it with clearer understanding of its nature.

William O. Douglas, c. 1930. Library of Congress Prints and Photographs Division. Photo by Harris and Ewing.

6. William O. Douglas

Cardozo wrote opinions quickly. Only one justice matched him in speed. That was Washington State's William O. Douglas. On the Court, replacing the retired Brandeis (Cardozo had passed away that year, and his seat went to Felix Frankfurter), Douglas was the next and perhaps most open advocate of reading law forward. His vision of the future was not as glowing as Cardozo's, but then, his past had not been as generous. Growing up in poverty, Douglas never trusted wealth. Uncomfortable in the city, Cardozo's preferred home, Douglas loved the solitude of the wilderness, and from it drew inspiration and solace. Brandeis refused to run for office, though offered support for it many times. Cardozo had to win his seat on the New York Supreme Court, and again in 1926 on the Court of Appeals, but he disliked politics. Douglas had no hesitancy in entertaining the idea of high office, even while he served on the High Court bench. Far from Brandeis's style of writing that looked like social science reports, and Cardozo's that mixed literary eloquence and common sense, Douglas's nonjudicial essays and judicial opinions were a combination of cryptic pronouncements and wide-ranging observations on law, society, and politics. Nevertheless, scattered in them were bright shining insights, seeing danger in the future and demanding law be reread to counter those dangers. Abe Fortas, who knew Douglas as a friend, ally, and mentor, believed that "throughout his life, Douglas fiercely occupied high ground." In Justice William Brennan's opinion, Douglas was "the only true genius" he had ever known.[1]

Douglas was born in rural Minnesota in 1898, and the family followed his father's ministry to California and then to Washington State. His father died when William was six years old, and the future justice grew to maturity in Yakima, Washington. His family was never wealthy; indeed he recalled penury always hovering about his childhood. But he was ambitious, energetic, and able in school. Early on he learned, and learned to despise, the unceasing differences between wealth and poverty, and the way that the rich burdened the poor. His abiding love of wilderness added a vividness to his recollections of early life. He went to high school in Yakima, and then to Whitman College, in Walla Walla, Washington, then to a stint at teaching high school. From there to Columbia Law and a brief spell in corporate law at Cravath Swain in New York City. It did not suit him, and he moved back to Yakima to practice law. Once again, the small town practice of law offered no joy, and like his family, he was once again on the move, back to New York City and teaching at Columbia. He shined in the classroom, and began to develop a reputation as a corporate law expert. Yale Law School reached out and he once again moved, this time from New York City to New Haven, Connecticut. His affection for Yale Law School was abiding, despite a long stint on the Securities and Exchange Commission during the New Deal. He would have become Yale's dean but for an appointment to replace the retiring Brandeis on the High Court.[2]

Douglas was to become an expert on business law, teaching it and writing a casebook on it. But it was almost by accident that he became an adept on the subject. He was literally on his way out the door at Columbia Law School when a chance to prepare a correspondence course in business law came his way. With characteristic confidence, he leapt at the opportunity, recalling later that it was a "formidable" one. Taking evenings and weekends away from his studies, he went to the library, read cases, and wrote chapters, finishing in six weeks—a foretaste of his work habits in years to come. He briefly taught Bankruptcy, Damages, and Partnership at the law school. He remained in New York City for six years, finishing his studies and practicing law with a major corporate firm, Cravath Swain. For the firm, he went to stockholders meetings and had a taste of the shenanigans he would later reveal in his term at the Securities and Exchange Commission. He could have stayed with the firm and become a corporate lawyer of great influence. He made friends—many of them lifelong—including some future federal judges, but he did not like living in the city.[3]

At Columbia Law School and later at Yale Law School, Douglas was part of a reform cadre of law professors. These were the Legal Realists, and they sought to free law from old forms of teaching and scholarship. Instead of ironclad rules passed down over the generations, they argued that law should be taught to students as it was practiced in the real world. "We were blunt and outspoken in our demands" for curriculum reform, Douglas recalled. Led by Underhill Moore and Walter Wheeler Cook, joined by Karl Llewellyn and Herman Oliphant, they stressed facts over doctrine and incorporated customs of the trades that lawyers served. Douglas, infuriated by opposition from then president of the university Nicholas Murray Butler, resigned. But a meeting with Dean Robert M. Hutchins of Yale Law School led to an appoint there, and a "happy time" in New Haven. It was also a productive time for a young law scholar. The project was the same as at Columbia, "to make the law relevant to life." It looked to a law that could solve future problems. For law "changes fast" and the lawyer's reading of the law had to be "readily adaptable to changing situations and problems." But the enthusiasm and the effort went to naught, as projects and programs lost their energy. Looking back fifty years later, he concluded, "my years at Yale disillusioned me concerning the law as an instrument of power for the social good."[4]

Nevertheless, the Yale years produced a body of scholarship at odds with Douglas's later dismal judgment of government intervention. The first of the former was the beginning of his collaboration with Yale Law School colleague Carroll Shanks, "Insulation from Liability through Subsidiary Corporations" (1929), followed by a casebook of business law Douglas and Shanks coauthored. In "Insulation," written before the great crash of 1929, the authors conceded that the subsidiary corporation was a matter of well-established fact in law and business. It served the interests of the corporate managers. But did it serve the interests of the stockholders, or of the public at large? The authors concluded that "The significance of this examination is that the concepts which the courts are using can be broken down and translated into the varying factual combinations which are found." There was a warning against fixed rules taken as sure guides: "From the foregoing it will be seen that where contractual rights are concerned the contents of any rules which may be stated to help in the work of prediction are but shifting and faintly outlined at the best, themselves uncertain subjects of predictability," but no guidance followed except a boilerplate warning: "Until the courts stop to analyze with more particularity the factors motivating their decisions before lapsing into phrases such as 'alter ego' or 'adjunct' or 'constructivisity' there seems little hope of making prediction more certain than the foregoing." The article rehearsed the case law, but there was little legal realism in it: that is, the larger context of the subsidiaries business, the way that the directors of the parent company behaved, the economic conditions of the practices were all absent. The case law would be largely incorporated into the body of the casebook. In the latter, the introduction (more than the body of the work) promised a new view of business law based on social and economic materials. The following pages, like the article, simply gave case after case, although there were references to sociological and academic economic scholarship.[5]

Douglas was beginning to find an answer to the legal realism puzzle: be real, but how to make this a standard for reading law? In Douglas's "Protective Committees in Railroad Reorganizations" (1934):

> Speaking generally, there has long been a need for reform and regulation of the practices of protective committees. This need has not been peculiar to railroads—in fact, it has probably been less acute there than in other types of reorganizations. The need for increased regulation has not been due primarily to the incompetency or to the fraudulent proclivities of committee members. Rather, the need has arisen because so often the committees have been constituted by the inside groups, those affiliated with or drawn from the old management or the financial interests associated with it.

The bottom line was clear: "Under these circumstances, the small security-holder stood little chance to gain the real protection which any legal system should afford him." How to afford this protection? New law. The prospect of a new law creating a securities exchange commission provided an answer: A *Yale Law Review* article coauthored with George Bates on the SEC frankly looked to the future. "At the present time one could not expect more far reaching effects. The economy under which we live is not static. Industry is not stabilized and under our present methods never can be. Competition and the progress of invention make it inevitable that many enterprises will fail. The toll of technology over a period of years is enormous." The new law must be read forward to prevent future chaos.

The presence of so many uncertainties serves to detract attention from the fundamental purpose of the Act: protection of investors. Nevertheless, in spite of the varied issues raised by the present battle over the Act, it cannot be denied that the principles embodied in the Act have become a permanent and integral part of our legal system. The present problem is not their abolition or retention but the discovery of ways and means of accomplishing expeditiously and efficiently their avowed purposes.

Douglas was now ready for the next step in his career, from a commission as a director of a study of the way in which the nation's securities brokers handled their clients' (and their own) finances, to membership on the SEC, to its chairmanship.[6]

As a New dealer and an FDR loyalist, Douglas believed that the federal government, and its "Alphabet" regulatory agencies, had a genuine place in American lawmaking. He also saw these agencies as a way to crack the Wall Street inner circle of corrupt financiers and investment bankers, first as the author of an eight-volume report on the abuses of the investment firms and their counsel, and then as a member, and finally as the head of the SEC. In this sense, he represented the western energy of progressivism and reform that complemented Brandeis and the Wilsonians. When he assumed the headship of the SEC at Roosevelt's behest (Wall Street and the Exchange cringed with horror at his appointment), he told his first press conference that he was for the investor, not for the broker and the deal makers. This was the little guy whose interests, Douglas believed, the SEC was meant to protect. The connection to Brandeis was clear. *Other People's Money* could have been Douglas's Bible, as he later wrote; the SEC act "was a restatement of the earlier creed of Brandeis that members of the financial oligarchy handling 'other people's money' are trustees." As Douglas recalled, under his own stewardship, "No agency [of the federal government] I think, ever accomplished so much in so little time, in getting programs that were new and complicated, accepted and reduced to practical procedures." For that was the job of the interpreter of laws—to look ahead and manipulate them into realistic instruments, in this case to manage the economy.[7]

But Douglas, like many westerners in Washington, DC, was also a maverick with a streak of independence. This he would show after 1939, when he went on the bench. Over time, he began to see intrusive big government as an enemy of individual rights. He would make a practice of leaving Washington, DC, for Goose Creek, Washington, taking with him or having him sent all the paperwork for the Court over the summer. The restlessness of his early years grew into travel abroad. He loved the unpopular cause and the defense of minority rights. He identified with the downtrodden, never trusted the establishment, and, while a patriot, never blindly followed the dictates of government. He tinkered with the idea of running for public office, and declined two invitations to join a presidential ticket, then publicly denied having any political aspirations. But like Brandeis, Douglas had no hesitation promoting the political ambitions of his friends.[8]

During his service at the Securities and Exchange Commission in Washington, DC, William O. Douglas was a frequent visitor to Brandeis's apartment-office in the city. The two men were very friendly, and Douglas later recalled that Brandeis had been one of his idols. Indeed, Douglas seemed to have gone to school on Brandeis more than once. The reference to *Other People's Money* was but one occasion of indebtedness. In a 1948 talk to the Yale Law School Association annual dinner, he adopted the theme of Brandeis's "Living Law": "If ever a generation was called upon in a few short years, or perhaps months, to shape the destiny of the world we live in, it is ours. Of all the people of this generation, it is the professional classes who should take a prominent place in shaping that destiny." Among those classes, lawyers—future lawyers in particular—were foremost. "For if the lawyer is to spend as much time shaping new community policies as he does interpreting the rules of a waning policy, his legal education ought at least to introduce him to that phase of his future career."[9]

Douglas thought that Brandeis supported Douglas for a seat on the High Court. This was so, although Brandeis may not have actually recommended Douglas to President Franklin D. Roosevelt. In personality, however, the two men could not have been further apart. Brandeis was cool and sometimes distant, but never uncivil. Douglas was capable of great kindness and genuine warmth, but ordinarily cold and curt, and sometimes arrogant and mean, something never true of Brandeis. Douglas never inspired the kind of adoration that Brandeis loyalists evidenced.[10]

On the Court, after a period of adjustment, Douglas came to adopt the role of public intellectual. His audience was as much public opinion and policy makers as it was the Brethren, and his view of law was as much in aid of current and future problem solving than of resolving past and present disputes. The central themes of his ringing defense of individualism and individual rights, while not always internally consistent, were clear. One cannot say that he valued doctrinal clarity (or precedent), but he had a broad-ranging jurisprudence. Like Brandeis, Douglas saw in American history the grounds for a rights-based constitutionalism. At the same time, he saw an ominous future of tyranny over people's minds and spirits. In this sense, his reading of law was a throwback to Jefferson's rather than to the Progressives or Populists.[11]

Indeed, no one who follows Douglas's career writes about the Douglas doctrine. For Douglas was not concerned with consistency so much as with issues. For Brandeis, reading law forward in judicial opinions took shape in the interstices of established law. Cardozo found the method congenial to a result-oriented process. For Douglas, the luminosity of the Bill of Rights threw its penumbras far into the future. Brandeis certainly read the First Amendment forward; Cardozo did the same with the common law; Douglas saw the entirety of the first ten amendments, along with the Fourteenth Amendment, as the centerpiece of the future Constitution. This was the proposition he set out in his *A Living Bill of Rights* (1961).[12]

The opening passage of *A Living Bill of Rights* echoed Brandeis: "the Constitution is not a dusty, obsolete historical document. It is the heart of our life as a nation." The threats to the Constitution, hence the need to read it forward, were the looming omens of infringement of the rights "of others" by government officials, or legislative majorities, "by oversight or design." Then it was that challenges came to the courts, where Douglas confronted them. Douglas found that reading law forward had a long and honorable past. "History teaches that the costs and dangers of suppressing ideas will always be greater than the real or the fancied risks of permitting their expression." Douglas and the Court had just run the gamut of the Second Red Scare, with state legislatures and Congress, inferior courts and prosecutors suppressing the speech and publication of Communists. Douglas, sometimes alone on the Court, fought for freedom to express ideas. He sounded like Jefferson, in his first Inaugural Address:

> During the contest of opinion through which we have passed [the bitterly contested election of 1800] the animation of discussions and of exertions has sometimes worn an aspect which might impose on strangers unused to think freely and to speak and to write what they think; but this being now decided by the voice of the nation, announced according to the rules of the Constitution, all will, of course, arrange themselves under the will of the law, and unite in common efforts for the common good. All, too, will bear in mind this sacred principle, that though the will of the majority is in all cases to prevail, that will to be rightful must be reasonable; that the minority possess their equal rights, which equal law must protect, and to violate would be oppression.

Douglas translated this as "In the final analysis freedom is the way we think about and treat a non-conforming neighbor, a dissenter, the holder of a minority view among us, and the liberty he actually enjoys." And underlying all of these was "the right to be let alone." The lesson of the past was clear: "The battle over the Bill of Rights is a never ending one."[13]

Douglas's Bill of Rights was an open-ended declaration of human freedom. When the Court misread the Constitution by looking backward, Douglas corrected it: "Today a white man stands convicted for protesting in unseemly language against our decisions invalidating restrictive covenants. Tomorrow a Negro will be hailed before a court for denouncing lynch law in heated terms." The list of future wrongs a restrictive view of the Bills of Rights would impose went on and on: "minority groups of all kinds" will be "caught in the mesh of" narrowed readings of the Bill of Rights. Over and over in his opinions, Douglas warned of a future of "gradual encroachments" on the freedom of citizens, a veritable "cancer on the body politic." The First Amendment had to be read as a document for the future, not merely a traditional and limited right. First Amendment rights required narrowly drawn statutes, or government agencies would take unconstitutional liberties to constrain freedom of speech and press.[14]

In particular, the "loyalty programs" of the twentieth century presented a new challenge, as new and more intrusive means to investigate individuals emerged. Present employees and applicants to government agencies hauled before legislative investigative committees enjoyed few of the rights to privacy Douglas believed the ordinary citizen enjoyed. The overbreadth and unlimited scope of these information trawls discouraged able men and women from seeking government jobs and from "expressing unorthodox ideas" once hired. These were among the most dangerous developments in Bill of Rights jurisprudence, for it suppressed the spirit as well as the voice of the people. For above all, for Douglas the right that preceded all others was the right of the individual to privacy. As he wrote in "The Right to Be Left Alone" in the third of the North Lectures at Franklin and Marshall College in 1957, published as *The Right of the People* (1958), the way to "rejuvenate America" was to take the right of privacy seriously.[15]

The Constitution did not mention privacy, much less a right to privacy. But "the individual needs protection from government itself." Douglas would fashion that right out of the penumbras of the Bill of Rights. In 1957, he found the right of privacy "sometimes explicit and sometimes implicit in the Constitution." But existing law, especially the Constitution, must be read in a forward-looking fashion. Although Douglas had to wait eight years to put his view of privacy into an opinion for the Court, the argument was already fully developed in the Franklin and Marshall talks. "Under modern conditions" privacy was under attack. The right to be let alone; the right to travel within the country; the right to conscience; the right to be safe in one's home— these "have suffered greatly in recent years." Worse would come if the Russian Communist example was any guide. For the assault on the minds and spirits—on the beliefs—of dissenters in government, private schools, and the academy was overwhelming in 1957, including loyalty oaths and secret investigations. The Court was coming around to Douglas's position, at least when dealing with legislative intrusions into private beliefs. But only a "brave employee" would be willing to hire a lawyer and bring suit against the government itself. And if the right to be left alone was under unceasing attack, it was even more to be "one of our great rallying points."[16]

Douglas's commitment to the right of privacy derived not from Brandeis's writing on privacy, although Douglas cited Brandeis's dissenting opinion in *Olmstead* in *The Right of the People* in case after case, but from Douglas's own experience. This was why Douglas always wrote of a "right to privacy" rather than Brandeis's preferred formulation of a right "of privacy." Privacy was not a property right but a personal right. In this way Douglas elevated privacy to the first rank of great rights of free people. A first hint came in his opinion in *Skinner v. Oklahoma* (1943): "This case touches a sensitive and important area of human rights. Oklahoma deprives certain individuals of a right which is basic to the perpetuation of a race, the right to have offspring. Oklahoma has decreed the enforcement of its law against petitioner, overruling his claim that it violated the Fourteenth Amendment. Because that decision raised grave and substantial constitutional questions, we granted the petition for certiorari." Not only did Douglas pointedly distinguish the case from *Buck v. Bell*, he ended the opinion for the Court with a reference to Brandeis: "if an excision were made, this particular constitutional difficulty might be solved by enlarging, on the one hand, or contracting, on the other (*cf.* Mr. Justice Brandeis dissenting, *National Life Ins. Co. v. United States*, 277 U.S. 508, 277 U.S. 534–535) the class of criminals who might be sterilized." It was one not-so-subtle effort to note the limitations of Brandeis's views and the expansion of his own.[17]

That recognition grew from the experience of dissenting in cases during the witch-hunts of the McCarthy Era but more so it was the translation into legal terms of his experience of solitary travel through the wilderness of the West. In 1965, after a series of short books on his wandering through American wilderness areas, he proposed an environmental Bill of Rights. The "Wilderness Bill of Rights" catalogued the tortious intrusion on the land and the waters of the country in what was perhaps the most forward looking of all his extrajudicial writings. Future prospects for conservation of natural spaces lay not in the old idea of resource management, but in the newer concept of "beauty" "desecrated" by development and exploitation of resources. Law, read forward, must protect access to wilderness without destroying the very qualities that made wilderness so important to the human spirit.[18]

A law with one eye on the future was the key to protecting wilderness, and Douglas's reading of the Constitution required the protection of "wilderness values." The Wilderness Act preserved some areas, as did various federal, state, and local attempts to preserve parkland, but "the laws are in the main incompatible with a Wilderness Bill of Rights." Even this was not enough to prevent further despoliation. "We need a new conservation ethic," Douglas concluded, making "conservation a civic cause." These were not mentioned in the Constitution, but for citizens to petition successfully to protect existing and expand wilderness areas current law was not enough. An office of conservation was needed to raise these concerns to the highest executive level. In Douglas's second iteration of basic rights, the trees and the land would be protected against timber, mining, and other extractive concerns, as well as against government agents who carried out the will of the corporate despoilers. The beauty of the "original America" would be protected as a matter of constitutional law. While the plea for individuals to come forward was stirring and the offer of a constitutional amendment was bold, Douglas knew that neither was a workable solution. Instead, throughout the book, in the midst of paeans to natural beauty and complaints about automobiles and loggers, Douglas relied on existing federal law. That law, read forward, provided real solutions, and he told the reader how those laws should be read forward. Five years later, in the National Environmental Protection Act, many of Douglas's proposals became reality.[19]

The fight for wilderness values was not easily won. Perhaps the best example of this commitment was Douglas's dissent in *Sierra Club v. Morton* (1972). A proposed site for a ski club on federal lands in the Sequoia National Forest had been challenged by the Sierra Club. The majority of the Court found that the club did not show any individualized harm to its members from the proposal, and so lacked standing to bring the suit. In his dissent, Douglas found a petitioner that did have standing, figuratively and literally.

The critical question of "standing" would be simplified and also put neatly in focus if we fashioned a federal rule that allowed environmental issues to be litigated before federal agencies or federal courts in the name of the inanimate object about to be despoiled, defaced, or invaded by roads and bulldozers, and where injury is the subject of public outrage. Contemporary public concern for protecting nature's ecological equilibrium should lead to the conferral of standing upon environmental objects to sue for their own preservation.

The notion that the trees should have the right to bring the suit was not Douglas's invention—in admiralty law ships were persons—but his argument that "So it should be as respects valleys, alpine meadows, rivers, lakes, estuaries, beaches, ridges, groves of trees, swampland, or even air that feels the destructive pressures of modern technology and modern life" made sense when one looked at the increasing and almost unstoppable incursion of modernity into wilderness lands. Older ideas like standing must give way to a new reading of law if the wilderness was to be preserved in the future. Who was to speak for the trees? For the forests? For the streams and the lakes? "Those who have that intimate relation with the inanimate object about to be injured, polluted, or otherwise despoiled are its legitimate spokesmen."[20]

Bringing one's personal experience to the law was not unheard of in writings on jurisprudence—Cardozo had written of it in his *Nature of the Judicial Process* (1921) and law professor Jerome Frank had carried it to an extreme in his book *Law and the Modern Mind* (1930), but even when Cardozo joined the Supreme Court in 1932 and Frank the Court of Appeals for the Second Circuit in 1941, they did not go as far as Douglas.

For Douglas reached into his love of wilderness solitude to fashion a sweeping defense of personal privacy as the right on which all other constitutional rights rested. Near the end of his life, Douglas wistfully recalled how, "I like to go in the woods at night and listen to the nocturnal sounds. . . . There is the lovely call of the loon that takes me back in memory to the lakes of Minnesota and Canada." He always felt closer to the "travelers of the air" than to those who walked "on the ground."

His opinions, like those birds, flew high above the doctrinal burdens the groundlings of the law carried on their backs.[21]

Douglas's view of the primacy of privacy as a legal right evolved over the course of his tenure on the Court. The first case in which he probed the question was *Public Utilities Commission v. Pollak* (1952). Passengers in a street car and bus company suit claimed that the piped-in music and advertising violated their right to privacy. The majority of the Court voted to dismiss the suit. Douglas dissented. It was a case "of first impression," in which the Court wrote "on a clean slate." While no one had a liberty right to still the street sounds of the city, no one could be compelled to attend church services or political gatherings against their will. With all sorts of political propaganda filling the airwaves, a person could turn off the unwanted information in his home or vehicle, but not when it was thrust at him in a public conveyance. "If liberty is to flourish, government should never be allowed to force people to listen to any radio program. The right of privacy should include the right to pick and choose from competing entertainments, competing propaganda, competing political philosophies." Hidden in Douglas's fustian against piped-in advertisements on buses was his recognition that more and more information would be thrust upon the unwilling. He had, in effect, seen the coming of the blogosphere, social media, and twitter bombing. Against the forerunner of these he raised the banner of privacy.[22]

The right to privacy was central to Douglas's opinion for the Court in *Griswold v. Connecticut*. It was not a case of first instance, as the Court had previously declined to deal with the precise issue in *Poe v. Ullman* (1961). A Connecticut statute made giving information on or providing the use of contraceptives a criminal offense. Appellants—the executive director of the Planned Parenthood League of Connecticut, Estelle Griswold, and its medical director, Lee Buxton, a licensed physician—were convicted as accessories for giving married persons information and medical advice on how to prevent conception and, following examination, prescribing a contraceptive device or material for the wife's use. Appellants claimed that the accessory statute as applied violated the Fourteenth Amendment. A state intermediate appellate court and the state's highest court affirmed the judgment. The US Supreme Court reversed, with a majority opinion by Douglas.[23]

There were two issues for Douglas in that case. The first was the indictment of Griswold and Buxton as accessories, as the statute made the woman seeking the outlawed birth control information the primary offender. Could they raise the constitutional issues that the married couple did not bring to court? That is, did they have "standing" to appeal their conviction under the statute? The second issue was the constitutionality of the statute itself. The charge was that "They gave information, instruction, and medical advice to *married persons* as to the means of preventing conception. [The appellants] examined the wife and prescribed the best contraceptive device or material for her use." The statute, a relic of the era of Anthony Comstock and the purity campaign after the Civil War, was no longer in force on the federal side, and little Comstock acts had been repealed in the rest of the country. The state itself was not eager to enforce it. Nevertheless, its language was broad. "Any person who uses any drug, medicinal article or instrument for the purpose of preventing conception shall be fined not less than fifty dollars or imprisoned not less than sixty days nor more than one year or be both fined and imprisoned." The accessory was similarly culpable. "Any person who assists, abets, counsels, causes, hires or commands another to commit any offense may be prosecuted and punished as if he were the principal offender."[24]

Griswold and Buxton appealed, basing their claim on the Fourteenth Amendment Due Process Clause. No state might deny Due Process to any citizen of the United States. "We think that appellants have standing to raise the constitutional rights of the married people with whom they had a professional relationship." The idea that a professional relationship, like the lawyer/client or doctor/client privity, had a special place in Due Process was in itself something of a novelty, although Douglas found precedent for it. As well, previously "we thought that the requirements of standing should be strict, lest the standards of 'case or controversy' in Article III of the Constitution become blurred." Here the criminal conviction clarified the issue. "Certainly the accessory should have standing to assert that the offense which he is charged with assisting is not, or cannot constitutionally be, a crime." Then, a marital relationship was also privileged under the Clause. "The rights of husband and wife, pressed here, are likely to be diluted or adversely affected unless those rights are considered in a suit involving those who have this kind of confidential relation to them." Douglas did not hesitate to treat novelties as though they were well-established parts of constitutional law. In the final analysis, despite the sometimes "elliptical," even "cryptic" and often repetitive nature of his opinions, it was his "vision" of the future and his reading of the law into that future that made his decisions "not only right for the day they were decided, they were equally right for today and for tomorrow."[25]

It was this style of writing opinions that simultaneously enabled and concealed Douglas's commitment to reading law forward. Like his personal view of privacy, it was implicit in his writing. In "coming to the merits, we are met with a wide range of questions that implicate the Due Process Clause of the Fourteenth Amendment." Douglas rejected the idea that the Court was a "super-legislature to determine the wisdom, need, and propriety of laws that touch economic problems, business affairs, or social conditions." This was the substantive due process of the *Lochner v. New York* (1905) majority. Then Douglas did exactly that in weighing the substantive impact of the Connecticut law. "This law, however, operates directly on an intimate relation of husband and wife and their physician's role in one aspect of that relation." Where was that subject in the Constitution? "The association of people is not mentioned in the Constitution nor in the Bill of Rights." Nor was "The right to educate a child in a school of the parents' choice—whether public or private or parochial—is also not mentioned. Nor is the right to study any particular subject or any foreign language. Yet the First Amendment has been construed to include certain of those rights." That is, in prior decisions the Court had impleaded those substantive relationships into the Bill of Rights, then imposed them on the states through the Fourteenth Amendment. Douglas proposed to continue that process into the future, but he concealed that plan by reciting precedent. What was new became old. He cited the cases wherein the Court had previously acted, as though they proved his proposition that "the State may not, consistently with the spirit of the First Amendment, contract the spectrum of available knowledge. The right of freedom of speech and press includes not only the right to utter or to print, but the right to distribute, the right to receive, the right to read and freedom of inquiry, freedom of thought, and freedom to teach indeed the freedom of the entire university community." Instead of pushing a new view, in the "spirit" of the First Amendment Douglas claimed to be only reaffirming older cases.[26]

Douglas could not conceal entirely what he was doing. He was marching into the future. "The First Amendment has a penumbra where privacy is protected from governmental intrusion. In like context, we have protected forms of 'association' that are not political in the customary sense but pertain to the social, legal, and economic benefit of the members." The penumbra of rights, rights yet unexplored, was a future of robust rights. The case citations did not mention penumbras, but for Douglas the right of assembly, of association, of belief "is more than the right to attend a meeting; it includes the right to express one's attitudes or philosophies by membership in a group or by affiliation with it or by other lawful means." The right existed, and "while it is not expressly included in the First Amendment its existence is necessary in making the express guarantees fully meaningful."[27]

What might be seen, at best, as Douglas's scattershot use of precedent and, at worst, as his indifference to precedent was in fact his vision of where the law should go. Although, as one of his former clerks has written, "Everyone knows that Douglas was impatient with and careless in his use of conventional legal doctrine," he knew where the law must go. "The foregoing cases suggest that specific guarantees in the Bill of Rights have penumbras, formed by emanations from those guarantees that help give them life and substance." Penumbras and emanations? His only source for that was his own dissenting opinion in *Poe v. Ullman*. But reading the law for its best outcome need not rest on precedent. Instead, "various guarantees create zones of privacy." A zone of privacy was not a metaphor. It was the legal version of Douglas's wilderness, a real time space in which the individual had the right to be let alone. There followed a list of suggested sources in the Amendments for this constitutionally protected zone, none of which was particularly on point (that is, none of which entailed connubial rights), but all of which, taken together, gave the opinion a conventional appearance of "penumbral rights." However did the penumbras coalesce into "penumbra rights"? That is, how did a conjectural noun become a conventional modifier? The answer was that these rights existed in a future of rights. The closest of Douglas's citations to these rights were the Fourth and Fifth Amendments as "described . . . as protection against all governmental invasions 'of the sanctity of a man's home and the privacies of life' . . . recently referred in *Mapp v. Ohio*, . . . to the Fourth Amendment as creating a 'right to privacy,' no less important than any other right carefully and particularly reserved to the people." Douglas added that the Court had seen "many controversies over these penumbral rights of 'privacy and repose,' " citing his own writings. "These cases bear witness that the right of privacy which presses for recognition here is a legitimate one."[28]

Having created the zone of privacy, Douglas populated it. "The present case, then, concerns a relationship lying within the zone of privacy created by several fundamental constitutional guarantees. And it concerns a law which, in forbidding the *use* of contraceptives rather than regulating their manufacture or sale, seeks to achieve its goals by means of having a maximum destructive impact upon that relationship." Again, the basis for constitutional repugnance was not precedent, but Douglas's own vision of future horrors: "Would we allow the police to search the sacred precincts of marital bedrooms for telltale signs of the use of contraceptives? The very idea is repulsive to the notions of privacy surrounding the marriage relationship." Brandeis had read the law forward to attach the privacy right to the home. Douglas extended it to the bedroom.[29]

One finds the same subtle forward reading of law in Douglas's concurrence in *Doe v. Bolton* (1973), the Georgia case joined with *Roe v. Wade* (1973). In *Roe* Texas criminal law made the performance of an abortion a crime. An unmarried pregnant woman sought injunctive relief from the federal courts against Texas, although the suit was filed against the Dallas district attorney. Joined in the suit was a doctor who would have been arrested for performing the abortion. A separate action, similar to that filed by the unmarried, pregnant woman, was filed by a married, childless couple, who alleged that, should the wife become pregnant at some future date, they would wish to terminate the pregnancy by abortion without fear of prosecution. The three-person panel on the district court (required when a petitioner wished an injunction against a state) found that the unmarried woman and the doctor had standing to sue; the right to choose whether to have children was protected by the Ninth Amendment and applied to the state through the Fourteenth Amendment; the Texas criminal abortion statutes were void on their face, because they were unconstitutionally vague and overbroad; but the application for injunctive relief should be denied. Both the state and the plaintiffs appealed the decision of the district court panel, and the US Supreme Court agreed with the district court's view of the rights of the unmarried pregnant woman.[30]

Justice Harry Blackmun wrote the opinion for the Court after two rounds of oral argument. He found that the state had a legitimate interest in protecting the health of the mother and, after a certain period in the pregnancy, the life of the fetus, but that the right to privacy (explained in Douglas's *Griswold* opinion) encompasses a woman's decision whether or not to terminate her pregnancy. What was more, and this would become a controversial portion of the opinion, the unborn are not included within the definition of "person" as used in the Fourteenth Amendment. Blackmun introduced a trimester test of these competing rights: prior to the end of the first trimester of pregnancy, the state may not interfere with or regulate an attending physician's decision, reached in consultation with his patient, that the patient's pregnancy should be terminated; until the point in time when the fetus becomes viable, the state may regulate the abortion procedure only to the extent that such regulation relates to the preservation and protection of maternal health; from and after the point in time when the fetus becomes viable, the state may prohibit abortions altogether, except those necessary to preserve the life or health of the mother.[31]

Douglas signed on to Blackmun's opinion, but added his own in a concurrence. The concurrence followed the companion case, *Doe v. Bolton* (1973). In that case, a Georgia law, modeled on the Model Penal Code's reform proposal, required that the abortion be performed by a duly licensed Georgia physician when necessary in "his best clinical judgment" because continued pregnancy would endanger a pregnant woman's life or injure her health, the fetus would likely be born with a serious defect, or the pregnancy resulted from rape. There were institutional requirements as well. A legal abortion could only be performed in a hospital accredited by the Joint Commission on Accreditation of Hospitals (JCAH); the procedure had to be approved by the hospital staff abortion committee; and the performing physician's judgment had to be confirmed by independent examinations of the patient by two other licensed physicians. The Supreme Court struck down the Georgia statute on the same Due Process grounds as it reversed the Texas law.[32]

For Douglas, the question was once again the right to be let alone. "The questions presented in the present cases go far beyond the issues of vagueness. . . . They involve the right of privacy, one aspect of which we considered in Griswold v. Connecticut . . . when we held that various guarantees in the Bill of Rights create zones of privacy." Douglas could have drawn support from Justice Arthur Goldberg's opinion in *Griswold*, based on the Ninth Amendment's unenumerated rights. He chose not to. "The Ninth Amendment obviously does not create federally enforceable rights. It merely says, 'The enumeration in the Constitution, of certain rights, shall not be construed to deny or disparage others retained by the people.'" Where might the right to be let alone then appear? Douglas found them in the "catalogue of these rights includ[ing] customary, traditional, and time-honored rights, amenities, privileges, and immunities that come within the sweep of 'the Blessings of Liberty' mentioned in the preamble to the Constitution." Nowhere in American constitutional law in the twentieth century was the "Blessings of Liberty" clause in the Preamble to the Constitution regarded as self-implementing. Abraham Lincoln was the last to argue something like that with respect to slavery, and his argument did not bear fruit until the ratification of the Thirteenth Amendment. Rather than state that the Preamble should be read forward and given self-sustaining authority, Douglas hid the claim in the "liberty" of the Fourteenth Amendment.[33]

But nothing in the Fourteenth Amendment mentioned "the autonomous control over the development and expression of one's intellect, interests, tastes, and personality." Douglas nevertheless found these rights "protected by the First Amendment and, in my view, they are absolute, permitting of no exceptions." The cases he cited referred to speeches, films, and religious beliefs, but nothing about intellect and personality. He was simply reading those precedents forward to apply them to reproductive rights. Their weight in his opinion in *Doe*, then, was not because they were on point, but because he had taken part in them and read them in a certain way. While some critics might dismiss the cases as window dressing at best and abusive mischief at worst, those critics would miss the point. Douglas, seeing bits and pieces in the precedents rather than cases as a whole, from those bits and pieces constructed his own reading of liberty interests. Those interests were fundamental. They included (because in *Griswold* he said they included) "The liberty to marry a person of one's own choosing . . . the right of procreation . . . the liberty to direct the education of one's children, . . . and the privacy of the marital relation."[34]

Quoting from his own concurrence in *Eisenstadt v. Baird* (1972), Douglas continued his commentary on his own opinion in *Griswold*:

> It is true that in *Griswold* the right of privacy in question inhered in the marital relationship. Yet the marital couple is not an independent entity with a mind and heart of its own, but an association of two individuals each with a separate intellectual and emotional makeup. If the right of privacy means anything, it is the right of the *individual*, married or single, to be free from unwarranted governmental intrusion into matters so fundamentally affecting a person as the decision whether to bear or beget a child.

Douglas, using Douglas's own prior words, moved the precedents' pieces forward.[35]

Douglas's view of the privacy right pushed the language of the Fourteenth Amendment far beyond where anyone else on the Court had pushed it. Or rather, he simply read it forward, into spaces that modern men and women already occupied. "That right includes the privilege of an individual to plan his own affairs," including "the freedom to care for one's health and person, freedom from bodily restraint or compulsion, freedom to walk, stroll, or loaf." And, as was his wont, there followed bits and pieces of precedent that did not exactly match his claims, but gave a burnish to the opinion.[36]

From which he could then assert, "The Georgia statute is at war with the clear message of these cases—that a woman is free to make the basic decision whether to bear an unwanted child." Look ahead, not in law, but in fact, and one finds that

> rejected applicants under the Georgia statute are required to endure the discomforts of pregnancy; to incur the pain, higher mortality rate, and aftereffects of childbirth; to abandon educational plans; to sustain loss of income; to forgo the satisfactions of careers; to tax further mental and physical health in providing child care; and, in some cases, to bear the lifelong stigma of unwed motherhood, a badge which may haunt, if not deter, later legitimate family relationships.

While the state had legitimate interests "to protect," and the birth of children was a "rightful concern of society" (Douglas's characteristic concessions), these may not outweigh the woman's right to privacy in an early abortion. For

> right of privacy has no more conspicuous place than in the physician-patient relationship, unless it be in the priest-penitent relationship. It is one thing for a patient to agree that her physician may consult with another physician about her case. It is quite a different matter for the State compulsorily to impose on that physician-patient relationship another layer or, as in this case, still a third layer of physicians. The right of privacy—the right to care for one's health and person and to seek out a physician of one's own choice protected by the Fourteenth Amendment—becomes only a matter of theory, not a reality, when a multiple-physician-approval system is mandated by the State.

The "liberty" in the Fourteenth Amendment included the right of privacy.[37]

In his opinions, written with lightning speed, often before the conference of the justices met and before he had a chance to read his colleagues' draft opinions, Douglas proved to be a bold and big thinker. He often agreed with the majority, but concurred to make his own point. He was not a legal scholar, despite the many citations in these concurrences and dissents, but he had a facile pen. Like Brandeis, who inventively brought social science and law review articles into his opinions, and Cardozo, who employed figurative language and metaphor, Douglas innovated by bringing comparative religion and environmental analogies into his opinions. His opinions lacked the weight of Brandeis's and the suggestiveness of Cardozo's but possessed strength and directness.

Douglas's reading of law forward was pointillist; one had to step back from the many dots of it to see the larger pattern. This was especially true of his speeches and essays. For unlike Brandeis, who after his elevation eschewed outside speaking engagements, Douglas not only accepted invitations to speak outside the court, but arranged to have these speeches published. One explanation is that he needed the advances from publishers to pay alimony, but another is that he saw the addresses and the publications as a way to say what he could not in his opinions. In the extrajudicial writings, one finds much of his activist reading of law scattered throughout like points of bright light. As he wrote to Dean Edmond Cahn, in 1962, preparing the James Madison Lecture, at the NYU School of Law, the Bill of Rights "are negative and do not generate the forces of freedom. . . . What may be needed for the development of freedom" was new and novel ways of reading law. He wanted to title the lecture, "A Bill of Rights Is Not Enough." As he told an audience at UCLA in 1964, "we need visionary programs" to match law to the novel challenges of the world. Otherwise, the "disease," "the power of government . . . to suffocate both people and causes" of the future, would fatally infect the laws. The cure was obvious: "The First Amendment, as I read it, was designed precisely to prevent that tragedy."[38]

Near the end of his career on the Court, Douglas took time to spell out some of those dangers. Law had become too complex, too burdened by precedent and doctrine. "Finding a right to correct a wrong is, however, the least of all the modern pressing problems. If poor and rich alike had lawyers to assert their claims, we would still be left with staggering problems." In this, the fundamental belief that the future of reform lay not with courts, Douglas agreed with Brandeis. A "great restructuring of our society" was needed. Of course, that restructuring must come from law, but not the law of meum and tuum. One could not sue or regulate one's way to a just world. Legislation on "the most explosive issues," those including racial discrimination, housing, food for the hungry, education," was Douglas's first priority. These legal remedies did not arise from the courts. They required the wholehearted effort of legislatures and presidents. Legislation must expand "the public sector," the "blueprint" for which was an economic bill of rights.[39]

But Douglas did not profess deference to legislative bodies or administrative agencies. As he dissented in *U.S. v. Richardson* (1974), about the top-secret classification of documents, concealing ordinary information from public scrutiny, "No greater crisis in confidence can be generated than today's decision. Its consequences are grave because it relegates to secrecy vast operations of government and keeps the public from knowing what secret plans concerning this Nation or other nations are afoot." As a result, "an individual's stake in the integrity of constitutional guarantees is undermined by deciding that the individual who seeks this knowledge has no standing to in a court of law." The mindless bureaucracy, often captured by the very corporations it was supposed to supervise, and indifferent to the individual in need, was as sore an affliction as need itself. Above all, law must be "responsive to human needs. . . . Laws must be revised so as to eliminate their present bias against the poor."[40]

I have written that Douglas's jurisprudence was pointillist, many brilliant dots of light scattered throughout his work, only forming a coherent image when one steps back from them. I believe that picture was for him a disturbing one. Bad law let loose the night monsters, in the army, in the schools, in the hitherto-sacred corners of individual life. The danger was a gradual slide into the police state, whose surveillance was everywhere and whose agents were willing collaborators. Douglas was not optimistic, as he saw "the Supreme Court . . . shoved more and more into the background."[41]

Growing old on the Court has never been a pleasant prospect. Some stayed far too long for their old powers, hearing, sight, and ability to concentrate gone before they were. David J. Fields, a picture of energy when he joined the Court, had to be persuaded by his son-in-law Justice David Brewer to retire; Taft, when president, lamented the failing capabilities of some on the Court, but refused to go quietly when his own abilities declined steeply. Brandeis retired when he believed his abilities were weakening, and Sandra Day O'Connor and Anthony Kennedy left when they felt it was time for them to go, but Ruth Bader held on to the end. After a paralyzing stroke, Douglas continued to come to court and, when he retired, continued to write opinions as the "tenth justice."[42]

In his thirty-six years on the Court, Douglas participated in 4501 cases, joining the majority in 2918, dissenting in 1181, concurring, concurring in the judgment, and raising jurisdictional objections in the remainder. Although I have focused on his environmental and privacy jurisprudence, he wrote on a wide variety of constitutional and common-law subjects. His passing, in 1980, was lamented by friends and former foes. All agreed he was an original. No one has, in the passing of time, quite matched his colorful legacy, and that would have pleased him. His contribution to a reading of the law forward is undeniable, taking it in ways that a more conventional jurist might not have assayed.

Stephen G. Breyer, 2006. Collection of the Supreme Court of the United States. Photo by Steve Petteway.

7. Stephen G. Breyer

In experience and temperament Stephen G. Breyer was as far from William O. Douglas as Douglas was from Benjamin N. Cardozo. Born to a wealthy family in San Francisco, Breyer attended Stanford for his undergraduate degree and then went to Oxford and finally to Harvard Law School. A cosmopolitan, his writing marked him as the epitome of a postmodern judge: technologically sophisticated and internationalist in viewpoint. In his balancing of interests and promotion of "active liberty," Breyer openly and repeatedly read the law forward.[1]

In Breyer's tenure on the federal courts, new legal issues had arisen that required a sophistication in economics and computer sciences that even the elite law schools had not, until recently, taught. At the same time, the justices' opinions grew longer and more complex as the Supreme Court docket shrank from about two hundred cases a session at the start of the twentieth century to around eighty cases per session in the twenty-first century. All of which made Breyer's mastery of detail and focus on alternative outcomes a highly appropriate skill set for the High Court.[2]

Breyer, like Douglas, was a law professor, a government servant, and an intellectual before he joined the Court of Appeals for the First Circuit. Like Douglas, Breyer kept before him the interests of the little guy, the individual, whose rights remained important even in the most complex appellate litigation. Like Douglas, Breyer was a westerner. He was born and raised in the San Francisco area and went to school there, then went east for law school, Harvard. Like Douglas, Breyer's opinions made him a lightning rod for criticism as well as praise. Unlike Douglas, he spent a long judicial apprenticeship on the Court of Appeals, becoming its chief judge, before President Bill Clinton nominated him to the US Supreme Court. The confirmation hearings were relatively smooth sailing and on July 29, 1994, the Senate voted 87 to 9 to confirm the president's choice. At Harvard Law School and again on the Court Breyer was something of a technocrat, a specialist in international and administrative law. Although thought by some to be pro–large corporate enterprises, hence belonging to the very group of conservative jurists that Douglas opposed, Breyer proved that assumption wrong. He was very much a pragmatist, demanding and mastering huge amounts of factual data, not only on the case at hand, but on related subjects. On the Court, he was soon a lynchpin of the liberal caucus, and would remain so for the next twenty-eight years.[3]

Before he put on the judge's robes, law professor Breyer specialized in copyright law. His 1970 article on that topic, written six years after his appointment to the Harvard faculty, hinted at his view of law's purposes and consequences. Copyright protection of literary works had a history as well as a well-defensed tradition. That is, it rested on the language of a series of copyright laws, a long history, and a tradition of protection. The subject of the essay was a revision of federal copyright law then under consideration by Congress. It would have strengthened and lengthened copyright protections. But Breyer argued that the underlying basis for such protections was logically and practically flawed. In fact, few authors (the exception being the trade press most popular authors) ever made back from royalties or sales nearly what they put into the books in time and effort. The book was not "property" in the sense that land or chattels were personal property. The advantage to the publisher was the other reason for copyright, and here the consumer of books gained great advantage if books could be copied freely. The article thus anticipated the web publication of "pirate" editions of textbooks and academic books at little or no cost to the browser who read the pirated edition online instead of buying even a used edition. The article did not see any reason why cost analysis should not replace more traditional and historical arguments for copyright—except perhaps that without copyright exclusivity, most manuscripts would never become books because most publishers would not remain in business. Instead, as he recognized, "the computer" and its progeny would allow the dissemination of knowledge without the obstacles of outside referees and the like.

This made sense when Breyer's means of publication was a student-edited law review underwritten by the tuition of Harvard Law School and a subvention from the university. The fact that the article was seventy-one pages long, a short book, was again possible because it was published by Breyer's own students. The article also failed to take into account that a pirate edition by a third party might not have an economic incentive at all, but simply be the pirate acting out of elee-mosynary motives or even revenge. Such a copyist does not "compete" for sales in any meaningful way. To argue that buyers might combine to defeat such copying, and thereby protect both original author and original publisher, again rests on the law school model, in which professors assign certain books to their classes and require their presence in the classroom. In fine, the article is not particularly convincing to a scholar who writes and tries to convince presses to publish their book, but is a very early example of Breyer trying to balance a variety of future interests as a way to read law; "advancing technology and changing economic circumstances" made reading law forward a must. Good law takes real world balancing acts into account.[4]

The Breyer of 1980 was already reading law forward, in the sense that he analyzed dispute resolution in a hypothetical future, rather than the present. All the speculative activity of his pre-judicial writings rested on the belief that a future balancing of interests among various stakeholders was a better way to solve present problems than reaching back into past solutions. This attitude was evident in his *Regulation and Its Reform* (1982), which describes how new problems faced the regulators and the regulations but their administrative ideas were rooted in the past.[5]

Regulation was actually a casebook designed to teach regulation "so that a student of the subject can understand more readily the problems facing a conscientious regulator." The format of the book gave Breyer, who based it on his teaching materials, the opportunity to bring together a variety of his own interests. In it, he combined law, economics, and government policy issues. The analytical framework complemented the subject matter—a policy paper written initially for a member of the US Senate and an ABA commission report had become a manual for future legislation. That is why "reform" was in the title. For it was evident to Breyer that in important ways government regulation of the economy, grown so large and so central to government, was a failure, at least insofar as "there is a perceived public demand for reform."[6]

More still was at stake in the success of the book. Going in a case-by-case method (again a parallel to the traditional casebook), Breyer meant to develop a probe to isolate failure in the regulatory regime and, from these failures, to help regulators and legislators "decide where and whether to design new regulatory programs and to rely instead upon alternatives to traditional systems of regulation—alternatives that tend to be less restrictive, and less intrusive, than full blown governmental regulation." In short, Breyer's plan was a program of forward reading of law—"to design new regulatory programs." The plan was applicable to all law: "determine the objectives, examine the alternative methods of obtaining these objectives, and choose the best method for doing so." The Administrative Procedure Act of 1946 provided the umbrella for all of this, and it had to be read forward for Breyer's plan to work. There was no need (in this book at least) to look for justifications of any particular program "in its authorizing statute," no need to go back to the historical or the political experience of the authorizing statute, for "often" these will not "change one's judgment" about "the *best* method" for reform. In the end, Breyer promised a useful "guide" to such reform.[7]

When Breyer did the research for *Regulation*, he was a law professor. When the book was published, he was a circuit judge on the Court of Appeals for the First Circuit. The method accompanied the appointment. Looking back at *Regulation* in a review of a later Breyer work, law professor Cass Sunstein weighed Breyer's methods. According to Sunstein, Breyer wanted to "evaluate theories of legal interpretation with close reference to their consequences." This was not exactly what Breyer had done—he was evaluating not legal theories (he had little use for them anyhow), but outcomes of legal decisions according to their anticipated consequences. For Sunstein, Breyer was a pragmatist. Sunstein equated this philosophical concept, that meaning lay in the real world application of words, with "purposivism." Sunstein's Breyer speaks in "thoroughly pragmatic terms, emphasizing the beneficial consequences of purposivism." Pragmatism and purposivism are not the same and should not be equated, however. Purposivism is judges reading texts to divine the purpose of the text's authors. While, Breyer said, legislative purpose is important to the judge, and one reason for deferring to legislatures, it did not trump looking at consequences.

"When Breyer asks judges to identify the purpose of reasonable legislators, he is inviting a degree of judicial discretion in the judge of what purposes are reasonable." That is, rather than simply quoting from the speeches of legislators on the floor of the assembly or their statements in legislative hearings, the term *reasonableness* introduced into the equation allows the judge to bend the record to their own use.[8]

Breyer sat on the US Court of Appeals for the First Circuit from 1980 to 1994, during which he was able to deploy his preferred jurisprudence in cases involving deference to legislatures, the purpose of legislation, and extralegal considerations of markets and competition. This was especially true in antitrust cases. Antitrust law was old— going back to English common law actions against restraint of trade. The first federal law to bring together ruling notions of free market competition was the Sherman Anti-Trust Act of 1890. As amplified by the Clayton Anti-Trust Act of 1914, to which Brandeis had made major contributions, the two acts generated much litigation. In one of these cases, *Barry Wright Corp v. ITT Grinnell* (1983), the petitioner argued that the defendant had cut it out of a contract by, among other things, undercutting its prices. Breyer, writing for the court, disagreed. "To understand the basis of our disagreement, one must ask why the Sherman Act ever forbids price cutting. After all, lower prices help consumers. The competitive marketplace that the antitrust laws encourage and protect is characterized by firms willing and able to cut prices in order to take customers from their rivals. And, in an economy with a significant number of concentrated industries, price cutting limits the ability of large firms to exercise their 'market power.'" Instead of relying on the text of the Sherman Act, written in 1890, Breyer looked to a future (in this case in the nuclear power plant industry) "quite different from that the anti-trust legislators occupied . . . at a minimum it likely moves 'concentrated market' prices in the 'right' direction—towards the level they would reach under competitive conditions."[9]

While price cutting was a monopolistic or oligopolistic maneuver in 1890, designed to crush competition, for Breyer it was quite the opposite. The fact that it was a mere power tool in the hands of the larger seller did not matter. Older interpretations of the rule based on its literal application must fall. "Thus, a legal precedent or rule of law that prevents a firm from unilaterally cutting its prices risk interference with one of the Sherman Act's most basic objectives: the low price levels that one would find in well-functioning competitive markets." The source for this was not precedent; it was (selective, market-oriented) textbooks on economics. Breyer conceded that "other courts" had read the effects of price cutting differently, but even if

> it drives competitors out of business, and later on it raises prices to levels higher than it could have sustained had its competitors remained in the market, without special circumstances there is little to be said in economic or competitive terms for such a price cut. Yet, how often firms engage in such "predatory" price cutting, whether they ever do so, and precisely when, is all much disputed—a dispute that is not surprising given the difficulties of measuring costs, discerning intent, and predicting future market conditions.

Thus the best result, the best way to read the Sherman Act, in this case and others like it, lay in law that assessed future market conditions.[10]

In *Kartell v. Blue Shield of Massachusetts* (1984) the court, in an opinion by Breyer, rejected doctors' claims of monopolistic behavior by a major health care provider. The district court had found that the defendant's barring of balance sheet billing was a restraint of trade under the Sherman Act. Breyer, and the court of appeals, reversed. Breyer again turned to the voice not of precedent, but of his Harvard Law School colleague Philip Areeda, an antitrust specialist who favored market rather than regulatory solutions to antitrust claims. "Ordinarily, however, even a monopolist is free to exploit whatever market power it may possess when that exploitation takes the form of charging uncompetitive prices. As Professor Areeda puts it, 'Mere monopoly pricing is not a violation of the Sherman Act.'" Is "free to exploit" a formula based not on the text of the act, but on the law professor's ideology? Areeda was not the only authority for this nontextual reading of text. "The reasons underlying this principle include a judicial reluctance to deprive the lawful monopolist (say a patent monopolist) of its lawful rewards, and a judicial recognition of the practical difficulties of determining what is a 'reasonable,' or 'competitive,' price." Here the citation was not only to Areeda; it was to "R. Bork, *The Antitrust Paradox*, 125–29 (1978)." Strange bedfellows, Breyer and Bork? The hidden persuader in the opinion was a future consideration, a consequence of upholding the district court finding. "The rising costs of medical care, the possibility that patients cannot readily evaluate (as competitive buyers) competing offers of medical service, the desirability of lowering insurance costs and premiums, the availability of state regulation to prevent abuse—all convince us that we ought not create new potentially far-reaching law on the subject. And, the parties have not seriously argued to the contrary." The rising costs and the increasing complexity of medical care meant that the customer lacked the expertise to make decisions about pricing. Good law took this into account, the old text of the 1890 antitrust act notwithstanding. Or rather, the old text had to be reread with the novelties of modern medical practice in mind.[11]

Town of Concord v. Boston Edison Co (1990) offered further evidence of Breyer's style of reasoning. Here the question was not price fixing but "price squeeze." Although precedent clearly found that the squeeze of an independent producer's prices by its supplier, who also sold directly to customers, was a violation of the Sherman Act, Breyer reasoned differently. "Our analysis of the likely effects of a price squeeze in a fully regulated industry leads us to conclude that the answer is no. Effective price regulation at both the first [original production] and second [sales] industry levels makes it unlikely that requesting such rates will ordinarily create a serious risk of significant anticompetitive harm." The act's purpose, Breyer believed, was to promote competition. "At the same time, regulatory circumstances create a significant risk that a court's efforts to stop such price requests will bring about the very harms—diminished efficiency, higher prices—that the antitrust laws seek to prevent." In short, the effect of regulation (via the antitrust laws) was inefficiency, and the proper way to read text—through its likely effects—was to avoid or diminish future inefficiency.[12]

Defenders of Breyer's record on the court of appeals found him a pragmatist. Using the term in a very loose fashion, this assessment found that Breyer "argues neither for nor against economic regulation, environmental regulation, or health and safety regulation." Instead, his goal was "improving the government's performance of regulatory missions." The way he did this was to weigh different approaches to regulation. Central also was the empiricism of his opinions, in which he offered different potential arrays of facts. Breyer himself anticipated the judgment with his own depiction of his methods. But Breyer was never merely or just a pragmatist. He was never just concerned with outcomes.[13]

To be sure, Breyer did not make this distinction as clear as he could have. In his own description of his aims during his confirmation hearing in 1994, as a judge who wanted to make law more democratic (shades of Brandeis—perhaps even more than shades, a clear borrowing), the way in which democracy played into law and economics/efficiency judging was not clear. His opening remarks were of a Brandeisan character.

> I believe that the law must work for people. The vast array of Constitution, statutes, rules, regulations, practices and procedures, that huge vast web, has a single basic purpose. That purpose is to help the many different individuals who make up America—from so many different backgrounds and circumstances, with so many different needs and hopes—its purpose is to help them live together productively, harmoniously, and in freedom. Keeping that ultimate purpose in mind helps guide a judge through the labyrinth of rules and regulations that the law too often becomes, to reach what is there at bottom, the very human goals that underlie Constitution and the statutes that Congress writes.

But in the long and distinguished dossier that followed his opening remarks, one could find a list of law review articles that revealed little democratic analysis and a lot of market-based efficiency. As he told the Senate panel,

> You know what Justice Holmes said. You are going to be disappointed, but what he said was this. He said, "You can regulate, you can regulate, you don't have to compensate, when you regulate. But, Government, you cannot go too far." What is too far? Indeed, ever since that time, the courts

have been trying to work out what is too far, and I don't think anyone has gotten a perfect measure of that. They look into factors, they say how important is the regulation, what kind of reliance has there been on this, has there been a physical, a physical occupation of property.

At the time one could ask which Breyer the Senate confirmed—the democratic enabler or the market efficiency expert? Whichever one chose, however, one would find Breyer reading law forward.[14]

One can find Breyer's reading law forward in a myriad of his opinions, particularly his dissents. Here he walked in the footsteps of Brandeis, Cardozo, and Douglas. Take, for example, his treatment of deference to the legislative branches. This was true in a series of dissents, including *U.S. v. Lopez* (1995). In this case, he saw Congress looking into the future, and worried that the Court was tying Congress's hands. In *Lopez*, it was the Gun Free Schools Act of 1990 that was at stake, and the majority thought that Congress had gone too far in its application of the Commerce Clause. Breyer disagreed. The danger (now proven all too common) of firearm deaths in schools was one that the law should anticipate, he argued, and the Court should expand the reach of the Commerce Clause to encompass it. He began with history, looking back, then looked ahead. "In my view, the statute falls well within the scope of the commerce power as this Court has understood that power over the last half century." Then a half-step forward, "the Constitution requires us to judge the connection between a regulated activity and interstate commerce, not directly, but at one remove. Courts must give Congress a degree of leeway in determining the existence of a significant factual connection between the regulated activity." Then into the likely future, "reports, hearings, and other readily available literature make clear that the problem of guns in and around schools is widespread and extremely serious." But the future held more than the promise of tragedy in the schools. It held the promise of heightened educational skills: "In recent years the link between secondary education and business has strengthened, becoming both more direct and more important." And this tied the Gun Free Schools Act to the Commerce Clause. What seemed on its face to be a mere preference for congressional action in this area became a vision of a safer and a more productive national future.[15]

Consider next his discussion of state sovereignty and congressional statutes in *College Savings Bank v. Florida* (1999):

> In today's world, legislative flexibility is necessary if we are to protect this kind of liberty. Modern commerce and the technology upon which it rests needs large markets and seeks government large enough to secure trading rules that permit industry to compete in the global market place, to prevent pollution that crosses borders, and to assure adequate protection of health and safety by discouraging a regulatory "race to the bottom." Yet local control over local decisions remains necessary. Uniform regulatory decisions about, for example, chemical waste disposal, pesticides, or food labeling, will directly affect daily life in every locality. But they may reflect differing views among localities about the relative importance of the wage levels or environmental preferences that underlie them. Local control can take account of such concerns and help to maintain a sense of community despite global forces that threaten it. Federalism matters to ordinary citizens seeking to maintain a degree of control, a sense of community, in an increasingly interrelated and complex world. Courts can remain sensitive to these needs when they interpret statutes and apply constitutional provisions.[16]

As his service on the Court came to a close, Breyer's reading law forward was even more evident. In *Area School District v. B. L.* (2021), Breyer wrote for an 8 to 1 majority. The opinion frankly read the law forward. The test of impermissible speech by a student was threefold. Schools might regulate certain kinds of student speech in certain circumstances: (1) "indecent," "lewd," or "vulgar" speech uttered during a school assembly on school grounds, (2) speech, uttered during a class trip, that promotes "illegal drug use," (3) and speech that others may reasonably perceive as "bear[ing] the imprimatur of the school," such as that appearing in a school-sponsored newspaper." In *Tinker v. Des Moines* (1969) the Court found that schools could regulate speech when it "materially disrupts classwork or involves substantial disorder or invasion of the rights of others." Nothing in Brandi Levy's vulgarity-filled Snapchat diatribe against her school's cheerleading coaches for

not letting her join the cheerleading squad touched any of the impermissible tests. The fact that the blast was carried to other students and
was accessible to the school administrators on the web raised problems
that older decisions did not face, but good law must anticipate and
resolve arising as well as established causes of action.

> Particularly given the advent of computer-based learning, we hesitate to
> determine precisely which of many school-related off-campus activities
> belong on such a list. Neither do we now know how such a list might vary,
> depending upon a student's age, the nature of the school's off-campus ac-
> tivity, or the impact upon the school itself. Thus, we do not now set forth
> a broad, highly general First Amendment rule stating just what counts as
> "off campus" speech,

as the Court of Appeals for the Third Circuit had done in its unanimous opinion for Levy. But it was clear to Breyer that the school did
not supplant the parents' off-campus responsibilities, including those
regarding children's speech, and in fact, that schools should be teaching the value of freedom of speech, even when it was unpopular, or
criticism of the school itself. This sort of case was surely going to arise
in the future, for social media had become the choice of communica-
tion for the young. When looking ahead, the First Amendment must
recognize that fact.[17]

Breyer's forward-looking jurisprudence obviously applied to the impact of computer uses. One finds it center stage in Breyer's opinion in
Google LLC v. Oracle America (2021). The two tech giants were battling
over 11,500 lines of source code that Google had taken from Oracle's
Java program to use on its Android communications system. Justice
Breyer wrote for a 6 to 2 majority. While Breyer found that the code
was copyrightable, he believed that the borrowing was a fair use exception under the copyright laws. At the time of the borrowing, "many
software developers understood and wrote programs using the Java
programming language, a language invented by Sun Microsystems."
For three years, "Google tailored the Android platform to smartphone
technology, which differs from desktop and laptop computers in important ways." Lower federal courts struggled to determine whether
Google could assert a fair use defense. Breyer looked to the purpose of

copyright law—to promote the progress of science and useful arts. He noted that the courts and Congress had limited the power of copyright, again in the interest of promoting new ideas. Then he looked to consequences. When copyright would "stifle" the very purpose for which it was created, courts should allow a limited fair use by a party that did not have a license or permission to copy. Because of the way that programmers used existing code, "Generically speaking, computer programs differ from books, films, and many other 'literary works' in that such programs almost always serve functional purposes. . . . In a word, [the Court] can carry out its basic purpose of providing a context-based check that can help to keep a copyright monopoly within its lawful bounds." Purpose and consequences were tests that lay outside the text of the copyright law. "The fact that computer programs are primarily functional makes it difficult to apply traditional copyright concepts in that technological world." Was Google creating something new? Did it alter and progress the older source language? Then it passed muster. Thus, did Breyer not only push copyright law into the future, he returned from the future to reenvision copyright law.[18]

Even when Breyer seemed to abandon forward-looking jurisprudence, and return to older, formalist methods, he read the law forward. One thinks of the powerful strict Calvinist sermons of Jonathan Edwards and George Whitefield in the 1730 and 1740s. Both men warned backsliding churchgoers that salvation lay entirely in the hands of a Supreme Being, and that Being was angry at Christians' stubborn sinfulness. But after hours of reducing the congregants to abject fear, both ministers left the door to salvation ajar. Their Creator loved them, and wanted them to repent. So in cases where he seemed to revert to something like originalism, Breyer ended by reading the law forward. Consider *Bush v. Gore* (2000). In *Bush*, the majority voted to take the Florida electoral vote from the legislature's mandated recount and the state's supreme court litigation, and give the electoral votes to Republican candidate George W. Bush. The division on the Court seemed to follow partisan political lines, as all of the majority had been appointed by Republican presidents. Two of the dissenters (David Souter and John Paul Stevens) were appointed by Republican presidents as well, and all four published separate dissents and joined in one another's. Breyer's dissent was particularly vigorous, given his expressed commitment to consensus judging. The issue was in part one of democracy—which side favored a democratic solution to the conundrum?[19]

Breyer's dissent included references to text, history, and tradition. "The Court was wrong to take this case. It was wrong to grant a stay. It should now vacate that stay and permit the Florida Supreme Court to decide whether the recount should resume." Why? Because the majority of the Court had announced to the country that the tribunal was a political one, not a legal one. "The political implications of this case for the country are momentous. But the federal legal questions presented, with one exception, are insubstantial." There really was no case or controversy for the Court to decide. All the issues brought before the Court challenging the legislative recount were matters that the legislature was supposed to handle, as the state's highest court had decided. Why not defer to the state in a matter which the Constitution had left to the state, or leave it to Congress under the Constitutional provisions therein? In other words, text, the text of state law and constitutional law, dictated the means for resolving the dispute. The majority had simply misread both federal and state law to reach an impermissible conclusion. There certainly was no reason to order the recount to stop. There was plenty of time under the law—text again—for the state to finish its recount.[20]

History dictated that the Court abstain.

> The Twelfth Amendment commits to Congress the authority and responsibility to count electoral votes. A federal statute, the Electoral Count Act, enacted after the close 1876 Hayes-Tilden Presidential election, specifies that, after States have tried to resolve disputes (through "judicial" or other means), Congress is the body primarily authorized to resolve remaining disputes.... The legislative history of the Act makes clear its intent to commit the power to resolve such disputes to Congress, rather than the courts.

Breyer followed with excerpts from the congressional debates, using the historical record to prove the constitutional point.[21]

Breyer had more to say about the thinking of Congress. "Congress was fully aware of the danger that would arise should it ask judges, unarmed with appropriate legal standards, to resolve a hotly contested Presidential election contest." A recitation of the history of the disputed 1876 presidential election followed, for it was the background of the 1877 electoral act that controlled the subject. Three states sent two slates of electors to Congress. Tilden, the Democratic candidate, was one electoral vote short of the needed 185 to win, while Hayes, his Republican opponent, could only win with all of the three states. Congress appointed a special commission to decide which set of electoral votes to count. It had five senators, five representatives, and five Supreme Court justices. Initially the Commission was to be evenly divided between Republicans and Democrats, with Justice David Davis, an independent, to possess the decisive vote. However, when at the last minute the Illinois Legislature elected Justice Davis to the US Senate, the final position on the Commission was filled by Supreme Court Justice Joseph Bradley. Here was the crucial fact: "The Commission divided along partisan lines, and the responsibility to cast the deciding vote fell to Justice Bradley. He decided to accept the votes of the Republican electors, and thereby awarded the Presidency to Hayes." What did that history prove? At the time, Bradley was accused of being partisan. "For present purposes, the relevance of this history lies in the fact that the participation in the work of the electoral commission by five Justices, including Justice Bradley, did not lend that process legitimacy." The analogy to the Supreme Court intervening in *Bush v. Gore* was obvious. "It simply embroiled Members of the Court in partisan conflict, thereby undermining respect for the judicial process. And the Congress that later enacted the Electoral Count Act knew it."[22]

Next came tradition. "Of course, the selection of the President is of fundamental national importance. But that importance is political, not legal." Tradition urged the Court to restrain itself. "The Constitution and federal statutes themselves make clear that restraint is appropriate. They set forth a roadmap of how to resolve disputes about electors, even after an election as close as this one. That roadmap foresees resolution of electoral disputes by *state* courts." Nowhere did the Constitution provide for "involvement by the United States Supreme Court."[23]

Text, history, and tradition all aligned. Where then was Breyer's forward-looking mandate? Was it only deployed when convenient? No—a forward reading of the law was still there, hidden in the interstices of the dissent. For he feared that the majority had foreclosed the democratic process, the Court inserting itself between the people's participation in the election and the state's officials. "The Court is not acting to vindicate a fundamental constitutional principle, such as the need to protect a basic human liberty. No other strong reason to act is present. . . . And, above all, in this highly politicized matter, the appearance of a split decision runs the risk of undermining the public's confidence in the Court itself. That confidence is a public treasure." Breyer more than hinted that the decision threatened American democracy in profound ways. Breyer had returned to a forward reading of the law from his tour through the history, tradition, and precedent, convinced even more strongly that looking back was not enough. It was a danger to the future of American electoral democracy that the majority's narrow reading of the case evoked.[24]

One can read the majority decision in *Bush v. Gore* as naked pragmatism. The country needed to move on from the election and the Court wanted to avoid a prolonged political struggle over the Florida balloting. Breyer's dissent rejected that kind of pragmatism. None of the opinions in *Bush v. Gore* mentioned the foremost advocate of that judicial pragmatism, Judge Richard Posner, but both he and Breyer surely recognized the connection. One of the founders of the law and economics school of jurisprudence during his teaching days at the University of Chicago School of Law, and in 2001 serving on the Court of Appeals for the Seventh Circuit, Posner was already a luminary among the law professor/federal judge corps. Considered by many a conservative, that appellation hardly captured the sophisticated and often highly complex nature of his judicial thinking.

Actually, Posner had fired the first shot in the duel with Breyer, writing in a summer 2000 law review article, "The legal profession's use of history is a disguise that allows the profession to innovate without breaching judicial etiquette, which deplores both novelty and a frank acknowledgement of judicial discretion and likes to pretend that decisions by nonelected judges can be legitimated by being shown to have democratic roots in some past legislative or constitutional enactment."

Whether Posner was already targeting Breyer, and Breyer knew it, Posner, in *Breaking the Deadlock: The 2000 Election, the Constitution, and the Courts* (2001), found that Breyer's dissent "missed the potential significance of overvotes" and his reading of the legislative record behind the Electoral Count Act of 1877 was simply wrong. Posner found other problems in Breyer's analysis of the case as well. But the most stinging rebuke, because it suggested that Breyer did not understand the complexity of the American legal system, came at the end of the book. "Many people refuse to think more deeply about the election and its aftermath. That refusal is dogmatic and simpleminded. Among the important things that it overlooks is that American democracy is an institutionally complex and historically determined set of laws and practices." This was a not very hard formula to decode for the importance of text, tradition, and history. But Posner had missed, either intentionally or by mistake, Breyer's own approach.[25]

Breyer revealed the subtlety of his forward reading of law in *Bush v. Gore*, along with an answer to Posner, in *Active Liberty* (2005). *Active Liberty* eschewed the vulgar defense of ends justifying means and the brute force of judicial activism in constitutional interpretation. Breyer refused to conclude that the law is whatever the courts say it is. Instead, his argument rested on a very sophisticated reading of a constitution fit for a truly democratic people. In fact, there are many antidemocratic instincts in our American people and its governors, so Breyer had to adjust his aim to fit realities. The key instead is "the freedom to participate in the government itself," which Breyer found in ancient polities. He assumed that the framers wanted this as well, rather than what he called "modern liberty," which restrains what government can do.[26]

For Breyer, the Court must "take greater account of the Constitution's democratic nature when they interpret constitutional and statutory texts." If the Constitution never mentions democracy as a program for judicial reading of texts (or in any other context), the notion of a democratic constitution was still energizing. "Through examples, my thesis illustrates how emphasizing the democratic objective can bring us closer to achieve the proper balance between" active and restrained constitutional interpretation, a method "by which judges, when they interpret a legal text, will yield better law—law that helps a community of individuals democratically find practical solutions to important contemporary social problems."[27]

For all the deference Breyer showed to constitutional history, Breyer believed that a better way to read law was to look to the future rather than backward. Perhaps still smarting from the failed dissent in *Bush v. Gore*, and Posner's comments on it, Breyer concluded that the good judge will "take account" of the text's "history, including history that shows what the language likely meant to those who wrote it." The bow to original intent was followed by "the likely consequences of the interpretive alternatives." Language, history, tradition, precedent, purpose, and consequences of a reading of text did not have equal weight in his estimation, however. For Breyer believed that purpose and consequence, the judge's own "emphasis" (not the judge's own bias), had to conform to the "relation between the Constitution's democratic objective and its other general objectives." Breyer was frank about how his "view can differ from the views of various others" by taking into account "broader provision[s]" and "basic objectives." His broad hint was that language, tradition, and history—the mantra of the originalists—"undervalue[] consequences," while his approach was "to focus increased attention upon the Constitution's democratic objective." Consequences, objectives, all these were the watchwords of reading the law forward. After all, had not the Court's "judicial 'philosophy'" itself changed over time?[28]

Breyer conceded that the judge still "must display that doubt, caution and prudence" that comes with not knowing everything. Active liberty required "judicial modesty." Nevertheless, the democratic objective in the Constitution requires the judge to think about expanding the realm of liberty, the "active liberty which resonates throughout the Constitution." This is a guide to reading the law. The judge should apply "a text in light of its purpose" and should "look to consequences." This is not the judge doing "whatever he thinks best," however, but finding the best purpose in the law. Good law, that is good reading of law, is an instrument to that end. In the end, however, Breyer still walked a tightrope back and forth, something akin to Brandeis's and Cardozo's refusal to generalize.[29]

The argument for constitutionally permissible "consequences" (or in the terminology of this essay, reading law forward) is not the past, but the future. The framers did not have a "basically democratic outlook" but that does not matter, unless one is an originalist, which Breyer definitely is not. But Breyer is not content with questionable history, and he continued, "as history has made clear, the original Constitution was insufficient." Here history is on his side. That is, it leads to active liberty. For that Constitution "did not include a majority of the nation." Whether the original "sowed the democratic seed" or not, it was open ended, allowing amendment, interpretation, and statutory interventions. In the first session of Congress, following the open-ended invitation of Article III, the Judiciary Act of 1789 created a structure of district and circuit federal courts, and imbued these with the authority to interpret text. The Bill of Rights, while not mentioning democracy, opened the way to freedoms now seen as central to a democratic republic. Breyer did not choose these examples, closing his account with the production of the document itself, but he is surely right to conclude that the history of the Constitution has been "a quest for workable government, workable democratic government."[30]

How did active liberty work in practice? Breyer offered six working examples. An intellectual heir to Brandeis and Douglas, Breyer included the right to privacy among the six. In this area of the law, technological advances, advances likely to grow in the future, posed special problems for judges. For Breyer, privacy meant individual control over what others might know about the individual. Search and seizure in the age of the web meant that unwanted gaze was almost impossible to avert. Both intimate and financial information was too easily exposed to third parties. Thus "privacy related legal challenges lie at the intersection of a legal circumstance [a particular case] and a technological circumstance [the method by which the information was gained or revealed to others]." Brandeis had seen it in wiretapping and Douglas in radio transmissions of paid informants. Now it was embedded in the very fabric of everyday life. Breyer admitted he had no solution, but he did have a plan: an "ongoing" campaign by individual litigants, legislators, and judges to "limit" intrusion "in ways now unforeseeable." Rather than adopting a one-size-fits-all constitutional rule, judges must continually revisit the issues with an eye on the future rather than a fixed point in the past. Do not confuse this with practicality, he warned. The method might look piecemeal, but it was process that mattered more than particular outcomes.[31]

Next came the First Amendment. Speech in modern America took many forms, oral, written, signed, coded, and electronic. All sorts of public and private interests were implicated in free speech questions. "To treat all these instances alike" would raise all kinds of dilemmas. Make the scrutiny too strong and the Court supplants the legislature. Make it too weak and one undermines the protections "necessary to maintain the health of our democracy." Again, as Brandeis and Douglas had advocated, the answer lay in looking forward. When a restriction applies to speech that affects public opinion, or policy, or elected officials, it must be strictly scrutinized. When the law restricts access to public forums, for example, during election cycles, or when it gives to a few a dominance over the opinions of the many, a different standard might apply. How to know when to allow and when to curb? There was no clear answer in language, history, or tradition, the trinity of originalism. "Remove our blinders," however, and an answer emerges: read the First Amendment as "seeking primarily to encourage the exchange of information and ideas necessary for citizens themselves" to shape public opinion.[32]

In areas of law that were not constitutional, Breyer's forward reading of law was just as clear. His own specialty (what he had taught at Harvard Law School, for example) was administrative law. With the twentieth-century explosion of administrative agencies in both federal and state government, these institutions have become a fourth branch of government. Congress created independent agencies and under the Administrative Agency Act of 1946 they had to hold public hearings. Their findings were appealable to the federal courts. The agencies still have considerable discretion in fact finding and public exposure, however. For Breyer, the more important question is "how can we reconcile democratic control of government with the technical nature of modern life?" Breyer did not have to say that experts and expertise have become more and more important as more and more often Americans express their distrust of expertise. The answer for the judge was a balanced delegation, but how much or how little remained "a mystery."[33]

Another answer that Breyer, modestly, did not assay in the book was that the judges, often with the aid of "masters" appointed by the court, can make themselves into experts. This is not usually done at the appellate level, but it is increasingly common at the trial or hearing level in tort, copyright, and civil rights cases. Of course, there are, however, noteworthy exceptions to this rule, as when the Court in the early stages of the *Brown v. Board of Education* hearings took time out to send counsel (and one of the justice's clerks) to examine the historical records. In other civil rights cases, for example, the Boston busing cases, the work of court-appointed experts was decisive in formulating a remedy for de facto segregated schools. [34]

Breyer concluded *Active Liberty* with a postscript (preceded by a recapitulation and followed by an epilogue). Titled "A Serious Objection," it ran longer than some of his chapters. Here he used the originalist position as a backdrop to restate his own views on purpose and consequences. The latter, rather than some version of originalism, "will help a judge better to understand and to apply specific provisions." Apply to what? Consequences were the "yardstick" by which the people's will was enabled. In other words, democracy itself required the judge to look ahead to "workable outcomes."[35]

But other scholars and judges insisted that language (aka textualism), history, and tradition were more important gauges of constitutionality than "real-world consequences." These jurists fear that the consequential will too easily become (or was already) the judge's personal or ideological notion of the good. Breyer found this line of reasoning, with all its cautions, misleading. For no version of text, history, or tradition provided a sure method of interpretation. Literalism of this kind ignored the existence of past controversies over the meaning of key texts. History taught that there was always subjectivity.[36]

Better by far was to tie a reading of consequences to the particular purpose of the text. Look ahead to bad consequences as well as good ones; avoid unnecessary divisiveness and conflict resulting from too narrow or too open-ended a decision; look closely at the context of each case; look to underlying contemporary values; remember that decisions are not just words, they are remedies. And remember that "no one but an expert historian" may know, or begin to know, the best answer to historical questions. Aim for "clear, workable rules." Note that the formula includes workable, not just clear. Bright-line hard-and-fast rules may ignore consequences. Above all, the judge was to explain their view in terms that the people can understand.[37]

Breyer is a greatly respected jurist among members of the legal academy. Partly for this reason, and partly because it appeared to directly challenge the jurisprudence of textualism and originalism, his *Active Liberty* was reviewed the year after publication in the *Yale Law Journal* by Richard A. Posner, among others. Judge Posner's review began with a concession. Whether it applies to him as well as Breyer is unclear, but "A Supreme Court Justice writing a book about constitution law is like a dog walking on his hind legs: the wonder is not that it is done well but that it is done at all." The adage has nothing to do with the book or with the review, but it must have seemed irresistible to Posner, whose criticism of the quality of the justices and their opinions had grown in recent years. He did not find Breyer's work "convincing." The references to active liberty in past writings were incomplete, or worse, misleading, as the example of ancient Athens proved. American liberty was neither negative nor active; it was republican. Posner, exercising the discretion of an author in a law review, did without footnotes to prove these points, and historians (T. H. Breen, Gary Nash, Alfred Young, and others) could have been found on the other side of the question, but the book and the review are not really part of the historical canon.[38]

Posner accused Breyer of a "loose instrumentalist approach" to the Constitution, but did not find that accusation damning. Posner meant instrumentalist as a synonym for pragmatic. Just lose the history, he suggested. There followed a condensed version of Posner's own book-manqué (i.e., how he would have revised Breyer). Posner did not find Breyer's speculation plausible in matters of free speech and campaign finances, his "weighing imponderables" were an oxymoron, and key terms "are so indefinite that they cannot guide decision." Broader "abstractions" like democracy and active liberty "are so vague and encompassing that they can be deployed on either side of most constitutional questions." The "coercive, one-sided dialogue" that Breyer proposed for dialogue with Congress would tie Congress "in knots." It was an olive branch to the democratically elected branch in any case. In the end, the "debate between conservatives like Scalia and liberals like Breyer is a semantic fog." The result is that justices "are forced back on personal elements" and "ideology." Were the book an essay, Posner would grade it a B-.[39]

But Breyer's work had its fans. Law Professor Kathleen Sullivan admired Breyer's enthusiasm and down-to-earth passion for public service. She approved of his commitment to working with legislative bodies, and saw these themes repeated, convincingly, in his *Active Liberty*. She noted his continuation of what she saw as Brandeis's tradition of eclecticism and flexibility, balancing legitimate interests "in the face of deep and seemingly intractable disagreement." She did not find Breyer lost in the "fog" at all. Instead, she lauded his opinions "in plain sentences" without footnotes.[40]

Paul Gewirtz was another admirer. He began where Breyer did, with a distinction between negative liberty—protecting the citizen from government interference—and active liberty, enabling people to share in the governmental process. This was a distinction that Breyer himself made early in the book, but then dropped. For Gewirtz, and for other "liberal" judges and jurisprudents, negative liberty was a guiding light. It was certainly Douglas's mantra. Gewirtz offered that the book did not advance a theory, for Breyer was not a theoretician, but a series of riffs on a theme (Breyer had himself played with the music analogy) that should be heard alongside Breyer's own opinions on the Court of Appeals and the Supreme Court (again, Breyer himself imported bits and pieces from his opinions). Gewirtz concluded that Breyer's process was pragmatic, not a very striking or original conclusion, as it happened. Breyer liked to build consensus, and thrived on collegiality.[41]

The penumbras of *Active Liberty* continued to reach out into legal academia in the next decade. Commenting on a 2011 conference featuring Breyer and Justice Antonin Scalia at his home law school of Texas Tech, professor Arnold Loewy approved of Breyer's inclusion of consequences in his tests of constitutionality. He found that a court of nine Breyers would thus be preferable to a court of nine Antonin Scalias because Scalia would not include consequences. Loewy recognized the vital importance of consequentialism but did not take the next step into a broader reading of law forward.[42]

In the meantime, Breyer did not respond directly or immediately to the Posner review, but he returned to the notion of workability in a series of talks and then a new book. Breyer was especially attuned to the reputation of the modern Court in the media and public opinion. His fear was that an "alarming trend" was gaining ground among the public. More and more, they thought that "judges simply decided cases according to their own preferences." In a system in which the legitimacy of the courts rests, at least in part, on public acceptance of judicial fairness, this trend was especially worrisome to the bench. Breyer thought that the solution lay in judges making an effort to explain how they reached their decisions. *Active Liberty* was an effort in this direction, and it clearly had mixed results, even among the cognoscenti. As a result, he spent a good bit of the essay on Hamilton's views of the judiciary, in support of judicial independence. Posner was not convinced.[43]

Breyer continued the indirect conversation with Posner in another book. *Making Our Democracy Work: A Judge's View* (2010) was something of an answer to Posner. The only mention of Posner came in the acknowledgments, but Posner's shadow fell over the entire work. Posner had questioned the clarity and utility of Breyer's jurisprudence in the review of *Active Liberty*. Breyer did not let the challenge go without a reply. In the new book, he opened by saying that the aim of the justices was to "ensure a *workable* constitutional democracy [italics in original]." The addition of the modifier was a response to Posner's review of *Active Liberty*, among other aims. Breyer chose the word *pragmatism*, but his pragmatism was not mere practicality. "I do not argue that all judges should decide all legal cases pragmatically. But I also suggest that by understanding that its actions have real-world consequence and taking those consequences into account, the Court can help make the law work more efficiently." The key terms were *consequences* and *efficiently*, both linked to future outcomes.[44]

Breyer attacked the issue from an angle that Posner had not defended: the need to have popular acceptance of the Court's output, even when many people did not agree with the decisions. So, when Breyer wanted to prove that his own jurisprudence captured the essence of democratic judging, the example he chose was *Bush v. Gore*, a case on which he and Posner disagreed in print. For a sitting appellate judge to criticize the opinion of a sitting justice of the Supreme Court is not unheard of, but surely Breyer had taken note of it. He did not mention Posner, but the silence was pointed.[45]

Breyer's out-of-court writings increasingly focused on the politicization of the Court, the subject of his dissent in *Bush v. Gore*. It was the political question that underlay both *Bush v. Gore* and the abortion rights cases, with consequences for the Court as well as for the democratic republic itself. It was these consequences that spurred Breyer to reach back into history, tradition, and text, as well as to look with concern to a future in which courts could no longer claim to be above politics.

True, the lurking danger of reading law forward is that it may incorporate partisanship. What if federal judges and judging is nothing more than a branch of politics? That would make any attempt to save the legitimacy of reading law forward a waste of effort. (It would also undermine the campaign of the originalists.) If the judiciary were just another political branch of government, no one would be surprised when judges import their politics into their jurisprudence. After all, was not that why they were appointed by the chief partisan in our system—the president? Before any of these unpalatable opinions lead to open resistance to the court, Breyer offered a solution: Trust us. Our deliberations (in conference) may be secret; our votes (in conference) may be concealed; we do not face the wrath of anyone (except for impeachment); and we are an elite unrepresentative of the populace. We are not even the most qualified of that elite by intellect at least and sometimes by physical capacity. But we are not just pols. Judge John Roberts told Congress at his confirmation hearing for the center seat on the High Court.

> I have no platform. Judges are not politicians who can promise to do certain things in exchange for votes. I have no agenda, but I do have a commitment. If I am confirmed, I will confront every case with an open mind. I will fully and fairly analyze the legal arguments that are presented. I will be open to the considered views of my colleagues on the bench, and I will

decide every case based on the record, according to the rule of law, without fear or favor, to the best of my ability, and I will remember that it's my job to call balls and strikes, and not to pitch or bat.

We are not partisan hacks, Justice Amy Coney Barrett told a Kentucky audience. We are not "junior league politicians," Justice Breyer continued to insist.[46]

In the last year and half of Breyer's tenure, the political question reared its head and roared. The appointments of Justices Brett Kavanaugh and Amy Coney Barrett brought the issue of abortion rights center stage. Breyer's jurisprudence was challenged by it. In *Women's Whole Health v. Hellerstedt* (2016) the Court, in an opinion by Breyer, had overruled the Fifth Circuit Court of Appeals (which had upheld a Texas law imposing restrictions on doctors performing abortions). Breyer had based his opinion on both adherence to the *Casey* standard and an appreciation of the dangers to pregnant women that the Texas law posed.[47]

Between 2016 and 2022 the composition of the Court had changed. Justice Anthony Kennedy, who had voted with the majority to strike down the law, retired, and his replacement, Judge Brett Kavanaugh, was on record as opposing abortion rights (although he assured members of Congress that *Roe v. Wade* was safe). The appointment of Kavanaugh was widely seen as a political one, President Donald Trump favoring the pro-life politics of his base. The Louisiana law in *June Medical Services v. Russo* (2021) was not only modeled on the Texas law, it was almost identical, and its sponsors in the state legislature stated that they hoped the change in the composition of the Supreme Court bench would reverse *Hellerstedt*. Everyone on the Court knew what everyone else knew—the case had major political consequences, much like *Bush v. Gore*. When Justice Ruth Bader Ginsburg died, her replacement, Amy Coney Barrett, was again seen as a political choice. She voted with the majority to overturn *Roe v. Wade* in the *Dobbs v. Jackson* (2022) case discussed below.

Breyer is a subtle, thoughtful jurist. Anyone following closely his participation in oral argument will see this. He is a teacher on the bench, and the lawyers presenting their briefs become his students. But he did not try to lecture them so much as ask them for greater precision in the presentation of their cases—in effect, to make them better lawyers. Thus the oral argument in *Russo* became something of a Socratic dialogue, similar to that in first-year law school courses. When counsel was obtuse or obdurate, however, Breyer was not so gentle. The best example and the most recent was his examination of lawyers for the state of Louisiana in *Russo*. The district court had enjoined enforcement of the law; the Court of Appeals for the Fifth Circuit quashed the temporary injunction and would have allowed the law to go into effect. When Louisiana's Elizabeth Murrill presented the case for the state law, requiring doctors to have admitting privileges at a hospital within twenty-five miles of where they performed abortions, Breyer grew impatient with her answers, like Socrates with any of his dialogue respondents. Plainly, what concerned him was less the law itself than the future of all abortion provisions if the Court upheld the state law. It was the future harm rather than findings of the present harm that mattered. (The "Does" in question were the doctors whose credentials, or lack thereof, were at stake.)[48]

Look more deeply into the dialogue and one sees what Breyer wanted and Murrill just did not get. He wanted her to see the future, the consequences. If she did, and honestly responded, it would be to say, yes—here is the future—no pregnant woman would be able to get a safe and legal abortion in my state. (And now that may be true.) He made this plain in his opinion for the Court in the case. Although it appeared that he was simply arguing that the Court should follow its own precedents, in particular the recently decided *Whole Women's Health v. Hellerstedt*, the meat of his opinion looked forward, not back. The state had argued, and the Court of Appeals for the Fifth Circuit had agreed, that there were some "minimal" benefits to the women seeking abortions, and that there was no substantially increased burden (the *Casey* standard of undue burden for women seeking an abortion) under the statute. Breyer's recitation rejected this interpretation of the facts. If he was right, one might conclude (as both pro-life and pro-choice organizations had revealed) that the origin and foundation of the Louisiana law were political. The state legislature and its governor wanted to rid the state of abortion providers. That would void a woman's ability to terminate a pregnancy in practice, while not challenging the right to an abortion openly. Breyer knew this, and hinted at his knowledge of it. "The evidence also shows that opposition to abortion played a significant role in some hospitals' decisions to deny admitting privileges. . . . Still other hospitals have requirements that abortion providers cannot satisfy because of the hostility they face in Louisiana." The response of the state was "that the record does not show that Act 620 will burden every woman in Louisiana who seeks an abortion." To Breyer, this was disingenuous, for the *Casey* standard was "a large fraction" of the women affected, not "every." In coming to the edge of this conclusion, but leaving it unspoken, Breyer upheld the notion that Court did not act as a political institution. It was above politics—or should be. But that was the very heresy that so worried Judge Robert Bork. Did reading the law forward lead to more rather than less politics on the Court?[49]

In 2021, Justice Breyer published a book designed to replenish public trust in the appellate judiciary. *The Authority of the Court and the Peril of Politics* (2021) addressed the question of why people should obey the courts. All authority in a democratic republic ultimately rests on the consent of the governed. Rarely is that consent direct, however, or current. Democracy can be messy. There are so many layers of government in our system that consent is often buried in party and interest group politics. Elections are not temporally related to events, and more and more often are occasions of obfuscation of issues rather than plain choices. The courts, particularly the federal courts, are the furthest from the people in terms of consent. What if the courts produce decisions that are unpopular? There is always the option of popular nullification of a decision, but that has its risks. Congress or the executive branch may step in, but the Court has the last word (at least according to the Court). Massive resistance is another possibility, and then there is always revolution.

Breyer gave his reasons to trust the Court. Although his Scalia memorial talk (the basis of the book) supposedly referred to all life tenured courts, the final suggestions actually grew from his experience on the Supreme Court. They were the adherence of the justices to rule of law, including precedent and the other categories of active liberty; "just do the job" rather than engage in politics itself; deliberation, a process beginning with the reading of briefs, hearing and participating in oral argument, discussion at the judicial conference on each case, and sharing drafts of opinions; compromise on the court, including the way that discussion among the justices and even dissents influenced the decision of the court; and finally incorporation of public response to issues. Given that Breyer, like Brandeis and Douglas, was more famous for his dissents and concurrences than for simply going along with the majority, and that all three wrote "outside" the confines of the court (or in Brandeis's case encouraged others to engage in political activities, and Douglas courted political office), there was something a little too "optimistic" in his concluding remarks. As Albion Tourgée wrote after one failed reconstruction of law, "The life of the Fool proper is full of the poetry of faith. He may run after a will-o'-the-wisp, while the Wise deride, but to him it is a veritable star of hope. He differs from his fellow-mortals chiefly in this, that he sees or believes what they do not, and consequently undertakes what they never attempt."[50]

Was Breyer ahead of everyone? Reading law forward, accused of being a betrayal of the judge's trust, actually undergirds it, for in it judges tell us what they are thinking. Breyer calls this "clarity" and it is that honesty that makes his preferred jurisprudence; no hiding ideology under a faux reading of text. If that is the best the judge can do, perhaps that is enough to save democratic judges and judging from the accusation of partisanship. Or not.[51]

As Breyer departed the Court, replaced by newly appointed Justice Ketanji Brown Jackson, it appears that the most recent abortion rights question has given an answer to the question of political judging that Breyer feared. More Americans than ever before believe that the Court is a political organ whose members are pols in robes. And the Court majority's opinions in *Dobbs v. Jackson Women's Health Organization* (2022) rests solidly on the originalist foundation that Breyer warned against.[52]

Breyer's jurisprudence was in step with Brandeis's, Cardozo's, and Douglas's. Although Breyer's flexibility and balancing tests might seem to set him apart, he was always looking into the future, where law must go and consequences mattered, always ready to reassess the meaning of current law. As he wrote in *Active Liberty*, his aim was "better law—law that helps a community of individuals democratically find practical solutions to important contemporary social problems." In 2022, Breyer stepped down from the bench, leaving behind over 550 opinions. He had served on federal appellate courts for over forty years. His contribution to legal thinking and the substantive body of law was varied and original. He surely belongs in the pantheon of great ones reading law forward.[53.]

Conclusion

The Making of a Democratic Jurisprudence

In the previous pages I have explored a jurisprudence of reading law forward, showing how, in the hands of a group of our foremost judges, that method improved our law. That is, a jurisprudence of reading law forward enabled courts to respond to the challenges of changing conditions. It kept law fresh. It enabled the growth of a democratic society. At the same time, various formulations of originalism have never lost their popularity. The two approaches came into sharp relief in the dueling opinions of Justices Breyer and Alito in *Hellerstedt*, *Russo*, and most recently *Dobbs*. It was justice Oliver Wendell Holmes Jr. who wisely wrote that hard cases make bad law. Certainly one can argue that abortion rights cases are among the hardest for today's judges to adjudicate. In the streets pro-life and pro-choice carry on their own contest, but in *Dobbs* it was once again Alito and Breyer. Their opinions demonstrate in stark relief the two varieties of jurisprudence traced in this book.[1]

Justice Samuel Alito's opinion for the Court in *Dobbs v. Jackson Women's Health Organization* (2022) showed that Justice Alito is a firm believer in original intent. He has long insisted that there is nothing in the Constitution that supported *Roe v. Wade*. At the same time, the common law system rests heavily on precedent, and *Roe* was surrounded by an armada of precedents, in particular *Casey v. Planned Parenthood of Pennsylvania* (1992). How could Justice Alito get around the precedents while still adhering to originalism? The answer was plain: use history to erase a portion of the past rather than explore it. Alito argued that constitutional rights must echo in the history and traditions of the country. He found nothing in the years up to the 1960s that generated a right to end a pregnancy. In fact, in most states it was a crime. He ignored the fact that the crime was not the violation of fetal life, but the danger to the prospective mother. (The state statutes did not make pregnant women a defendant.) More important, he ignored the fact that the rule of history is not stasis but change, and that change in the context of *Roe* was the rise of the new feminism, women's rights to their reproductive careers, and a rising tide of leading medical and legal authorities agreeing that the old laws were unjust.[2]

Alito wrote,

We hold that Roe and Casey must be overruled. The Constitution makes no reference to abortion, and no such right is implicitly protected by any constitutional provision, including the one on which the defenders of Roe and Casey now chiefly rely—the Due Process Clause of the Fourteenth Amendment. . . . Until the latter part of the 20th century, such a right was entirely unknown in American law. . . . Roe was egregiously wrong from the start. Its reasoning was exceptionally weak, and the decision has had damaging consequences. And far from bringing about a national settlement of the abortion issue, *Roe* and *Casey* have enflamed debate and deepened division.

The result was that "26 States have expressly asked this Court to overrule Roe and Casey and allow the States to regulate or prohibit previability abortions." They too had looked back with longing at a time when women did not have the right (in law at least) to end a pregnancy at any stage. The conclusion—the past speaking in firm tones to the present—was clear. "It is time to heed the Constitution and return the issue of abortion to the people's elected representatives." Justice Alito did not need to put the two pieces together; it was clear that, in at least the twenty-six states, the rights of pregnant women would either vanish or be severely restricted.[3]

One may criticize Justice Alito's version of history. Setting aside questions of factual accuracy, he had arbitrarily canceled a vital recent portion of the long history of the abortion rights debate by erasing the legal precedents to which that debate had led. No precedents, no history. Moreover he had dismissed without discussion the years of struggle for abortion rights that had led to *Roe*. By eliding that portion of the case's history, he had silenced the voices of the new feminists, the doctors, and the law professors who had argued for reform of the abortion laws in the 1960s. But that is exactly what constitutional litigation should be about—the rise over time of new ideas about law. Using a heckler's veto argument, he reversed fifty years of feminism and equal rights advocacy. He suggested that sending the issue of abortion rights back to the states would not end the controversy, of course, as he surely knows it wouldn't, and as the furor surrounding *Dobbs* has demonstrated. But these kinds of criticisms could be applied to Justice Breyer's use of history in *Active Liberty*. It is beyond controversy that judicial use of history rarely rises to the level that professional historians demand of one another.[4]

By contrast, Justice Breyer's dissent in *Dobbs* looked both back to precedent and forward to envision a world in which pregnant women faced awful choices and dire physical and mental dangers. Unlike the majority opinion, the dissent recovered the years leading up to *Roe*. "To hear the majority tell the tale, *Roe* and *Casey* are aberrations: They came from nowhere, went nowhere—and so are easy to excise from this Nation's constitutional law. That is not true. . . . they are rooted in—and themselves led to—other rights giving individuals control over their bodies and their most personal and intimate associations." Writing for the three dissenters, Breyer warned,

> Today, the Court. . . . says that from the very moment of fertilization, a woman has no rights to speak of. A State can force her to bring a pregnancy to term, even at the steepest personal and familial costs. An abortion restriction, the majority holds, is permissible whenever rational, the lowest level of scrutiny known to the law. And because, as the Court has often stated, protecting fetal life is rational, States will feel free to enact all manner of restrictions.

By discarding the long conversation, in and out doors, over women's rights, the Court not only discarded well-established precedent; it paid no heed to a future of distress and harm for pregnant women. It was the very opposite of reading law forward to seek the best outcome for the pregnant woman and her potential child.

> Some States have enacted laws extending to all forms of abortion procedure, including taking medication in one's own home. They have passed laws without any exceptions for when the woman is the victim of rape or incest. Under those laws, a woman will have to bear her rapist's child or a young girl her father's—no matter if doing so will destroy her life. So too,

after today's ruling, some States may compel women to carry to term a fetus with severe physical anomalies.

There were even direr possibilities.

A State can of course impose criminal penalties on abortion providers, including lengthy prison sentences. But some States will not stop there. Perhaps, in the wake of today's decision, a state law will criminalize the woman's conduct too, incarcerating or fining her for daring to seek or obtain an abortion. And as Texas has recently shown, a State can turn neighbor against neighbor, enlisting fellow citizens in the effort to root out anyone who tries to get an abortion, or to assist another in doing so.[5]

Deciding which of the two sets of opinions in *Dobbs* is the better way to view our constitutional regime is not my purpose. But the contrast between the two jurisprudences imbedded in those opinions could not be more striking. One looks back, albeit seeing only the past that it wishes to see, and the other looks back, considering precedent and text, but also forward, weighing future harms and seeking future progress. I let the reader decide.

Here the skeptical reader may ask, is mine not a consequentialist defense of consequentialism? An instrumental defense of instrumentalism? A pragmatic defense of pragmatic readings of law? In sum, is it not circular? My answer is that the historical approach takes us out of the endless and unrewarding controversy over philosophies of law into the real world, where law functions—or does not function. There one finds that judges who read the law forward were able to surmount the obstacles that a law frozen in time imposed. Changes in society, in politics, in commercial life, and in culture were accommodated by reading law forward.

At the outset of this essay, I suggested that reading law forward was the default jurisprudence of the revolutionaries. Today, it keeps that revolutionary energy and purpose alive. The judge and the jurisprudence that only look backward in a world that is moving rapidly forward may make the law seem irrelevant. As the popular response to *Dobbs* has demonstrated, when the majority of ordinary people in a democratic republic like ours cannot understand judicial rulings, when opinions are cloaked in language and repeat concepts older than we are, we rightly ask, where is our consent? How can we have given it when we do not understand what the judge tells us? In this era of highly contested appointments and confirmation hearings, a judicial process that ordinary people can understand is increasingly valuable. Linking current textual meanings to future opportunities and anticipated problems, then returning with enlightened vision to existing law, lessens this problem. Then and perhaps only then can the law truly rest on the consent of the governed.

Acknowledgments

I am grateful to Mark Graber, N. E. H. Hull, Williamjames Hull Hoffer, William Nelson, Edward Purcell, Logan Sawyer III, Mark Tushnet, and Melvin Urofsky for agreeing to read and comment on the manuscript. Senior Editor David Congdon at the University Press of Kansas supported the author and the project throughout with good humor and patience. Kelly Chrisman Jacques and Robert Demke, respectively, were my production editor and copyeditor at the press, and to them I am greatly indebted. David Tanenhouse and an anonymous reader refereed the manuscript for the press favorably, and their kind and helpful criticism improved it greatly. The American Founding Group at the University of Georgia commented on the introduction and the first chapter. I am grateful to Keith Dougherty, Michael Taylor, Nathan Chapman, Harrison Frye, Ted Rossier, and the other members of the group for their suggestions. Remaining errors are mine alone.

In the epilogue to his *Cardozo: A Study in Reputation* (1990), Judge Richard A. Posner called for more "critical judicial stud[ies]" like his of Cardozo. Posner might justly become the subject of such a study in the future. A public intellectual as well as a law professor, a social scientist (one of the founders of the school of law and economics), and a long-serving federal appellate judge, he has written brilliantly on subjects as disparate as pornography, plagiarism, impeachment, and the federal courts. In the final chapter of this volume, Posner jousts with US Supreme Court Justice Stephen G. Breyer. Breyer is another law professor-public intellectual on the bench, the author of luminous studies of regulation, international law, and the judicial process. The two men have not only raised the level of judicial discourse; they hold aloft a standard of impartiality and thoughtfulness on and off the bench. This volume is dedicated to them.

Notes

1. Ronald Dworkin, *Law's Empire* (Cambridge, MA: Harvard University Press, 1986), 239 and after (Hercules), 185 (integrity); Dworkin, *Freedom's Law* (Cambridge, MA: Harvard University Press, 1996), 10 (past and future); Gregory C. Keating, "Justifying Hercules: Ronald Dworkin and the Rule of Law," *American Bar Foundation Research Journal* 12 (1987): 525 (reputation of Hercules); "Other judges": Judge Learned Hand quoted in G. Edward White, *The American Judicial Tradition: Profiles of Leading American Judges*, 3rd ed. (New York: Oxford University Press, 2007), 217. White recognized the dilemma of Hercules as a common one for judges, and also for anyone (himself including) writing about judges (xxiv). He concluded that there was no way to determine absolutely if a judicial opinion was subjective.

The origin of modern jurisprudence in America is Roscoe Pound, "The Scope and Purpose of Sociological Jurisprudence," *Harvard Law Review* 24 (1911): 591–619; 25 (1911–1912), 140–168; and 25 (1911–1912): 489–516. On Pound and sociological jurisprudence, see N. E. H. Hull, *Roscoe Pound and Karl Llewellyn: Searching for an American Jurisprudence* (Chicago: University of Chicago Press, 1997), 76–124.

2. Stephen G. Breyer, *Active Liberty: Interpreting our Democratic Constitution* (New York: Knopf, 2005), 3, 5, 6. On the insider vs. outsider question in jurisprudence, see, e.g., R. Kent Greenawalt, "Too Thin and Too Rich," in *The Autonomy of Law: Essays on Legal Positivism*, ed. Robert P. George (Oxford: Oxford University Press, 1996), 19–24. I believe there is another place where one can find a version of this ideal of everyone wins jurisprudence—equity. For more on this, see Peter Charles Hoffer, *The Law's Conscience: Equitable Constitutionalism in America* (Chapel Hill: University of North Carolina Press, 1990).

3. For Richard A. Posner's view of legal "everyday" pragmatism, see Posner, *Law, Pragmatism, and Democracy* (Cambridge, MA: Harvard University Press, 1990), especially 9, 59–61. On consequentialism, see Stephen Darwell, ed., *Consequentialism* (Malden, MA: Blackwell, 2003). The classic definition of instrumentalism is Morton Horwitz, *The Transformation of American Law, 1780–1860* (Cambridge, MA: Harvard University Press, 1977), 16–30. For an example of qualifications and complexities, see Richard A. Posner, "Pragmatism

versus Purposivism in First Amendment Analysis," *Stanford Law Journal* 54 (2002): 737–752; on squishy definitions, see Posner, "Pragmatic Adjudication," *Cardozo Law Review* 18 (1996): 2.

4. Robert M. Cover, "Forward: Nomos and Narrative," *Harvard Law Review* 97 (1983): 10, 16 (I suppose Cover favored the latter; Owen Fiss, *Pillars of Justice: Lawyers and the Liberal Tradition* [Cambridge, MA: Harvard University Press, 2017], 159–160); Edmund Jackson v. Wendell Phillips and Others, 96 Mass 539, 568 (1867) (Gray, J.).

5. Antonin Scalia, *A Matter of Interpretation*, new ed., ed. Akhil Amar (Princeton: Princeton University Press, 1997), 7; Dobbs v. Jackson's Women's Health, 597 U.S. ___ 19–1392, slip opinion, 5, 8, 9, 11, 12, 14, 24 (Alito, J.); New York State Rifle & Pistol Association, Inc., et al. v. Bruen, Superintendent of New York State Police, et al., 20–843, p. 8 (2022) (Thomas, J.).

6. Robert Bork, *The Tempting of America (the Political Seduction of the Law)* (New York: Free Press, 1989), 1.

7. Posner, *Law, Pragmatism, and Democracy*, 84–85; INS v. Chadha, 462 U.S. 919, 959 (1983) (Burger, C.J.); School District of Abington Township v. Schempp, 374 U.S. 203, 294 (1963) (Brennan, J.); Swann v. Charlotte-Mecklenburg Board of Education, 401 U.S. 1 (1971). The doctrine of strict adherence to original texts of the law is called originalism or original intent. *Black's Law Dictionary*, 6th. ed. (St. Paul, MN: West, 1991), p. 1133. The literature on originalism is explored in Jack M. Balkin, *Living Originalism* (Cambridge, MA: Harvard University Press, 2011). Balkin's work was reviewed by Lawrence Solum, an expert on the subject, in "Construction and Constraint," *Jerusalem Review of Legal Studies* 7 (2013): 17–34. In a sophisticated linguistic essay Solum sees originalism as a "family" of theories, though the term "clade" might be more appropriate, all of which concern (but none settle) the vexing question of constraining the discretion of judges. A new start on the problem is William Baude, "Is Originalism Our Law," *Columbia Law Review* 115 (2015): 2349–2408. A more orthodox exposition of that jurisprudence is Antonin Scalia, *The Essential Scalia* (New York: Crown, 2020), 15 and after. Was Dworkin himself an originalist? See Lawrence A. Alexander, "Was Dworkin an Originalist?," in *Legacy of Ronald Dworkin*, ed. Wil Waluchow and Stefan Sciaraffa (Oxford: Oxford University Press, 2016), 299–322.

8. I am not asking for something along the lines of David Hume's prescription for metaphysics, however: "Does it contain any experimental reasoning, concerning matter of fact and existence? No. Commit it then to the flames: for it can contain nothing but sophistry and illusion." Hume, *An Enquiry Concerning Human Understanding* (1777; Chicago: Open Court, 1921), 176. Nor

do I want to emulate the knight of a new jurisprudence who proves his merit by cracking the skulls of advocates of competing theories. See Felix S. Cohen, "The Problems of a Functional Jurisprudence," *Modern Law Review* (June 1937): 5. But I do ask the functionalist question "how does this or that legal rule work in practice?" (6).

9. Prigg v. Pennsylvania 41 U.S. 539, 621, 623, 625 (1842) (Story, J.). See the fuller discussion herein on pages 53–62.

10. Hynes v. New York Central R.R 231 N.Y. 229, 233 (1921) (Cardozo, J.). See the discussion on pages 123–125 herein. See also the comment in Richard A. Posner, *Cardozo: A Study in Reputation* (Chicago: University of Chicago Press, 1990), 53.

11. The result would be a more comprehensive list and a much bigger book, but the problem of selection would not change. See, for example, White, *America Judicial Tradition*, 5, 6: "These judgments on coverage were based not on an implicit ranking of the stature or importance of the subjects but on a desire to provide fresh perspectives on the mind-set of individuals judges. . . . a far more systematic set of criteria than the above would still not insure an infallible selection process."

12. A last caveat, for historians: Am I guilty of a version of presentism, the evil that David Hackett Fischer's now classic *Historians' Fallacies* condemned as "a complex anachronism" in which only those parts of the past that have survived are included in our historical narratives? Fischer, *Historians' Fallacies: Toward a Logic of Historical Thought* (New York: Harper, 1970), 135. The epithet "presentist" was commonly and conveniently hurled at left-wing historians by their critics in the 1970s and 1980s, and has reappeared periodically. It means that the only important history is the version that provides evidence for present social and political aims. Colleen Flaherty, "Presentism, Race, and Trolls," *Inside Higher Education*, August 22, 2022, quoting concerns raised by American Historical Association president Richard Sweet, in "Is History History? Identity Politics and Teleologies of the Present," American Historical Association, *Perspectives on History*, August 17, 2022: "This new [social justice] history often ignores the values and mores of people in their own times, as well as change over time, neutralizing the expertise that separates historians from those in other disciplines. The allure of political relevance, facilitated by social and other media, encourages a predictable sameness of the present in the past. This sameness is ahistorical, a proposition that might be acceptable if it produced positive political results. But it doesn't." Judges who read the law forward are not interpreting the past through the lens of the present, however. They are not historians, who can at least convince themselves into thinking

that they are living and thinking in the past. Judges are dispute resolvers and problem solvers. They have to live and think in the present.

CHAPTER ONE. JOHN MARSHALL

1. Peter Charles Hoffer, *Law and People in Colonial America*, 2nd ed. (Baltimore: Johns Hopkins University Press, 2019), 163–164. Portions of this chapter are adapted, from Peter Charles Hoffer, *Daniel Webster and the Unfinished Constitution* (Lawrence: University Press of Kansas, 2021); and Peter Charles Hoffer, Williamjames Hull Hoffer, and N. E. H. Hull, *The Federal Courts: An Essential History* (New York: Oxford University Press, 2016).

2. Alexis de Tocqueville, *Democracy in America* (1836), trans. Henry Reeve, 4th ed. (New York: Henry Langley, 1845), 1:303; Peter Charles Hoffer and Williamjames Hull Hoffer, *The Clamor of Lawyers: The American Revolution and Crisis in the Legal Profession* (Ithaca, NY: Cornell University Press, 2018), 152–155; G. Edward White, *Law in American History*, vol. 1 (New York: Oxford University Press, 2012), 52–53.

3. Joseph Galloway, *A Candid Examination of the Mutual Claims of Great-Britain and the Colonies* (New York: Rivington, 1775), 1; Eric Nelson, *The Royalist Revolution: Monarchy and the American Founding* (Cambridge, MA: Harvard University Press, 2014), 146–183. Noted in passing: this view of law was the precursor of originalism.

4. Mary Sarah Bilder, *Madison's Hand: Revising the Constitutional Convention* (Cambridge, MA: Harvard University Press, 2015), 168.

5. Peter Charles Hoffer, Williamjames Hull Hoffer, and N. E. H. Hull, *The Supreme Court: An Essential History*, 2nd ed. (Lawrence: University Press of Kansas, 2018), 51; "Honors to Judge Marshall," *Niles Weekly Register*, July 18, 1835; Thomas Hart Benton, *Thirty Years View: or, A History of the Workings of the American Government, from 1820 to 1850* (New York: Appleton, 1854), 2:681; Herbert A. Johnson, ed., *The Papers of John Marshall* (Chapel Hill: University of North Carolina Press, 1977), 2:161–178; R. Kent Newmyer, *John Marshall and the Heroic Age of the Supreme Court* (Baton Rouge: Louisiana State University Press, 2001), 407. But see Paul Finkelman, *Supreme Injustice: Slavery in the Nation's Highest Court* (Cambridge, MA: Harvard University Press, 2018), 26 and after (Marshall owned slaves on plantations managed by others in his family).

6. George Lee Haskins and Herbert A. Johnson, *Foundations of Power: John Marshall, 1801–1815, Oliver Wendell Holmes Devise History of the Supreme Court of the United States*, vol. 2 (New York: Macmillan, 1981), 382–389.

7. William E. Nelson, *Marbury v. Madison: The Origins and Legacy of*

Judicial Review (Lawrence: University Press of Kansas, 2000), 71 (take the court out of politics). But see the argument for "A full scale war over the courts" in these years: Jed Handelsman Shugerman, *The People's Courts: Pursuing Judicial Independence in America* (Cambridge, MA: Harvard University Press, 2012), 34. On the Jeffersonians' backward looking, see Drew R. McCoy, *The Elusive Republic: Political Economy in Jeffersonian America* (Chapel Hill: University of North Carolina Press, 1982), 252–253; Leo Marx, *The Machine in the Garden*, 2nd ed. (New York: Oxford University Press, 2000), 74 (Jefferson's pastoral ideal); and Gordon S. Wood, *Empire of Liberty: A History of the Early Republic, 1789–1815* (New York: Oxford University Press, 2009), 10 (the ploughman will understand liberty better than the professor).

8. G. Edward White, *The Marshall Court and Cultural Change, Oliver Wendell Holmes Devise History of the Supreme Court*, vol. 3 (New York: Cambridge University Press, 2009), 179–180. There is a large and growing literature that downgrades the significance and the originality of *Marbury*'s claims and the scope of its version of judicial review. See, e.g., Jack Rakove, "The Origins of Judicial Review: A Plea for New Contexts," *Stanford Law Review* 49 (1997): 1039–1040; Robert Lowery Clinton, *Marbury v. Madison and Judicial Review* (Lawrence: University Press of Kansas, 1989), *passim*; and Michael J. Klarman, "How Great Were the 'Great' Marshall Court Decisions?," *Virginia Law Review* 87 (2001): 1111, 1113.

9. A fire in the Capitol in 1898 "destroyed many of the Supreme Court's original jurisdiction case files." Jonathan W. White, *Guide to Research in Federal Judicial History* (Washington, DC: Federal Judicial Center, 2010), 45. The docket books still exist in RG 267, in the National Archives. After a "flurry" of suits involving citizens of one state suing another state was ended by the adoption of the Eleventh Amendment, only a handful of original jurisdiction suits graced the early Supreme Courts' dockets. Maeva Marcus et al., eds., *Documentary History of the Supreme Court* (New York: Columbia University Press, 1998), 6:4.

10. Marbury v. Madison, 5 U.S. 137, 177 (1803) (Marshall, C.J.).

11. 5 U.S. 170 (Marshall, C.J.). The "abstention doctrine" in Marshall's dictum here is prudential, that is, judge-made, law. Abstention shifted or left cases in the state courts, refused to hear cases that were moot, were unripe, did not present a matter that the courts could resolve, or were brought by parties having no standing to sue in the first place, as well as abstaining in pending state criminal cases—except when states act in bad faith, when they violate the federal Constitution, and "other unusual situations calling for federal intervention" (Younger v. Harris, 401 U.S. 37, 53 [1971] [Black, J.]). The

underlying question is whether courts have discretion to exercise the full extent of jurisdiction granted them by Congress. See, e.g., Martin H. Redish, "Abstention, Separation of Powers, and the Limits of the Judicial Function," *Yale Law Journal* 94 (1985): 78 and after.

12. The story of the trial is told in Peter Charles Hoffer, *The Treason Trials of Aaron Burr* (Lawrence: University Press of Kansas, 2008), 146–171. Burr was acquitted on charges of treason but a better case could have been made for conspiracy to commit a federal crime. The lapsed Sedition Act of 1798 had provisions against conspiracy, but the Federal Crimes Act of 1790, under which Burr was indicted, did not.

13. T. Carpenter, comp., *The Trial of Col. Aaron Burr on an Indictment of Treason* (Washington, DC: Westcott, 1807), 129.

14. Carpenter, 134; David Robertson, *Reports of the Trials of Colonel Aaron Burr . . .* (Philadelphia: Hopkins and Earle, 1808), 1:254. The issue did reappear, most notably in the impeachment hearings against president Richard M. Nixon, and Judge John Sirica ruled along the same lines as Chief Justice Marshall. His opinion was upheld by the US Supreme Court: U.S. v. Nixon, 418 U.S. 683, 704 (1974) (Burger, C.J.): "Notwithstanding the deference each branch must accord the others, the 'judicial Power of the United States' vested in the federal courts by Art. III, § 1, of the Constitution can no more be shared with the Executive Branch than the Chief Executive, for example, can share with the Judiciary the veto power, or the Congress share with the Judiciary the power to override a Presidential veto. Any other conclusion would be contrary to the basic concept of separation of powers and the checks and balances that flow from the scheme of a tripartite government."

15. The facts appear in Charles Hobson, *The Great Yazoo Lands Sale: The Case of* Fletcher v. Peck (Lawrence: University Press of Kansas, 2016), 84–92, 137–139, and in Fletcher v. Peck, 10 U.S. 87 (1810), 135, 136 (Marshall, C.J.).

16. 10 U.S. at 128 (Marshall, C.J.).

17. 10 U.S. at 129 (Marshall, C.J.).

18. 10 U.S. at 129–130 (Marshall, C.J.).

19. Edward Kaplan, *The Bank of the United States and the American Economy* (Santa Barbara, CA: ABC-CLIO, 1999), 67–70.

20. Quotations from Mark R. Killenbeck, *McCulloch v. Maryland: Securing a Nation* (Lawrence: University Press of Kansas, 2006), 122 and after.

21. McCulloch v. Maryland, 17 U.S. 316, 431–434 (1819) (Marshall, C.J.).

22. Cohens v. Virginia, 19 U.S. 264 (1821) (the U.S. Supreme Court is the final authority on the constitutionality of state court criminal prosecutions); Letters of Algernon Sydney, *Richmond Enquirer*, May 25, 1821; *Debates on the*

Federal Judiciary: A Documentary History (Washington, DC: Federal Judicial Center, 2013), 1:181–198.

23. Osborn v. Bank of the United States, 22 U.S. 738, 818, 819 (1824) (Marshall, C.J.); Bank of the United States v. Planters Bank, 22 U.S. 904, 905 (1824) (Marshall, C.J.).

24. Herbert A. Johnson, *Gibbons v. Ogden, John Marshall, Steamboats, and the Commerce Clause* (Lawrence: University Press of Kansas, 2010), 21–30. See also Maurice G. Baxter, *The Steamboat Monopoly: Gibbons v. Ogden, 1824* (New York: Knopf, 1972); and Thomas H. Cox, *Gibbons v. Ogden: Law and Society in the Early Republic* (Athens: Ohio University Press, 2009). Note for here and hereafter—monopoly did not have the stigma in the popular mind that it gained after the railroad era and into the twentieth century. Charles R. Geisst, *Monopolies in America: Empire Builders and Their Enemies from Jay Gould to Bill Gates* (New York: Oxford University Press, 2000), 2–3. In Darcy v. Allein, 74 ER 1131, the Court of Kings Bench declared a monopoly in the production of goods (here playing cards) was a violation of the common law provisions for freedom of trade. The exceptions were monopolies created for the common good and patents for a term of years. B. Zorina Khan, *The Democratization of Invention: Patents and Copyrights in American Economic Development, 1790–1920* (New York: Cambridge University Press, 2005), 82–84. The narrative here is again redacted from Hoffer, *Daniel Webster and the Unfinished Constitution*, 73–93.

25. I have assumed that the issue was riverine commerce rather than the omnipresent and hidden issue of slavery. There is no doubt that slaves worked on riverboats and riverboats were the means of transit for much of the interstate slave trade. Walter Johnson, *River of Dark Dreams: Slavery and Empire in the Cotton Kingdom* (Cambridge, MA: Harvard University Press, 2013), 5 and after. Nor that many commentators see slavery behind just about every Marshall opinion. See, e.g., Charles Warren, *The Supreme Court in United States History* (Boston: Little, Brown, 1922), 2:627–628. But Associate Justice William Johnson's concurring opinion in the case may have been a parting shot in the dispute over the South Carolina Negro Seaman's Act, which he had declared unconstitutional. See David Golove, "Treaty Making and the Nation: The Historical Foundations of the Nationalist Conception of the Treaty Power," *University of Michigan Law Review* 98 (2000): 1221–1222.

26. Hendrik Hartog, *The Trouble with Minna: A Case of Slavery and Emancipation in the Antebellum North* (Chapel Hill: University of North Carolina Press, 2018), 113–114.

27. Johnson, *Gibbons*, 30–31.

28. Johnson, *Gibbons*, 16–20, 32–34. On Kent's opinion, see Thomas P. Campbell Jr., "Chancellor Kent, Chief Justice Marshall, and the Steamboat Cases," *Syracuse Law Review* 25 (1974): 506–512.

29. Johnson, *Gibbons*, 31–47, 60–61, 72–73.

30. Daniel Webster, brief for Gibbons, 5–6, in Gibbons v. Ogden, 22 U.S. 1 (1824).

31. Webster, brief for Gibbons, 22, 24. This is the dormant version of the Commerce Clause, a version of concurrent regulatory authority that does not impede interstate commerce. Webster did not argue against all state regulations; only those that affected interstate commerce. Marshall would adopt this distinction in his opinion. Kent's reputation was such that Webster sent him the published brief in Dartmouth, and he never failed to praise the chancellor. John T. Horton, *James Kent: A Study in Conservatism, 1763–1847* (New York: Appleton, 1939), 267; Robert V. Remini, *Daniel Webster: The Man and His Time* (New York: Norton: 1997), 186–187. The roads question referred to the Bonus Bill, a federal project to fund roads and canals as internal improvements that Congress passed in 1816 and outgoing president James Madison vetoed as beyond the limited powers of Congress. In using the analogy, Webster was staking the case for internal improvements against Republican ideas of limited federal government.

32. Webster, brief for Gibbons, 11–12.

33. 22 U.S. at 187 (Marshall, C.J.).

34. 22 U.S. at 188 (Marshall, C. J.).

35. 22 U.S. at 189, 190 (Marshall, C.J.).

36. 22 U.S. at 192–193 (Marshall, C.J.).

37. 22 U.S. at 195 (Marshall, C.J.). On the conflict between realism and positivism, see Hendrik Hartog, "Pigs and Positivism," *Wisconsin Law Review* (1985): 899–937.

38. 22 U.S. at 198, 199, 203 (Marshall, C.J.).

39. 22 U.S. at 206, 207 (Marshall, C.J.). The internal slave trade was hugely profitable and moved some two million slaves around the country from 1820 to 1860. Robert H. Gudmestad, *A Troublesome Commerce: The Transformation of the Interstate Slave Trade* (Baton Rouge: Louisiana State University Press, 2002), figures from p. 9 and appendix on 210–211; Walter Johnson, *Soul by Soul: Life inside the Antebellum Slave Market* (Cambridge, MA: Harvard University Press, 2000), 16–17, 104–105.

40. 22 U.S. at 209 (Marshall, C.J.). In short, exceptions do not prove a rule.

41. See, e.g., Finkelman, *Supreme Injustice*, 26–75; David Waldstreicher,

Slavery's Constitution: From Revolution to Ratification (New York: Hill and Wang, 2009), 57–106; and Alan Taylor, *Thomas Jefferson's Education* (New York: Norton, 2019), 37 and after.

CHAPTER TWO. JOSEPH STORY

1. R. Kent Newmyer, *Supreme Court Justice Joseph Story: Statesman of the Old Republic* (Chapel Hill: University of North Carolina Press, 1979), 37–73.

2. Joseph Story, Address to the Members of the Suffolk Bar, September 10, 1821, in Story, *Miscellaneous Writings* (Boston: Monroe, 1830), 406.

3. Joseph Story to William Wetmore Story, January 1, 1831, in Joseph Story, *Life and Letters of Joseph Story*, ed. William Wetmore Story (Boston: Brown, 1851), 1:5–15. Hereinafter Story, *Life and Letters*.

4. Story, *Life and Letters*, 1:23, 90; Story to Fay, September 6, 1798, in *Life and Letters*, 1:71; Story to Fay, September 15, 1801, in *Life and Letters*, 1:72, Story, "Autobiography," in *Life and Letters*, 1:74.

5. Story, "Autobiography," in *Life and Letters*, 1:96; Story, December 23, 1830, "Introductory Lecture to Families of Harvard Faculty," in *Miscellaneous Writings*, 135; Story, Inauguration of the Author as Dane Professor, August 25, 1829, in *Miscellaneous Writings*, 440.

6. Newmyer, *Story*, 70–71; The Brig Alexander (Cir Ct Mass 1813) (Story, J.), in John Gallison, ed., *Cases Argued and Determined in the First Circuit* (Boston: Wells and Lilly, 1815), 1:543–544.

7. Martin v. Hunter's Lessee, 14 U.S. 304 (1816). On the suspect role of Marshall in *Martin*: R. Kent Newmyer, *John Marshall and the Heroic Age of the Supreme Court* (Baton Rouge: Louisiana State University Press, 2001), 363.

8. 14 U.S. at 324, 325 (Story, J.).

9. 14 U.S. at 325 (Story, J.).

10. 14 U.S. at 326 (Story, J.). James Madison, "liquidation," *Federalist*, No. 37: "all new laws, though penned with the greatest technical skill, are considered as more or less obscure and equivocal, until their meaning be liquidated and ascertained by a series of particular discussions and adjudications."

11. 14 U.S. at 327 (Story, J.).

12. 14 U.S. at 327 (Story, J.). On making law versus finding it, compare Stephen E. Sachs, "Finding Law," *California Law Review* 107 (2019): 527–585 (judges can still find law) with Hon. Jack G. Day, "Why Judges Must Make Law," *Case Western Reserve Law School* 26 (1976): 563–596.

13. 14 U.S. at 328 (Story, J.).

14. 14 U.S. at 331 (Story, J.).

15. 14 U.S. at 335 (Story, J.).

16. 14 U.S. at 338 (Story, J.).

17. 14 U.S. at 343 (Story, J.).

18. 14 U.S. at 344, 345 (Story, J.).

19. 14 U.S. at 348 (Story, J.).

20. 14 U.S. at 356 (Story, J.).

21. 14 U.S. at 348, 356, 361 (Story, J.).

22. Joseph Story, *Commentaries on the Constitution* (Boston: Hilliard and Gray, 1833), 1:vi.

23. Story, *Commentaries*, 1:289, 290–291.

24. Story, *Commentaries*, 1:408, 410.

25. Story, *Commentaries*, 2:123, 143, 369.

26. Joseph Story, *The Constitutional Class Book* (Boston: Hilliard, Gray, 1834), 10, 14, 27, 31, 240; on Indian removal, see, e.g., Claudio Saunt, *Unworthy Republic* (New York: Norton, 2021), 84 and after; on John C. Calhoun and the compact theory of the Constitution, see John Niven, *John C. Calhoun and the Price of Union* (Baton Rouge: Louisiana State University Press, 1988), 71, 194.

27. Story, *Class Book*, 100, 49, 140.

28. Story, *Class Book*, 127, 142, 151.

29. Joseph Story, "Charge to the First Circuit Grand Jury in Boston, October 1819," in Story, *Life and Letters*, 1:336.

30. U.S. v. The Kitty 26 F. Cas. 791, 792 (D.C. S.C. 1808) (Bee, J.). "Bee to South Carolina Senate Delegation supporting increased pay for federal judges handling admiralty cases," February 3, 1800, Thomas Bee Papers, Columbiana Collection, University of South Carolina Library, Columbia, SC; Story, Charge to Boston grand jury, 1819, in Story, *Life and Letters*, 1:341.

31. U.S. v. Schooner Amistad, 40 U.S. 518, 592 (1841) (Story, J.). On the notoriety of the case, see, e.g., Bruce A. Ragsdale, "The Amistad: The Mende Slave Revolt," Federal Judicial Center, www.fjc.gov/history/cases/famous-federal -trials/amistad-mende-slave-revolt.

32. 40 U.S. at 394 (Story J.).

33. 40 U.S. at 393, 394 (Story, J.).

34. 40 U.S. at 395 (Story, J.).

35. 40 U.S. at 396 (Story, J.).

36. 40 U.S. at 397 (Story, J.).

37. Prigg v. Pennsylvania, 41 U.S. 539 (1842); Joseph Story, *Commentaries on the Conflict of Laws* (Boston: Hilliard and Gray, 1834), 138; U.S. v. *Le*

Jeune Eugenie (Cir Ct. MA 1822) (Story, J.), quoted in Story, *Life and Letters*, 1:350. The story of the state act and the case is told in H. Robert Baker, *Prigg v. Pennsylvania, Slavery, the Supreme Court, and the Ambivalent Constitution* (Lawrence: University Press of Kansas, 2012). Baker finds a certain kind of forward reading of law in Story, to whit that recaption was a "'new and positive right' granted by the Constitution independent of any other legal source" (149). Such a grant by Congress was *expedient* rather than textualist. Story supposedly wanted a uniform rule and thought that Congress did too. But this does not conform to Story's own view of slavery, and although he deferred to Congress in many ways, it was not necessary to grant exclusivity to Congress to defer to it.

38. Paul Finkelman, "Story Telling on the Supreme Court: *Prigg v. Pennsylvania* and Justice Joseph Story's Judicial Nationalism," *Supreme Court Review* (1994): 247–294.

39. 41 U.S. at 609 (Story, J.).

40. 41 U.S. at 610, 611 (Story, J.).

41. 41 U.S. at 611 (Story, J.).

42. 41 U.S. at 611 (Story, J.). See Peter Karsten, "Revisiting the Critiques of Those Who Upheld the Fugitive Slave Acts in the 1840s and '50s," *American Journal of Legal History* 58 (2018): 297–300; and compare Sean Wilentz, *No Property in Man* (Cambridge, MA: Harvard University Press, 2018), 228, with Noah Feldman, *The Broken Constitution* (New York: Farrar, Straus and Giroux, 2021), 66.

43. 41 U.S. at 612 (Story, J.).

44. 41 U.S. at 612 (Story, J.).

45. 41 U.S. at 612, 613 (Story, J.).

46. 41 U.S. at 614 (Story, J.).

47. 41 U.S. at 614, 615 (Story, J.).

48. 41 U.S. at 615, 616, 617 (Story, J.).

49. Swift v. Tyson, 41 U.S. 1 (1842).

50. Michael Williams, *Americans and Their Forests: A Historical Geography* (New York: Cambridge University Press, 1992), 133–136.

51. Alan Taylor, *Liberty Men and Great Proprietors: The Revolutionary Settlement on the Maine Frontier, 1760–1820* (Chapel Hill: University of North Carolina Press, 1990), 109.

52. 41 U.S. 1, 2 (1842) (Story, J.); Tony Freyer, *Harmony and Dissonance: The Swift and Erie Cases in American Federalism* (New York: New York University Press, 1981), 1–43.

53. 41 U.S. at 38, 39, 40, 41, 18 (1842) (Story, J.). Note that Swift did not impose federal law on the states in similar fact patterns—their courts were still free to find their own judgments on state law grounds.

54. 41 U.S. at 19 (Story, J.).

55. Story, address to the Suffolk Bar, in *Miscellaneous Writings*, 431.

CHAPTER THREE. LEMUEL SHAW

1. Leonard W. Levy, *The Law of the Commonwealth and Chief Justice Shaw* (Cambridge, MA: Harvard University Press, 1957), 3.

2. White, *The American Judicial Tradition*, 37–64; Shaw quoted in Newmyer, *Story*, 252; Earl Maltz, *Fugitive Slave on Trial: The Anthony Burns Case and Abolitionist Outrage* (Lawrence: University Press of Kansas, 2010), 22–23; Alexandra Lahav and R. Kent Newmyer, "The Law Wars in Massachusetts," *American Journal of Legal History* 58 (2018): 327–358.

3. Levy, *Shaw*, 3–21; Frederick Hathaway Chase, *Lemuel Shaw, Chief Justice of the Supreme Judicial Court of Massachusetts, 1830–1860* (Boston: Houghton Mifflin, 1918), 3–57.

4. Shaw, Fourth of July Speech, 1815, in Chase, *Shaw*, 65; Elijah Adlow, "Lemuel Shaw and the Judicial Function," *Massachusetts Law Quarterly* 52 (1960): 52–69.

5. Chase, *Shaw*, 274–289; Kenneth S. Lynn, "Lemuel Shaw and Herman Melville," *Constitutional Comment* 5 (1988): 411–428.

6. Commonwealth v. Kneeland, 37 Mass. 206, 214, 217, 221 (Shaw, C.J.); Levy, *Shaw*, 51–52.

7. Roberts v. City of Boston, 59 Mass. 198, 205, 206, 208, 209 (Shaw, C.J.). Plessy v. Ferguson, 163 U.S. 537 (1896). See Robert Cottrol et al., *Brown v. Board of Education: Caste, Culture and the Constitution* (Lawrence: University Press of Kansas, 2003), 17–18, 28–33.

8. Charles G. Sellers, *The Market Revolution: Jacksonian America, 1815–1848* (New York: Oxford University Press, 1992), 43–44; Levy, *Shaw*, 325; Christopher Tomlins, *The State and the Unions* (Chapel Hill: University of North Carolina Press, 1985), 44; Alfred Konefsky, "As Best to Subserve Their Own Interests: Lemuel Shaw, Labor Conspiracy, and Fellow Servants," *Law and History Review* 7 (1989): 220–221.

9. Norway Plains Company v. Boston and Maine Railroad, 67 Mass. 263, 267 (1854) (Shaw, C.J.).

10. Commonwealth v. Alger, 61 Mass. 53, 64, 79, 83, 85 (1851) (Shaw, C.J.); William J. Novak, *The People's Welfare: Law and Regulation in Nineteenth-Century*

America (Chapel Hill: University of North Carolina Press, 1996), 7–8, and after.

11. Farwell v. Boston and Worcester R.R., 45 Mass. 49, 57, 58, 59 (Shaw, C.J.).

12. Levy, *Shaw*, 119, 178–179; Morton J. Horwitz, *The Transformation of American Law, 1780–1860* (Cambridge, MA: Harvard University Press, 1977), 209, 210.

13. Commonwealth v. Hunt, 45 Mass. 111, 129, 130, 134 (1842) (Shaw, C.J.); Eric Foner, *Free Soil, Free Labor, Free Men: The Ideology of the Republican Party before the Civil War*, reprint ed. (New York: Oxford University Press, 1995), 27. On the struggle of later scholars to reconcile the two cases, see Konefsky, "Subserve Their Own Interests," 233 (Shaw's ideas of individual virtue and responsibility infuse both cases).

14. Lemuel Shaw, "Slavery and the Missouri Question," *North American Review* 10 (1820): 141.

15. Commonwealth v. Aves, 35 Mass. 193, 207 (1836) (Shaw, C.J.).

16. 35 Mass at 208, 210 (Shaw, C.J.).

17. 35 Mass at 211 (Shaw, C.J.).

18. 35 Mass. at 212 (Shaw, C.J.).

19. 35 Mass. at 216 (Shaw, C.J.). In support Shaw quoted Joseph Story's conflict of laws jurisprudence: to the forum state belonged the final judgment of whose laws to adopt.

20. 35 Mass. at 217–218 (Shaw, C.J.).

21. 35 Mass. at 222 (Shaw, C.J.).

22. Sims Case, 61 Mass. 285, 291, 293 (1851) (Shaw, C.J.); Levy, *Shaw*, 78–83, 88.

23. 61 Mass. at 296, 304 (Shaw, C.J.); White, *The Judicial Tradition in America*, 61.

24. Shaw, Address to the Massachusetts Bar, August, 1860, in Chase, *Shaw*, 268, 269. On the lawyers and the coming of the Civil War, see Peter Charles Hoffer, *Uncivil Warriors: The Lawyers' Civil War* (New York: Oxford University Press, 2018), 1–47.

CHAPTER FOUR. LOUIS D. BRANDEIS

1. Horwitz, *Transformation*, 253, 254, 255. Just who the formalists were, however, remains a matter of controversy. See, e.g., William P. LaPiana, *Logic and Experience: The Origin of Modern American Legal Education* (New York: Oxford University Press, 1994), 188.

2. Thomas M. Cooley, *The General Principles of Constitutional Law in the*

United States (Boston: Little, Brown, 1880), 23, 25; Christopher Columbus Langdell, preface to *Selection of Cases on the Law of Contracts* (Boston: Little, Brown, 1871), vi. See, generally, William M. Wiecek, *The Lost World of Classical Legal Thought: Law and Ideology in America, 1886–1937* (New York: Oxford University Press, 1998).

3. David Rabban, *Law's History: American Legal Thought and the Transatlantic Turn to History* (New York: Cambridge University Press, 2013), 320.

4. Governor Stone quoted in Alan F. Westin, "The Supreme Court, The Populist Movement, and the Election of 1896," *Journal of Politics* 15 (1953): 8. William Jennings Bryan quoted in Edward A. Purcell Jr., *Litigation and Inequality, Federal Diversity Jurisdiction in Industrial America, 1870–1958* (New York: Oxford University Press, 1992), 26; George Sheldon quoted in "Raps the Federal Courts," *New York Times*, September 13, 1907, 6; Theodore Roosevelt, Message to Congress, December 3, 1906, *Congressional Record*, 59th Cong., 2d Sess., 1906, 41, pt. 1:22. Here and after, I owe a debt to Dan Holt, *Debates on the Federal Judiciary: A Documentary History*, vol. 2, *1875–1939* (Washington, DC: Federal Judicial Center, 2013).

5. Roscoe Pound, "The Causes of Popular Dissatisfaction with the Administration of Justice," Address to the Annual Meeting of the American Bar Association, August 30, 1906, p. 4, https://law.unl.edu/RoscoePound.pdf. On sociological jurisprudence and the legal realists, see Laura Kalman, *Legal Realism at Yale, 1927–1960* (Chapel Hill: University of North Carolina Press, 1986); N. E. H. Hull, *Roscoe Pound and Karl Llewellyn: Searching for an American Jurisprudence* (Chicago: University of Chicago Press, 1997); and John Henry Schlegel, *American Legal Realism and Empirical Social Science* (Chapel Hill: University of North Carolina Press, 1995).

6. Melvin I. Urofsky, *Louis D. Brandeis: A Life* (New York: Pantheon, 2009), 3–102. Brandeis's life has attracted attention for his role as an advocate, his judicial decisions, and his Jewishness. Among the many book-length accounts of that life, in addition to Urofsky, Alpheus Mason, and Philippa Strum, cited throughout this chapter, one can find Gerald Berk, *Louis D. Brandeis and the Making of Regulated Competition, 1900–1932* (New York: Cambridge University Press, 2009); Robert A. Burt, *Two Jewish Justices: Outcasts in the Promised Land* (Berkeley: University of California Press, 1988); and Allon Gal, *Brandeis of Boston* (Cambridge, MA: Harvard University Press, 1980). Articles attesting to Brandeis's contributions to American jurisprudence include Louis L. Jaffe, "Was Brandeis an Activist?: The Search for Intermediate Premises," *Harvard Law Review* 80 (1967): 986; Edward A. Purcell Jr., "The Judicial Legacy of Louis Brandeis and the Nature of American Constitutionalism," *Touro Law*

Review 33 (2017): 5–50; and Clyde Spillenger, "Reading the Judicial Canon: Alexander Bickel and the Book of Brandeis," *Journal of American History* 79 (1992): 125–151.

7. Philippa Strum, *Louis D. Brandeis, Justice for the People* (New York: Schocken, 1984), 96; Bernard Schwartz, "Supreme Court Superstars: The Ten Greatest Justices," *Tulsa Law Journal* 31 (1995), 122–126; Purcell, "Brandeis," 6–8, 9. For the criticisms, see, e.g., G. Edward White, "The Canonization of Holmes and Brandeis: Epistemology and Judicial Reputations," *New York University Law Review* 70 (1996): 610–616.

8. Urofsky, *Brandeis*, 573–574.

9. Brandeis to Norman Hill White, July 6, 1907, in Melvin I. Urofsky and David Levy, eds., *Letters of Louis D. Brandeis* (Albany: SUNY Press, 1971), 2: 7; Strum, *Brandeis*, 74–93; Woodrow Wilson, *The New Freedom, A Call for the Emancipation of the Generous Energies of the People* (Garden City, NY: Doubleday and Page, 1921), a collection of campaign speeches influenced by Brandeis on individualism and democracy. For example, in the very first pages, the Brandeis mantra: "Our life has broken away from the past" (3).

10. Louis Brandeis, "The Opportunity in the Law" (1905), in Philippa Strum, ed., *Brandeis on Democracy* (Lawrence: University Press of Kansas, 1995), 53.

11. Louis Brandeis and Samuel Warren, "The Right to Privacy," *Harvard Law Review* 4 (1890): 193.

12. Brandeis, "The Opportunity in the Law," *Commonwealth Law Review* 3 (1905): 22–30.

13. Brandeis, "Opportunity," 22.

14. Brandeis, "Opportunity," 22–23.

15. Brandeis, "Opportunity," 24.

16. Brandeis, "Opportunity," 25.

17. Brandeis, "Opportunity," 26.

18. Brandeis, "Opportunity," 27–28.

19. Brandeis, "Opportunity," 29–30.

20. Brandeis, Address at Faneuil Hall, July 4, 1915, https://cis.org/Possess-National-Consciousness-American-Louis-Brandeis-July-4-1915; Strum, *Brandeis*, 60, 61, 67, 71–72, 79, 80, 81, 99–100, 179–180, 181–182.

21. Alpheus T. Mason, *Brandeis: A Free Man's Life* (New York: Viking, 1956), 126; Brandeis to Frankfurter, January 28, 1913, Melvin I. Urofsky and David W. Levy, eds., *Half Brother, Half Son: The Letters of Louis D. Brandeis to Felix Frankfurter* (Norman: University of Oklahoma Press, 1991), 22; Brandeis to Frankfurter, January 28, 1928, in Urofsky and Levy, 317.

22. Mason, *Brandeis*, 371–385; Urofsky, *Brandeis*, 372–376, 379–384.

23. Louis D. Brandeis, Address to the Chicago Bar Association, January 3, 1916, in Strum, *Brandeis on Democracy*, 59–66.

24. Brandeis, "Chicago Bar Association," 60.

25. Brandeis, "Chicago Bar Association," 61.

26. Brandeis, "Chicago Bar Association," 62.

27. Brandeis, "Chicago Bar Association," 63.

28. Brandeis, "Chicago Bar Association," 64.

29. Brandeis, "Chicago Bar Association," 64.

30. Brandeis, "Chicago Bar Association," 65; Brandeis to Frankfurter, January 28, 1913, in Urofsky and Levy, "*Half Brother, Half Son*," 22.

31. Urofsky, *Brandeis*, 430–459; Urofsky and Levy, *Letters of Louis D. Brandeis* 4:iii–xv; *Nomination of Louis D. Brandeis, Hearings. . . .* 64th Cong, 1st session (Washington, DC: Government Printing Office, 1916), appendix, 234.

32. Urofsky, *Brandeis*, 459; Burnet v. Coronado Oil and Gas, 285 U.S. 393, 408 (1932) (Brandeis, J. dissenting); Strum, *Brandeis*, 364. Was Brandeis a liberal or a conservative on the Court? The question would have puzzled him, as he did not view his job in these terms. Nevertheless, historians have divided on this question.

Brandeis continued a good deal of "extrajudicial" activity, largely through intermediaries. He suggested that others write articles and go to meetings, give speeches, and propose resolutions. These included his role in the American Zionist movement, Harvard Law School, and various public concerns. See, e.g., Urofsky, *Brandeis*, 460, and much of the correspondence with Felix Frankfurter in *Half Brother, Half Son*.

33. Brandeis to Felix Frankfurter, May 25, 1924, Urofsky and Levy, *Half Brother, Half Son*, 168; Brandeis to Frankfurter, December 17, 1924: "Prest. [president James Rowland] Angell [of Yale] asked me to give the Dodge Lectures. Of course, I refused." Urofsky and Levy, *Half Brother, Half Son*, 186.

34. Urofsky, *Brandeis*, 47–48.

35. Urofsky, *Brandeis*, 30, 48, 207, 477–478; U.S. v. Moreland, 258 U.S. 433, 441 (1922) (Brandies, J. dissenting). Here as elsewhere the debate over Brandeis's judicial activism is misplaced. These were not terms he used; rather they are the coinage of his clerks and legal academics. See, e.g., Louis Jaffe, "Was Brandeis an Activist?: The Search for Intermediate Premises," *Harvard Law Review* 80 (1967): 988: Brandeis was more "positive" about judicial abstention than restraint. He preferred "the sermon to the sword" and would have let more democratic institutions, for example, state legislatures, reform the law (989).

36. Strum, *Brandeis on Democracy*, 21, 415; Edward Purcell Jr., *Brandeis and the Progressive Constitution: Erie, Judicial Power, and the Power of Federal Courts in Twentieth-Century America* (New Haven: Yale University Press, 2000), 120; New State Ice Company v. Liebmann, 285 U.S. 262, 311 (1931) (Brandeis, J. dissenting).

37. New York Central v. Winfield, 244 U.S. 147, 161, 162, 163, 164, 165 (1917) (Brandeis, J. dissenting).

38. Urofsky, *Brandeis*, 601–605.

39. Truax v. Corrigan, 257 U.S. 312, 355, 357 (1921) (Brandeis, J. dissenting).

40. Urofsky, *Brandeis*, 556–570; Philippa Strum, *Speaking Freely: Whitney v. California and American Speech Law* (Lawrence: University Press of Kansas, 2015), 93–96, 112–122. The following passages are adapted from Hoffer, Hoffer, and Hull, *Supreme Court*, 213–216.

41. Espionage Act of 1917, 40 Stat. 217; Sedition Act of 1918, 40 Stat. 553.

42. Schenck v. U.S., 249 U.S. 47, 52 (1919) (Holmes, J.); David Rabban, *Free Speech in Its Forgotten Years, 1870–1920* (New York: Cambridge University Press, 1997), 280–285.

43. 249 U.S. at 52 (Holmes, J.).

44. Debs v. U.S., 249 U.S. 211, 214, 215 (1919) (Holmes, J.).

45. Frohwerk v. U.S., 249, U.S. 204, 208 (1919) (Holmes, J.).

46. Richard Polenberg, *Fighting Faiths: The Abrams Case, The Supreme Court, and Free Speech* (Ithaca, NY: Cornell University Press, 1998), 95–102, 218–228; Thomas Healy, *The Great Dissent: How Oliver Wendell Holmes Changed His Mind* (New York: Holt, 2013), offers the best account, but it remains conjectural.

47. Abrams v. U.S., 250 U.S. 616, 620–621 (1919) (Clarke, J.).

48. 260 U.S. at 626, 628, 630 (Holmes, J. dissenting).

49. 260 U.S. at 630 (Holmes, J. dissenting).

50. Gilbert v. Minnesota, 254 U.S. 325, 335, 336 (1920) (Brandeis J. dissenting).

51. 254 U.S. at 336 (Brandeis, J. dissenting).

52. 254 U.S. at 339, 340, 341 (Brandeis, J. dissenting).

53. 254 U.S. at 340, 341 (Brandeis, J. dissenting). There is a striking similarity to Justice William O. Douglas's penumbra of rights emanating from various part of the Bill of Rights leading to the right of privacy in *Griswold v. Connecticut* (1965). As we shall see, Douglas "went to school" on Brandeis's belief in the fundamental right to be left alone, then ventured beyond it.

54. Marc Lendler, *Gitlow v. New York: Every Idea an Incitement* (Lawrence: University Press of Kansas, 2012), 112–123. Incorporation of other parts of the Bill of Rights did not come until much later, to be sure.

55. Whitney v. California, 274 U.S. 357, 373 (1927) (Brandeis, J. concurring). Brandeis's contribution was more than incorporation. It has become known as the Brandeis rule of "counter speech." Instead of suppression, including drowning out speech we do not favor, Brandeis proposed "If there be time to expose through discussion, the falsehoods and fallacies, to avert the evil by the processes of education, the remedy to be applied is more speech, not enforced silence." 274 U.S. at 377 (Brandeis, J. concurring).

56. 274 U.S. at 375 (Brandeis, J. concurring).

57. 274 U.S. at 376, 377 (Brandeis, J. concurring).

58. 274 U.S. at 378 (Brandeis, J. concurring).

59. Urofsky, *Brandeis*, 302; Olmstead v. U.S. 277 U.S. 438 (1928).

60. Warren and Brandeis, "The Right to Privacy," 193, 194, 195.

61. 277 U.S. at 471 (Brandeis, J. dissenting).

62. 277 U.S. at 472, 473 (Brandeis, J. dissenting).

63. 277 U.S. at 478 (Brandeis, J. dissenting).

64. 277 U.S. at 490 (Brandeis, J. dissenting).

65. Brandeis to Felix Frankfurter, January 16, 1921, in Urofsky and Levy, *Half Brother, Half Son*, 61; Brandeis joined the Court's opinion, by Holmes, in Buck v. Bell, 274 U.S. 200 (1927), and the all-white primary, Grovey v. Townsend, 295 U.S. 45 (1935); and in separate but equal cases, Gong Lum v. Riche, 275 U.S. 78 (1927); and South Covington and Cincinnati Street Railway C. v. Kentucky, 252 U.S. 399 (1290), he voted to uphold Jim Crow laws. Edward Purcell has reminded the author that a "living constitution" need not be an egalitarian one.

66. Brandeis to Frankfurter, October 5, 1925, in Urofsky and Levy, *Half Brother, Half Son*, 215; Baltimore and Ohio RR v. U.S. 298 U.S. 349, 381 (1936) (Brandeis, J. concurring).

67. Joel K. Goldstein and Charles A. Miller, "Brandeis: The Legacy of a Justice," *Marquette Law Review* 100 (2016): 464, 468–471; Erie v. Thompkins, 304 U.S. 64 (1938). This is not to say that one should share Felix Frankfurter's disenchantment with the man who for many years was his mentor and patron; see Purcell, *Progressive Constitution*, 203–212.

CHAPTER FIVE. BENJAMIN N. CARDOZO

1. Richard Polenberg, *The World of Benjamin Cardozo: Personal Values and the Judicial Process* (Cambridge, MA: University of Harvard Press, 1997), 5, 86; White, *American Judicial Tradition*, 206; Posner, *Cardozo*, 150 (Cardozo a

superstar); Paul Freund, quoted in Posner, *Cardozo*, 19. Not everyone agreed with this assessment. Jerome Frank complained that Cardozo looked at law from above rather than below, in the trenches. Frank quoted in Polenberg, *Cardozo*, 163–164. Grant Gilmore, *The Ages of American Law*, 2nd ed. (New Haven: Yale University Press, 2014), 67, conceded that those who knew Cardozo "tell us of a man of compelling personal charm as well as of great sweetness of character." But Gilmore found "everybody praised" but "nobody read" Cardozo's *The Nature of the Judicial Process* (1922). Gilmore's judgement of Cardozo's Storrs lectures, published as *The Nature of the Judicial Process*, appeared in Gilmore's own Storrs lectures of 1975—Gilmore, *The Ages of American Law* (New Haven: Yale University Press, 1975), 67.

2. G. Edward White, *Tort Law in America*, expanded ed. (New York: Oxford University Press, 2003), 120.

3. On the pilpul see Micah Gottlieb, *The Jewish Reformation: Bible Translation and Middle-Class German Judaism as Spiritual Enterprise* (New York: Oxford University Press, 2021), 80–82. Cardozo was a member of a traditional Sephardic congregation, had a Bar Mitzvah, and took part in the life of the temple. The pilpul is a method of Talmudic discourse deeply ingrained in Jewish culture. Andrew L. Kaufman, *Cardozo* (Cambridge, MA: Harvard University Press, 1998), 69; Polenberg, *Cardozo*, 17.

4. Kaufman, *Cardozo*, 49; Kaufman, "The First Judge Cardozo, Albert, Father of Benjamin," *Journal of Law and Religion* 11 (1994): 271–315.

5. Kaufman, *Cardozo*, 37, 49, 55, 57–58, 61.

6. Kaufman, *Cardozo*, 191, 193, 195.

7. Kaufman, *Cardozo*, 117–119, 121, 127–128, 130–131, 132, 135, 136, 139, 141, 142. In a study published in 1990 (Posner, *Cardozo*, 90–91), the author found that Cardozo opinions from the New York years made it into torts and contracts casebooks far more often than his contemporaries, an astounding ratio of 13 to 1. The problem with this statistic is that some casebooks go through many editions, and the same old case cites are thus repeated. A classic case like *MacPherson* is going to bias the ratio of citations. But the point is well taken. A count of law review references to "Benjamin Cardozo" from the Hein Online Law Journal Library in November 2021 turned up just short of thirty thousand cites in articles, notes, and reviews.

8. MacPherson v. Buick Motor Co., 217 N.Y. 382, 384, 385 (1916) (Cardozo, J.); Kaufman, *Cardozo*, 270–275; White, *Tort Law*, 120–121; Edward Levi, *An Introduction to Legal Reasoning* (Chicago: University of Chicago Press, 1949), 24.

9. 217 N.Y. at 387, 391 (Cardozo, J.).

10. Hynes v. New York Central R.R. 231 N.Y. 229, 233, 234 (1921) (Cardozo, J.); Richard H. Weisberg, "Law, Literature, and Cardozo's Judicial Poetics," *Cardozo Law Review* 1 (1979): 324–326.

11. 231 N.Y at 234, 235, 236 (Cardozo, J.).

12. Benjamin N. Cardozo, *The Nature of the Judicial Process* (New Haven: Yale University Press, 1922), 10, 28, 40, 67. On the enthusiastic reaction to the lectures and the book among the legal cognoscenti, see White, *American Judicial Tradition*, 210–211.

13. Cardozo, *Judicial Process*, 101, 116, 122, 123.

14. Cardozo, *The Growth of the Law* (New Haven: Yale University Press, 1924), 2, 6, 11, 46.

15. Cardozo, *Growth*, 19, 21, 22, 27, 40–41, 43. No doubt, Cardozo was also indulging his other intellectual passion—the history of ideas. The many quotations from legal theorists, political theorists, and philosophers were testimony to his wide reading in these fields.

16. Cardozo, *Growth*, 66, 78, 79, 127, 133; State of Washington v. Dawson & Co. 264 U.S. 219, 236 (Brandeis, J. dissenting). Posner, *Cardozo*, 3–4, 28, 30, finds that Cardozo favored a "pragmatic . . . policy oriented jurisprudence."

17. Polenberg, *Cardozo*, 170–171.

18. Nixon v. Condon, 286 U.S. 73, 81 (Cardozo, J.); Charles Zelden, *The Battle for the Black Ballot: Smith v. Allwright and the Defeat of the Texas All White Primary* (Lawrence: University Press of Kansas, 2004), 42, 43.

19. 286 U.S. at 83 (Cardozo, J.); Zelden, *Black Ballot*, 54–61.

20. 286 U.S. at 84–85 (Cardozo, J.). On the Court's revision of the state action doctrine, see Heart of Atlanta Motel v. U.S., 379 U.S. 241 (1964).

21. Carter v. Carter Coal Co., 298 U.S. 238 (1936). On Cardozo and the New Deal, see Barry Cushman, *Rethinking the New Deal Court: The Structure of a Constitutional Revolution* (New York: Oxford University Press, 1998), 3 and after, a pointillist exploration of Cardozo's "wise and liberal" style; Kaufman, *Cardozo*, 495–538, a case-by-case analysis; Polenberg, *Cardozo*, 195–203; and William E. Leuchtenberg, *The Supreme Court Reborn: Constitution Revolution in the Age of Roosevelt* (New York: Oxford University Press, 1995), a political interpretation of the Court, in which Cardozo plays a supporting role as part of the liberal bloc.

22. 298 U.S. at 326 (Cardozo, J. dissenting).

23. 298 U.S. at 326 (Cardozo, J. dissenting).

24. 298 U.S. at 328 (Cardozo, J. dissenting).

25. 298 U.S. at 328 (Cardozo, J. dissenting).

26. 298 U.S. at 329 (Cardozo, J. dissenting).

27. 298 U.S. at 331 (Cardozo, J. dissenting).

28. 298 U.S. at 331, 332 (Cardozo, J. dissenting).

29. 298 U.S. at 333 (Cardozo, J. dissenting).

30. 298 U.S. at 333 (Cardozo, J. dissenting).

31. 298 U.S. at 334 (Cardozo, J. dissenting).

32. 298 U.S. 335 (Cardozo, J. dissenting).

33. 298 U.S. at 338 (Cardozo, J. dissenting); National Labor Relations Board v. Jones and Laughlin Steel Corp., 301 U.S. 1 (1937).

34. Steward Machine Co. v. Collector, 301 U.S. 548, 574 (1937) (Cardozo, J.).

35. 301 U.S. at 578 (Cardozo, J.).

36. 301 U.S. at 580 (Cardozo, J.).

37. 301 U.S. at 582 (Cardozo, J.).

38. 301 U.S. at 584 (Cardozo, J.).

39. 301 U.S. at 585, 586 (Cardozo, J.).

40. 301 U.S. at 588 (Cardozo, J.). On the futurist uses of the Preamble, see Peter Charles Hoffer, *For Ourselves and Our Posterity: The Preamble to the Federal Constitution in American History* (New York: Oxford University Press, 2013), 135–149.

41. Palko v. Connecticut, 302 U.S. 319, 325 (1937) (Cardozo, J.).

42. 302 U.S. at 322 (Cardozo, J.).

43. 302 U.S. at 324 (Cardozo, J.).

44. 302 U.S. at 325 (Cardozo, J.).

45. 302 U.S. at 325 (Cardozo, J.); see Galloway v. United States, 319 U.S. 372, 397 (1943) (Black, J.): "The founders of our government thought that trial of fact by juries rather than by judges was an essential bulwark of civil liberty. For this reason, among others, they adopted Article III, § 2 of the Constitution, and the Sixth and Seventh Amendments." On trial by jury in founding era: James Oldham, *Trial by Jury* (New York: New York University Press, 2006), 5.

46. 302 U.S. at 326 (Cardozo, J.).

47. 302 U.S. at 328 (Cardozo, J.).

48. Polenberg, *Cardozo*, 234–238.

CHAPTER SIX. WILLIAM O. DOUGLAS

1. Abe Fortas quoted in Melvin I. Urofsky, "William O. Douglas as a Common Law Judge," *Duke Law Journal* 41 (1991): 133; William Brennan quoted in Adam M. Sowards, "Protecting American Lands with Justice William O. Douglas," *George Wright Forum* 32 (2015): 173. A very different picture, highly unflattering, appears in White, *American Judicial Tradition*, 367:

"quickly partisan on issues, and disinclined to attribute impartiality to his colleagues," irresponsible, irritable, and dismissive of others' opinions, he was the "anti-judge."

2. William O. Douglas, *Go East, Young Man: The Autobiography of William O. Douglas, the Early Years* (New York: Dell, 1974), 47, 54, 63, 306–307; James F. Simon, *Independent Journey: The Life of William O. Douglas* (New York: Harper and Row, 1980), 139–196.

3. Douglas, *Go East*, 135, 136, 137, 150, 152, 154, 156–157.

4. Douglas, *Go East*, 160–161, 163, 164, 166, 169, 170.

5. Simon, *Independent Journey* 125, William O. Douglas and Carroll Shanks, "Insulation from Liability through Subsidiary Corporations," *Yale Law Journal* 39 (1929): 210, 217, 218; Douglas and Shanks, *Cases and Materials on the Law of Management of Business Units* (Chicago: University of Chicago Press, 1931), preface.

6. Douglas, "Protective Committees in Railroad Reorganizations," *Harvard Law Review* 47 (1934): 567; Douglas and George Bates, "The Federal Securities Act of 1933," *Yale Law Journal* 43 (1933): 172, 173; Simon, *Independent Journey*, 139–161.

7. William O. Douglas, "Forward," *George Washington Law Review* 28 (1959): 2, 4.

8. Simon, *Independent Journey*, 353; Melvin Urofsky, ed., *The Douglas Letters* (Bethesda, MD: Adler and Adler, 1987), 213–214; Douglas to Felix Frankfurter, July 2, 1940, Urofsky, *Douglas Letters*, 215; Douglas to Harry S. Truman, July 31, 1948, Urofsky, *Douglas Letters*, 219.

9. William O. Douglas, "Law in Eruption: A Concept of Lawyers' Duty in a Time of Change," *American Bar Association Journal* 34 (1948): 674.

10. Melvin Urofsky, "Getting the Job Done: William O. Douglas and Collegiality in the Supreme Court," in *"He Shall Not Pass This Way Again": The Legacy of William O. Douglas*, ed. Stephen L. Wasby (Pittsburgh: University of Pittsburg Press, 1990), 33–49; Urofsky, *Brandeis*, 750; Douglas, *Go East*, 306–307; Brandeis to Felix Frankfurter, October 8, 1937, in Uroksky and Levy, *Half Brother, Half Son*, 602; Urofsky, *The Douglas Letters*, 43n1.

11. Simon, *Independent Journey*, 353–354; Norman Dorson, "Douglas and Civil Liberties," in Wasby, *"He Shall Not Pass,"* 66.

12. William O. Douglas, *A Living Bill of Rights* (New York: One Nation Library, 1961).

13. Douglas, *A Living Bill of Rights*, 10, 27–28, 24, 25, 32, 61. When he needed authority for these views, he turned back to Brandeis's concurrence in Whitney v. California (28).

14. Beauharnais v. Illinois, 343 U.S. 250, 286 (1951) (Douglas, J. dissenting); Laird v. Tatum, 408 U.S. 1 18, 29 (1971) (Douglas, J. dissenting); United States Civil Service Commission v. National Association of Letter Carriers, 413 U.S. 548, 598 (1973) (Douglas, J. dissenting).

15. Douglas, *A Living Bill of Rights*, 34–35, 38; Douglas, *The Right of the People* (New York: Doubleday, 1958), 12.

16. Douglas, *The Right of the People*, 87, 90, 107, 113, 118, 165.

17. Skinner v. Oklahoma, 316 U.S. 535, 536, 543 (1942) (Douglas, J.).

18. Douglas, *A Wilderness Bill of Rights* (Boston: Little, Brown, 1965), 3, 4, 21.

19. Douglas, *Wilderness*, 25, 26, 38, 92, 109, 175.

20. Sierra Club v. Morton, 405 U.S. 727, 741, 742, 473 (1972) (Douglas, J. dissenting).

21. On the centrality of privacy in Douglas's jurisprudence, see Nadine Strossen, "The Religion Clause Writings of Justice William O. Douglas," in Wasby, *"He Shall Not Pass,"* 94–95; Dorothy J. Glancy, "Douglas' Right of Privacy: A Response to His Critics," in Wasby, *"He Shall Not Pass,"* 157; Douglas, *The Right of the People*, 124, 150; Douglas, *The Court Years: The Autobiography of William O. Douglas, 1939–1975* (New York: Random House, 1980), 392.

22. Dorothy J. Glancy, "Douglas' Right of Privacy: A Response to His Critics," in Wasby, *"He Shall Not Pass,"* 155; Public Utilities Commission v. Pollak, 343 U.S. 451, 467, 469 (1952) (Douglas, J. dissenting). See also On Lee v. United States 343 U.S. 747, 762 (1952) (Douglas, J. dissenting): "I now more fully appreciate" the "right to be let alone."

23. Poe v. Ullman, 367 U.S. 497 (1961) (as Connecticut was not enforcing the criminal statute against dissemination of birth control, the Court found no case or controversy to decide); Griswold v. Connecticut, 381 U.S. 479 (1965); David J. Garrow, *Liberty and Sexuality, the Right to Privacy and the Making of Roe v. Wade* (Berkeley: University of California Press, 1994), 196–269.

24. 381 U.S. at 480 (Douglas, J.).

25. 381 U.S. at 481 (Douglas, J.); Steven A. Duke, "Douglas and the Criminal Law," in Wasby, *"He Shall Not Pass,"* 142, 143.

26. 381 U.S. at 482 (Douglas, J.).

27. 381 U.S. at 483 (Douglas, J.).

28. William Cohen, "Douglas as Civil Libertarian," in Wasby, *"He Shall Not Pass,"* 121; 381 U.S. at 484, 485 (Douglas, J.).

29. 381 U.S. at 485, 486 (Douglas, J.).

30. N. E. H. Hull and Peter Charles Hoffer, *Roe v. Wade: The Abortion Rights Controversy in America*, 3rd ed. (Lawrence: University Press of Kansas, 2020), 113–179.

31. Roe v. Wade, 410 U.S. 113 (1973).

32. Hull and Hoffer, *Roe*, 127–129, 159–161.

33. Doe v. Bolton, 410 U.S. 179, 210 (1973) (Douglas, J. concurring).

34. 410 U.S. at 213 (Douglas, J. concurring).

35. 410 U.S. at 213 (Douglas, J. concurring) quoting from Eisenstadt v. Baird, 405 U.S. 438, 453 (1972) (Douglas, J. concurring).

36. 410 U.S. at 214 (Douglas, J. concurring).

37. 410 U.S. at 414, 415, 417 (Douglas, J. concurring).

38. Branzburg v. Hays, 408 U.S. 665, 724 (1972) (Douglas, J. dissenting). See, e.g., Urofsky, *Douglas Letters*, 106; Simon, *Independent Journey*, 332; Douglas to Edmond Nathaniel Cahn, January 10, 1962, in Urofsky, *Douglas Letters*, 151, 150; William O. Douglas, Lecture, December 4, 1964, at UCLA, www.youtube .com/watch?v=dGzKWNB1xgA.

39. William O. Douglas, *Points of Rebellion* (New York: Random House, 1969), 63, 64, 67.

40. Douglas, 83, 92; U.S. v. Richardson, 418 U.S. 166, 201–202 (1974) (Douglas, J. dissenting).

41. Douglas, *Court Years*, 391.

42. Simon, *Independent Journey*, 448–454; David N. Atkinson, *Leaving the Bench: Supreme Court Justices at the End* (Lawrence: University Press of Kansas, 1999).

CHAPTER SEVEN. STEPHEN G. BREYER

1. Ken I. Kersh, "Stephen Gerald Breyer," in *Biographical Encyclopedia of the Supreme Court*, ed. Melvin Urofsky (Washington, DC: CQ Press, 2006), 75–88.

2. Shrinking Supreme Court Docket: Ryan J. Owens and David A. Simon, "Explaining the Supreme Court's Shrinking Docket," *William and Mary Law Review* 53 (2012): 1219–1285.

3. See, e.g., Alan Morrison, "A Conversation with Justice Stephen Breyer," *Journal of Legal Education* 66 (2017): 357–371.

4. Stephen Breyer, "The Uneasy Case for Copyright," *Harvard Law Review* 84 (1970): 283, 288, 302, 337. Some of his speculation was off base. Take, for example, "In my view, a modest fall in college text publishing revenue should not cause must concern" (309) because college professors who write these books would turn to writing more articles and competition would cause book output to expand rather than contract. In fact, there is no increase in remuneration or therefore incentive for academics to turn from books to articles—except

among law professors, who rarely write books—and the arrival of "free-ware" or pirated textbooks killed more textbook publishing companies than it helped. Gone or absorbed by other publishers were textbook giants D. C. Heath, Addison-Wesley, Schocken, McGraw-Hill, Prentice-Hall, Houghton Mifflin, and the list goes on, felled by the very forces that Breyer lauded. The jobs lost were in the thousands, including those of many history majors and graduate students who elected to work in the textbook publishing business. Job losses were not included in Breyer's analysis. (An example of the absence of transactional costs from the Ronald Coase Theorem?)

5. Stephen Breyer, *Regulation and Its Reform* (Cambridge, MA: Harvard University Press, 1982), 191, 194, 195 (where the mismatch causes future harm to competition, and prefers antitrust, taxation, etc.). See Cass R. Sunstein, "Justice Breyer's Democratic Pragmatism," *Yale Law Journal* 115 (2006): 1719, 1780.

6. Breyer, *Regulation*, 5, 4.

7. Breyer, *Regulation*, 5, 8, 9, 11.

8. Sunstein, "Pragmatism," 1719, 1720, 1721, 1729.

9. Barry Wright Corp. v. ITT Grinnell Corp. 724 F.2d 227, 231 (1983) (Breyer, J.).

10. 724 F.2d at 232 (Breyer, J.).

11. Kartell v. Blue Shield of Massachusetts, 749 F.2d 922, 928 (1st Cir 1984) (Breyer, J.).

12. Town of Concord, Massachusetts v. Boston Edison Co., 915 F.2d 17, 19 (1st Cir. 1990) (Breyer, J.).

13. Richard J. Pierce Jr., "Justice Breyer: Internationalist, Pragmatist, and Empiricist," *American University Administrative Law Journal* 8 (1995): 749; Breyer, *Regulation and Its Reform*, 368.

14. Stephen G. Breyer, Testimony before the Senate Committee on the Judiciary, *Hearings before the Committee on the Judiciary of the United States Senate*, July 12, 1994, 103rd Cong., 2nd Sess. (Washington, DC: Government Printing Office, 1995), 20–21, 111.

15. U.S. v. Lopez, 514 U.S. 549, 615, 619 (1995) (Breyer, J. dissenting).

16. College Savings Bank v. Florida, 527 U.S. 666, 703 (1999) (Breyer, J. dissenting).

17. Mahanoy Area School District v. B. L., 594 U.S. ___ (2021) 5, 6, 7 (Breyer, J.).

18. Breyer, *Active Liberty*, 106; Breyer, "Copyright," 340–343; Google LLC v. Oracle America Inc., No. 18–956, 593 U.S. ___ (2021), 2, 3, 11, 13, 16, 17, 24, 35 (Breyer, J.).

19. David G. Savage, "How the Two Justices from California Are Moving the Supreme Court to the Left," *Los Angeles Times* June 29, 2016, www.latimes .com/nation/la-na-court-breyer-kennedy-center-20160628-snap-story.html; Bush v. Gore, 531 U.S. 98 (2000); Charles L. Zelden, *Bush v. Gore: Exposing the Growing Crisis in American Democracy*, 3rd ed. (Lawrence: University Press of Kansas, 2020), 178–180.

20. 531 U.S. at 145, 152 (Breyer, J. dissenting).

21. 531 U.S. at 154 (Breyer, J. dissenting).

22. 531 U.S. at 155, 156 (Breyer, J. dissenting).

23. 531 U.S. at 153 (Breyer, J. dissenting).

24. 531 U.S. at 157 (Breyer, J. dissenting). On the Court as a political body, see Richard A. Posner, in an October 25, 2016 interview recorded on C-Span and reprinted for the online ABA Journal *Above the Law*: "Posner said a weak federal judiciary can be blamed on appointing politicians who are more interested in politics rather than in good judges." www.abajournal.com/news /article/posner_says_supreme_court_is_awful_top_two_justices_are_okay _but_not_great. See also Joseph J. Ellis, "The Supreme Court Was Never Meant to Be Political," *Wall Street Journal*, September 14, 2018 (Brett Kavanaugh nomination); Ilya Shapiro, "Just Accept It, the Supreme Court Has Always Been Political," *Cato Institute*, September 26, 2020 (Amy Barrett nomination).

25. William Domnarski, *Richard Posner* (New York Oxford University Press, 2016); Richard A. Posner, "Post-Dependency, Pragmaticism, and Critique of History in Adjudication and Legal Scholarship," *University of Chicago Law Review* 67 (2000): 581 (the article did not mention Breyer); Richard A. Posner, *Breaking the Deadlock: The 2000 Election, the Constitution, and the Courts* (Cambridge, MA: Harvard University Press, 2001), 79–80n43; 144–145; 253.

26. Breyer, *Active Liberty*, 4.

27. Breyer, *Active Liberty*, 3, 5, 6.

28. Breyer, *Active Liberty*, 7, 9, 10, 12.

29. Breyer, *Active Liberty*, 5, 6, 18, 37.

30. Breyer, *Active Liberty*, 32, 33, 34. On the Judiciary Act of 1789 and its transformative impact, see Hoffer, Hoffer, and Hull, *The Federal Courts*, 30–40. On the Bill of Rights, see Akhil Amar, *The Bill of Rights: Creation and Reconstruction* (New Haven: Yale University Press, 1998), 45–46.

31. Breyer, *Active Liberty*, 66, 67, 72, 73, 74.

32. Breyer, *Active Liberty*, 41, 42, 45, 46, 47.

33. Breyer, *Active Liberty*, 102, 103.

34. Hoffer, Hoffer, and Hull, *Federal Courts*, 410.

35. Breyer, *Active Liberty*, 115.

36. Breyer, *Active Liberty*, 116.

37. Breyer, *Active Liberty*, 126, 127, 128, 134.

38. Richard A. Posner, "Justice Breyer Throws Down the Gauntlet," *Yale Law Journal* 115 (2006): 1699, 1700, 1702. For examples arguing that among the founders were advocates of active liberty, see T. H. Breen, *American Insurgents, American Patriots: The Revolution of the People* (New York: Hill and Wang, 2010); Gary B. Nash, *The Unknown American Revolution: The Unruly Birth of Democracy and the Struggle to Create America* (New York: Penguin, 2006); and Alfred F. Young, *Liberty Tree, Ordinary People in the American Revolution* (New York: New York University Press, 2006).

39. Posner, "Breyer," 1705, 1706, 1708, 1717.

40. Kathleen M. Sullivan, "Tribute to Justice Stephen G. Breyer," *New York University Law Review* 64 (2008): 28, 31.

41. Paul Gewirtz, "The Pragmatic Passion of Stephen Breyer," *Yale Law Journal* 115 (2006): 1675, 1675, 1677, 1678.

42. Arnold H. Loewy, "A Tale of Two Justices (Scalia and Breyer)," *Texas Tech Law Review* 43 (2011): 1208.

43. Breyer, "Judicial Independence," *Georgetown Law Journal* 95 (2007): 903, 905, 906.

44. Breyer, *Making Our Democracy Work: A Judge's View* (New York: Knopf, 2010), xiv. The target was Posner's *Law, Pragmatism, and Democracy*, and the choice of the word *pragmatic* was, in the context of the debate between the two men, more of an infra dig than an admiring adoption.

45. Breyer, *Making Our Democracy Work*, ix, 233.

46. Confirmation Hearing on the Nomination of John G. Roberts . . . September 15, 2005, 109 Cong., 1st Sess., www.govinfo.gov/content/pkg/GPO-CHRG-ROBERTS/pdf/GPO-CHRG-ROBERTS.pdf, p. 56; Amy Coney Barrett, September 12, 2021, speech at Mitch McConnell Center at University of Louisville, www.cbsnews.com/news/amy-coney-barrett-supreme-court-justices-partisan-hacks/; Stephen G. Breyer, September 13, 2021, talk at *Washington Post*, www.washingtonpost.com/washington-post-live/2021/09/13/authority-court-peril-politics-with-justice-stephen-g-breyer.

47. Whole Women's Health v. Hellerstedt, 579 U.S. ___ (2016); Hull and Hoffer, *Roe*, 324–332.

48. *June Medical Services v. Russo* 18–1323 and 18–1460. Oral argument transcript at www.supremecourt.gov/oral_arguments/argument_transcripts/2019/18-1323_1lo2.pdf. Audio at www.supremecourt.gov/oral_arguments/audio/2019/18-1323.

49. June Medical Services v. Russo, 591 U.S. ___ (2020) (Breyer, J.).

50. Stephen G. Breyer, *The Authority of the Court and the Peril of Politics* (Cambridge, MA: Harvard University Press, 2021), 64–91, 100; Albion Tourgée, *A Fool's Errand* (1879; New York: Harper Torch, 1961), 5.

51. Breyer, *Authority of the Court*, 66–67.

52. Dobbs v. Jackson Women's Health Organization, 19–1392 (2022).

53. Breyer, *Active Liberty*, 6.

CONCLUSION: THE MAKING OF A DEMOCRATIC
JURISPRUDENCE

1. Among legal academics, there is the (expected) dispute over whether *Dobbs* is a genuine originalist opinion. For example, does Justice Alito do justice to the textual analysis of the three clauses in the Fourteenth Amendment on which one might base an abortion right, or rather, does the absence from those clauses of anything like a guarantee of abortion rights undermine his logic? The problem is that the absence of text may preclude any of the varieties of originalist interpretation of text. For the first shots in the debate, see, e.g., J. Joel Alicea, "An Originalist Victory," *City Journal*, Eye on the News, June 24, 2022, www.city-journal.org/dobbs-abortion-ruling-is-a-triumph-for-originalists.

2. See, e.g., Hull and Hoffer, *Roe v. Wade*, 89–134. The more serious underlying problem is the uncertainty in "history and tradition"—which history and whose tradition is the judge relying on? American history and tradition are replete with injustice to minorities, for example, the removal of the Indigenous peoples, the anti-Asian immigrant legislation of the Gilded Age, and the long regime of Jim Crow. Would these justify a judge citing those examples as a reason to discriminate against minorities?

3. Dobbs v. Jackson Women's Health Organization, 597 U.S. ___ 6 (2022) (Alito, J.).

4. Often dismissed as "law office history," forays into historical events and ideas in judges' opinions, friends of the court briefs, and "expert" historians' testimony characteristically lack the nuance and objectivity of professional historical writing. See, e.g., Peter Charles Hoffer, *Past Imperfect*, 2nd ed. (New York: PublicAffairs Press, 2007), 124–127.

5. Dobbs, 597 U.S. ___ 6, 2, 3 (Breyer J. dissenting).

Index